The Paris Commune, 1871

TURNING POINTS
General Editor: Keith Robbins
Vice Chancellor, University of Wales Lampeter

This ambitious new programme of books under the direction of Professor Keith Robbins (already General Editor of Longman's very successful series Profiles in Power) *will examine moments and processes in history which have conventionally been seen as 'turning points' in the emergence of the modern world. By looking at the causes and long-term consequences of these key events, the books will illuminate the nature of both change and continuity in historical development. There are numerous titles in active preparation, and the following are already available:*

The End of the Ottoman Empire, 1908–1923
A.L. Macfie

The Paris Commune, 1871
Robert Tombs

The Paris Commune
1871

ROBERT TOMBS

LONGMAN
London and New York

Pearson Education Limited
Edinburgh Gate,
Harlow, Essex CM20 2JE,
United Kingdom
and Associated Companies throughout the world.

*Published in the United States of America
by Pearson Education Inc., New York.*

First published 1999

ISBN 0–582–30915–8 CSD
ISBN 0–582–30903–4 PPR

Visit Addison Wesley Longman on the world wide web at http://www.awl-he.com

British Library Cataloguing in Publication Data

A catalogue entry for this title is available from the British Library

Library of Congress Cataloging-in-Publication Data

Tombs, Robert.
The Paris Commune, 1871 / Robert Tombs.
p.   cm. — (Turning points)
Includes bibliographical references and index.
ISBN 0–582–30915–8 (hbk). — ISBN 0–582–30903–4 (pbk)
1. Paris (France)—History—Commune, 1871.   I. Title.
II. Series: Turning points (Longman (Firm))
DC316.T65   1999
944.081′2—dc21   99–13460
                                              CIP

Set by 35 in 10/12pt Baskerville
Produced by Addison Wesley Longman Singapore (Pte) Ltd.,
Printed in Singapore

Contents

List of Tables and Figures

PROLOGUE

The Episode, 18 March–28 May 1871

Before daybreak on 18 March, several thousand French regular troops trudged up the steep streets of Montmartre to capture by surprise hundreds of cannon parked on top of the hill by dissident units of the Paris National Guard, the citizen militia. To capture these heavy weapons was to be the first step towards reimposing the national government's authority on the militarized and unruly capital. Since the beginning of the war with Germany the previous July, which had led to a four-month siege of the city, the arming of its population, hunger, bombardment and finally capitulation to the Germans in January, Parisians had become increasingly dissaffected from their rulers. The end of the war had left Paris ungovernable, as most of the regular army was demobilized while the National Guard kept its guns. The newly elected National Assembly was far away in Bordeaux. The government it appointed, led by Adolphe Thiers, intended to assert its authority over Paris. The Montmartre expedition was the outcome.

It led to one of the most famous, and fateful, scenes in French history. Thousands of local National Guards, women and children turned out to obstruct and argue with the nervous, outnumbered and obviously unenthusiastic soldiers. The streets became jammed with people, horses and cannon. A few shots were fired by both sides, but generally the soldiers ignored their officers' orders to force back the crowds. Some handed over their rifles and went off 'arm in arm, fraternizing and singing' with the civilians. Officers were manhandled, and several were arrested by the crowd. Similar scenes took place elsewhere in the city. The commander of the troops at Montmartre, General Lecomte, and the hated former commander-in-chief of the Paris National Guard, Clément Thomas, grabbed by the crowd, were later shot in a garden on top of the hill by National Guards, army deserters and local civilians.

1

Across the city, people threw up barricades in a ritual of revolution, as in 1848 and 1830. The government and the army high command, convinced that they had lost control, retreated with all available troops to Versailles, 10 miles south-west of Paris, where the National Assembly arrived from Bordeaux on 20 March. The Central Committee of the Republican Federation of the Paris National Guard – an unofficial body set up in February to coordinate the activity of the militia battalions, hence their popular name of 'Fédérés' – established a provisional authority at the Hôtel de Ville, the city hall. A hostile demonstration by the conservative 'Friends of Order' was easily dispersed by National Guard gunfire on 22 March.

At first a negotiated settlement seemed likely. When the city's *arrondissement* mayors, its National Assembly deputies and the Central Committee all agreed to call elections for 26 March, people across the political spectrum supposed that an elected Parisian council would strike a deal with the Versailles government. Yet although many urged compromise, it is far from clear what it could have consisted of. Even moderates in Paris insisted that Versailles should formally accept the permanence of the Republic and the 'rights of Paris'. But the majority of the National Assembly was royalist, and intent on a restoration. The 'rights of Paris' would mean the city becoming a state within the state, with its own government and army. However reasonable this seemed to many Parisians, the National Assembly would never consent to it willingly. Thiers declared that Paris must be governed 'like Lyons, like Marseilles . . . like the other towns of France . . . there will be only one law, and no privilege . . . any attempted secession . . . will be energetically repressed in France as it has been in America'. On both sides there were loud voices opposing negotiation as a betrayal, all believing that they had might as well as right on their side. Paris had its National Guard, well armed and numerous. Versailles had the regular army, admittedly weak and demoralized, and counted on the support of the majority of the country, and if necessary the Germans.

The Paris elections of 26 March had the unintended consequence of snuffing out the dwindling possibility of compromise. The turnout was reasonable – over a quarter of a million – but many conservatives and moderates had left the city or boycotted the vote. So revolutionaries – veteran democrats from 1848, radical journalists, labour militants, patriotic National Guards – few of whom had held elected office before, won 73 seats to the moderates' 19. This result appeared to consecrate the 18 March insurrection as the culmination of the 'revolutionary tradition' which had revived during the last years of the Second Empire and been amplified by the German siege of Paris. 'The people', and not the political elite, had triumphed after a generation of Bonapartist authoritarianism. Popular patriotism had been victorious in the wake of a shameful surrender by professional politicians and soldiers. The new city council took the revolutionary title of Paris Commune, and was proclaimed amid euphoric scenes on 28 March. All National Guard battalions were ordered to parade at the Hôtel de Ville to make the occasion 'solemn'. The huge cheering, singing and marching crowds believed that 'the Free City of Paris' would begin a new era as a 'democratic and social republic'. Every previous insurrection that had successfully gained control of Paris had gone on to rule France.

Its prospects seemed improved by sympathetic revolts that had already broken out in France's other great cities and in several smaller towns in the southern half of the country, some of which had shown radical reflexes as quick as Paris. At Lyons and Marseilles, Communes were proclaimed on 23 March; at Le Creusot, Saint-Etienne and Narbonne on the 24th; at Toulouse on the 25th. However, in no case did these uprisings last longer than a few days, or even hours. The leaders hesitated to engage in open conflict with the Versailles government, and the rank and file, especially the local National Guard, stayed at home. Thereafter, although the Paris Commune and its supporters continued to call for armed support or at least political intervention from the provincial cities, and even from the countryside, Paris and Versailles were left to fight their duel. There are several reasons for this. The provincial cities lacked the military forces Paris had built up during the German siege. Many republicans were suspicious of Parisian extremism and found themselves genuinely torn between supporting a popular revolution and obeying a government elected by universal suffrage, especially after Thiers assured them that he would safeguard the Republic. Versailles used its legal powers to forbid coordinated action between the various local authorities, and its police hampered efforts by Commune envoys to make their point of view heard.

In the background was a far more powerful and potentially decisive third force: the German army, camped on the outskirts of Paris. The Commune, however anti-German its sentiments and patriotic its origins, was determined not to risk a clash, and assured the Germans of its peaceful intentions. The Versailles government, however eager to sign a peace treaty with Germany, was unwilling to let the Germans interfere in a French quarrel. Consequently, they remained throughout literally as spectators. They occupied the northern and eastern approaches to Paris, so fighting was confined to the western and southern sides. It was also possible to travel to and from Paris by road and rail through the German-occupied sector. Merchandise, letters and foodstuffs circulated. Women, men not of military age and foreigners with passports were able to go in and out of the city fairly easily. They included diplomats, foreign journalists, who sent frequent reports to their newspapers from inside Paris, and Versaillais spies.

Foreigners, whether resident, visiting or observing from afar, maintained at first a certain detachment from what seemed a very French and hence incomprehensible quarrel. The German Chancellor, Bismarck, declared that the Commune's demands for municipal liberties were 'not so unreasonable'. Given expectations of what revolutions were like, this one seemed remarkably calm, even somnolent, at first. Noted one visiting Englishman, 'The first thing that struck me on my arrival was the extreme tranquillity of the streets.' A notable exception to this detachment was Karl Marx, busy in London sending advice to contacts in Paris and formulating reasons why the Commune was an event of historic significance.

The city's tangible calm was partly because much of the administrative machinery ran as usual. It was also because many thousands of middle-class Parisians had left. Others continued to flee, especially men of military age determined to avoid fighting for the Commune or taking the risk of opposing it: some bribed sentries to let them shin down the city ramparts. Others kept off the streets. Consequently, the city centre and residential western quarters were indeed quiet, like 'August of a very hot year', thought Jules de Goncourt, or even, wrote a British visitor, like 'London on a wet Sunday'. Theatres found their usual audiences thin on the ground, and performers turned to running concerts to raise money for the National Guard wounded. A group of National Guard officers and a *Times* correspondent, trying to maintain old-style 'gay Paree' nightlife on the boulevards in May, were arrested by a National Guard patrol and sent to dig trenches. For Marx, this tranquillity was proof of workers' capacity for government, and evidence that criminality had left for Versailles with the bourgeoisie that inspired it.

It is harder to find contemporary impressions of working-class districts where the Commune had most of its supporters. An English journalist, after stressing the emptiness of the city centre, described Montmartre as 'full of life, the shops open, and the streets thronged with women and children' – many men would have been on military duty. At the Place du Trône the usual Gingerbread Fair was held, with 'nearly as many booths as usual, and acrobats, conjurers, fat ladies and other monstrosities were not wanting'.[1]

It is an illusion to think that one can reconstruct a sense of what Paris was 'like', except as a kaleidoscope of individual impressions.[2] It was the best of times, it was the worst of times: exciting and dull; hopeful and frightening; free and oppressive; a time of relative wealth and relative poverty. For many revolutionaries it was the high point of their lives. For businesses it was a time when customers were short: 'We see no one, we sell absolutely nothing,' wrote a draper from the Rue Saint-Denis. For many – both supporters and opponents of the Commune – it was a time of constant worry. For Paris had almost immediately to face a civil war of increasing intensity: this was the dominating fact of life during the Commune. Wary manoeuvres by both sides' troops in the no-man's-land between Paris and Versailles led to skirmishes on 2 April which inaugurated a second siege of seven weeks.

Most of the Commune's economic and social decrees grew out of this emergency, which came on top of the backlog of problems left by the war with Germany. The Commune had urgently to find money to pay the National Guards and meet the large costs of civil war. It had also to deal with problems inherited from the German siege: debt, rent arrears, the pawning of household articles and tools. It encouraged – with some reservations – production of armaments and equipment by workers' cooperatives of men and women. This was seen by some at the time (and by many later commentators) as a social experiment of great significance. It had also to ensure food supplies, though for this it depended both on the confidence of suppliers outside Paris and on the attitude of the Versailles government and the Germans. Although both contemplated imposing a blockade, it was never seriously implemented. Food therefore remained available at only slightly higher prices, and Parisians were not again reduced, as under the German siege, to horsemeat and rats.

The political history of the Commune also revolved round the civil war. Although some ideological and personal divisions existed

---

1. Vizetelly (1914), pp. 183, 178.
2. There is a vast quantity of individual impressions. Vivid accounts by Communards include Barron (1889), Sutter-Laumann (1891), Lissagaray (1886), Allemane (1981), Vallès (1972), Vuillaume (1971) and Brocher (1977). Many of the most picturesque and detailed impressions are from foreign observers writing for a foreign audience: a good guide to these is Horne (1965), and for more sober foreign reactions, Schulkind (1972).

from before 1871, they were exacerbated by the impossible burdens imposed on the Commune leaders. Failure to defeat Versailles – which seemed at first possible – and then realization that the defence of the city was going badly led to a series of replacements, dismissals and resignations to try to shore up a deteriorating military situation. A first Executive Commission appointed on 29 March was replaced by a second on 20 April, and that in turn on 1 May by a first then a second Committee of Public Safety, which was intended to bring dictatorial dynamism to the Commune government. This issue led to the principal political division within the Commune. The Commune's first War Delegate, General Cluseret, was appointed on 3 April when the fighting started to bring professional experience to the National Guard, but when he failed to stem the Versaillais advance he was arrested on 1 May and replaced by another soldier, the youthful Colonel Rossel. He resigned after a few days in office, complaining publicly that 'everyone discusses, no one obeys', and accusing the Commune of being 'the obstacle' because of its 'weakness'. He was replaced by a veteran civilian politician, Charles Delescluze.

Moreover, the Commune's plans to build a democratic political system and carry out social reforms were pushed into the background by military events beyond their control. Serious debates on social affairs were repeatedly interrupted by news of emergencies. Yet much of this was unknown to the general public: Commune debates were not regularly published, and sensitive matters were decided in secret session. Meanwhile, communiqués and press reports continued to announce victories.

At grass-roots level too, especially in the working-class districts where nearly all able-bodied men were in uniform, life was punctuated by military activity: ceremonial parades and flag-raising, band concerts held to raise money for the wounded and dependents, elections of officers, guard duty on public buildings, street patrols and spells in barracks. Drum-calls summoned the men for tours of duty at the ramparts and trenches. Ceremonial funerals of fallen comrades were often attended by large numbers. Heavy casualties, which could weigh unevenly on certain battalions and districts, caused anger and alarm. The surprise night attack on the Moulin Sacquet redoubt on 3 May, in which a large number of Fédérés were slaughtered, caused a horrified reaction in their home districts.

Economic life went on rather as it had for eight months, since the beginning of the German siege. The peacetime economy remained largely suspended, especially building and the skilled manufacturing trades (such as furniture, jewellery, clothing) that were the hallmark of Parisian industry. Most workers (except some employed in the food trades, transport and public utilities) were therefore dependent for their livelihood on National Guard pay of '30 sous' per day and rations, or on employment in war-related industries (making uniforms or munitions); or else they had to scratch a living by a variety of expedients – or leave the city. Popular and accepted though the Commune was at its height, fewer men served as Fédérés than had served against the Germans, and increasing efforts had to be made to muster the troops. Many people decided to keep out of what increasingly seemed a risky adventure. This was confirmed by a low turnout for Commune by-elections on 16 April.

Social life too revolved round politics and war, as it had since the beginning of the German siege. Local political clubs continued to meet in dancehalls, meeting rooms and (as during the 1790s) churches. They outspokenly debated political and social reforms and ways of winning victory. Much of the activity of the Commune was local. Decrees passed centrally had to be left largely to the authorities of the 20 municipal *arrondissements*, their police commissaires and their National Guard legions to execute, often with the intervention of self-appointed activists from local political clubs and committees. Hence, different *quartiers* had very different experiences, depending on the political and social composition of their population, and their proximity to centres of power or to the fighting. There was similar difference in the zeal shown in enrolling men for National Guard service. By May, there were some street roundups of men of military age, and it was probably risky to be seen in the street, especially in working-class districts, not wearing National Guard uniform and moreover not wearing a battalion number on the kepi. Pressure to do one's duty probably always came more effectively from friends and neighbours rather than from the Commune authorities.

Though most activity was local, some events had a city-wide impact. They probably enabled people to form some conception of what the revolution was and how it was developing; and afterwards, by remaining in people's memories, they affected how it was retrospectively understood. The 18 March events, which seemed to show Paris triumphing with ease over its oppressors in an almost bloodless victory, brought crowds out to build barricades and not infrequently to have themselves photographed in groups on top of them triumphantly brandishing their rifles. The proclamation of the Commune on 28 March assembled the largest number of people and has often been interpreted as a symbolic repossession of the city centre by the people of the working-class suburbs. Large concerts given in the Tuileries Palace and gardens, attended by some 15,000 people, showed that the setting of Second Empire court entertainment was now open to the people.

Certain episodes in the civil war had a similarly widespread impact. The first outbreak of fighting in the western suburbs on 2 April brought out crowds of spectators, and thousands of men were involved in a counter-attack on 3 April – a largely spontaneous reaction reminiscent of 18 March. When the civil war became a matter of routine, only occasional striking incidents became matters of general awareness and comment: for example, a ceasefire to evacuate the suburb of Neuilly, brought about by a large demonstration by Freemasons on 29 April, which at first seemed to promise a general end to hostilities; the fall of the key position of Fort Issy on 9 May; and the various arrests and resignations.

But fighting was taking place well outside the city walls, in the western and southern suburbs, and few people seem to have had a clear idea of what was happening. Shells fell only in the largely middle-class and partly evacuated western districts (which suffered far more than during the Prussian siege). The main centres of Communard support were on the other side of the city, and had direct experience of the fighting only when their men served a spell in the trenches. The most easily available news came from the Communard press and from official announcements posted up by the authorities, which were resolutely optimistic. Those sceptical of the official version were painfully aware of how little they knew about what was going on. Letters could still be sent, usually by posting them in the German-occupied suburb of Saint-Denis, but not received inside Paris. It was therefore difficult for those living through it to grasp the experience as a whole, just as it is difficult to summarize it: there was no single shared chronology. Broadly, however, during April it must have seemed that Paris was in no serious danger, whereas from early May onwards there were many signs that the military position was deteriorating.

Acts of ceremonial destruction were staged to signal the defeat – at least symbolic – of the people's enemies, and these became more spectacular as the situation deteriorated and morale needed a boost. On 6 April, National Guards from the La Roquette district burnt the guillotine taken from its shed near the local prison. Several churches were systematically wrecked, mainly by Commune police officials. An exhibition in May at Saint-Laurent church of human remains discovered in the crypt and said to be those of girls raped

and murdered by the priests (see p. 99) – one of several occur-
rences of anticlerical street-theatre – attracted crowds of sightseers.
On 15 May Thiers's house was demolished by decree of the Commune as a reprisal for Versaillais bombardment of the city. On 16
May occurred the most spectacular demolition, which caused world-
wide interest: that of the Vendôme Column, in the centre of the
city, which commemorated Napoleon I's victories. The Commune's
official justification was that it was 'a monument to barbarity [and]
militarism', but it was clearly an expression of the anti-Bonapartism
that had built up during the Second Empire and been confirmed
by the defeat of the imperial army by Germany. After long preparations, the column was pulled over by ropes and winches. Large
crowds turned out and many groups of Fédérés had themselves
photographed posing proudly beside the wreckage. The next day
occurred a no less spectacular demolition, which many suspected
was a Versaillais reprisal: the explosion of a munitions factory at the
Avenue Rapp, near the Seine. The blast was heard throughout the
city and sent up a large mushroom of smoke. This incident – blamed
on Versaillais agents though probably accidental – brought home
to Parisians that the civil war was fast approaching.

Life during the Commune has often been portrayed as either
chaos or festival, which may be different ways of describing the
same things. First, the absence of usual routines linked with work,
due to the suspension of the city's economic life and the subsistence of most of its working-class population on National Guard pay
and rations. Except for usually brief periods of duty, this left most
men with free time for socializing, politics and (an accompaniment
to both) drinking. Second, the weakness or absence of conventional
authority from above, as public order was largely in the hands of the
National Guards themselves and their elected officers. This meant
an overturning of the usual hierarchy: middle-class people could be
ordered around by workers, which sometimes involved harassment
by the officious, the bullying and the drunk. It also meant a much-
criticized level of disorganization and confusion, with a great deal
of arguing and milling around. But it also meant an unprecedented
level of freedom and equality. Third, the decentralization of initiative created a wonderful opportunity for political enthusiasts to make
speeches, to run clubs, committees and newspapers, and to take
practical action – whether starting cooperatives, opening schools or
wrecking churches. Fourth, ignorance of much that was happening
inside and especially outside the city meant that both friends and
enemies of the Commune had little notion of how long it would

last and what the outcome of the conflict might be. For all these reasons, the period from March to May seemed outside normal time. The sentimental way of describing it after the event was as 'le temps des cerises' – 'cherry time' – the title of a song written by a member of the Commune, Jean-Baptiste Clément.

Cherry time came brutally to an end on 21 May, when the first Versaillais troops clambered over the battered south-western ramparts. By the next morning, over 100,000 men had overrun the western districts of the city, capturing thousands of Fédérés almost without resistance. The troops were acclaimed as liberators by throngs of mainly middle-class residents, who showered them with money, food and wine. This was the beginning of what was to be known as 'la semaine sanglante' ('Bloody Week'), the most deadly and destructive few days in the history of Paris, the most ferocious outbreak of civil violence in Europe between the French Revolution of the 1790s and the Bolshevik revolution of 1917, and an episode that would give the Commune a new legend and meaning. From being a rather timid, incompetent and verbose municipal revolution, it became an epic of popular heroism and sacrifice. A sympathetic critic put it bluntly: 'The Commune, which would have sunk amid ridicule, took on a tragic dignity.'[3] In Richard Cobb's memorable phrase, it was like an appalling level-crossing accident at the end of a school outing to the seaside.

The Commune issued on '2 Prairial Year 79' a grandiloquent call to arms:

> The People who dethrone kings, who destroy Bastilles, the people of '89 and '93, the people of the Revolution, cannot lose in a day the fruit of the emancipation of 18 March . . . To arms, then, to arms! Let Paris bristle with barricades, and behind these improvised ramparts let it again shout its war-cry to its enemies, a cry of pride, a cry of defiance, but also a cry of victory: for Paris with its barricades is impregnable.

The response of most Parisians was quite the opposite: to put up the shutters and take shelter in the cellars. But all over the city, National Guard companies did muster whatever men they could – and women too – and began to prepare for the onslaught, building hundreds of barricades. Against them were nearly 130,000 troops drawn up on a continuous front across the city from north to south, and advancing slowly and cautiously from west to east. Thousands

---

3. The radical Henri Maret, in *Revue Blanche*, vol. 12 (1897), p. 261.

died fighting or were summarily shot as rebels captured carrying weapons. Often, being wounded, having a recently fired gun, a bruised right shoulder, gunpowder stains or any other suspicious characteristic meant the same fate.

Partly to block the way of the advancing troops, and also as symbolic acts of defiance, the Fédérés began to set buildings on fire: the Tuileries, the Palais Royal and the Louvre, symbols of monarchy; the Prefecture of Police and the Palais de Justice, symbols of oppression; Notre Dame, symbol of superstition; the Ministry of Finance, symbol of the fiscal power of the state; the Legion of Honour building, symbol of official status. Banks, shops and factories were left alone. The Hôtel de Ville itself, headquarters of the Commune and symbol of the power of the people of Paris, was burnt to prevent its capture, a gesture of defiance and an admission of irremediable defeat. The blaze in the centre of the city was visible from 20 miles away. It made an unforgettable impression on those who saw it. Remembered an American girl, 'I was often frightened during the Commune, but I do not remember anything more terrifying than the fires.'[4] Most of the Louvre and the Palais Royal were saved by advancing troops. Notre Dame was saved by a local Fédéré battalion. The Sainte-Chapelle (in the Palais de Justice) survived by chance. The Tuileries, the Hôtel de Ville and the rest were gutted. These huge fires caused panic on both sides.

Rumours spread that the Communards had planned to destroy the whole city, and that women fire-raisers – *pétroleuses* – were burning private houses. This – along with pent-up fear and anger the Commune had inspired over the previous weeks – led to an even more savage reaction against Communard prisoners and suspects. Neighbours denounced each other to the troops; landlords denounced tenants, and shopkeepers customers. Convoys of Fédéré prisoners were mobbed as they were marched off to Versailles. Thousands were shot on capture or after hasty court martial. Some Fédérés also shot some prisoners – most famously the Archbishop of Paris – in reprisal for the Versaillais carnage, and also, as with the material symbols, as an act of despairing defiance and posthumous vengeance.

The last few thousand combatants were surrounded in the working-class eastern districts. Those who tried to escape through the German lines beyond the eastern ramparts were turned back. Fighting fizzled out in the late afternoon of 28 May, though mass

4. *Macmillan's Magazine*, vol. 45 (1892), p. 66.

execution of prisoners in public parks, behind prison walls and most notoriously in the Père Lachaise cemetery against the 'Fédérés' Wall', continued for some days. In these eastern districts, the lives of thousands of families were devastated by death and imprisonment; even the Versaillais authorities, however unsympathetic, were forced to provide food for hungry children whose parents had been killed or captured. Elsewhere in the city, a kind of normality was quick to return. Thomas Cook organized trips to view the ruins. Goncourt noted on 6 June that on the boulevards 'crowds reappear [and] for the first time it begins to be difficult to make your way through the lounging of the men and the solicitation of the women'.[5]

The following chapters try to explain different aspects of this unique episode, the biggest popular insurrection in modern European history, and which came to epitomize 'revolution' as a spontaneous popular act. Chapters 1 and 2 explore the origins of the Commune as a Parisian event, and as a consequence of war. Chapter 3 examines how the Commune worked as a government. Chapter 4 looks at different ways of identifying its supporters, their reasons for participating and their understanding of what was happening. Chapter 5 examines how, and how effectively, the Commune mobilized its partisans for war, and why people were willing to risk their lives in the conflict. Chapter 6 discusses how the Commune has been remembered and interpreted. Running through them all is a common theme: the place of the Commune in the history of revolutions, and how from these various viewpoints it might have been a turning point, or more precisely a number of different turning points. For, to use Jacques Rougerie's metaphor, 1871 may have been both dusk and dawn.[6]

5. Goncourt (1978), p. 315.   6. Rougerie (1964), p. 241 and (1971), p. 6.

CHAPTER ONE

Paris, Bivouac of the Revolution

Paris in the era of Revolutions, 1789–1871

Whatever conclusions we shall reach about the meaning of the Commune in European and even world history, our starting point is its significance as the final episode in the cycle of political conflict that centred on Paris between 14 July 1789, when the Bastille was stormed, and 28 May 1871, when, a mile and a half to the north, the last Communard combatants were killed, captured or dispersed. Contemporaries were perfectly conscious of continuities from the past. The very name 'Commune' echoes the revolutionary Paris city government of 1792, as that of Fédérés (commonly given to the Communard National Guards) recalls their revolutionary predecessors; keen revolutionaries in 1871 adopted the 1793 revolutionary calendar, which placed them in Year 79; and the Commune's most open ideological split occurred over whether to set up a Committee of Public Safety inspired by that of 1793.

Paris had been a political powder-keg since the middle of the eighteenth century. First, the basic, age-old difficulty was supplying food to an outsize urban population when transport was slow and surplus agricultural production unreliable: dear bread meant trouble. This was only, and incompletely, solved in the middle of the nineteenth century by railways, commercial development and agricultural improvements: the price of bread was still in the 1860s a matter of serious concern to governments as well as consumers. Second, it was materially very difficult to maintain order among a mobile, growing and sometimes turbulent population. The civilian police force was much smaller than in London until the mid-1850s, and its back-up forces could do more harm than good: the part-time

National Guard was less than wholly reliable, and to use regular troops was to risk inflaming the situation.

Third was the element that distinguished Paris from other large cities, its unique political significance. During the eight decades that followed the fall of the Bastille, Paris was the arena in which the outcome of France's internal struggles had repeatedly been decided by fighting in the streets. There were several reasons for the capital's primacy. Political power had been concentrated there since the king and National Assembly had been forcibly brought from Versailles in October 1789. To this was added the centralization of administration carried out by the First Republic and Napoleon I. Cultural life, including publishing, the theatre and the visual arts, was largely Parisian. It was the national information centre from which books and newspapers went out to inform and instruct *la province*: 'opinion is made in Paris,' wrote Balzac; 'it is manufactured with ink and paper'. Paris enjoyed exceptional economic and cultural importance as France's only very large centre of population. By 1850 it contained 1.2 million people, more than the other 14 large towns combined, and it accounted for one-quarter of the country's total wealth.

Consequently, since 1789 it had acquired an ascendancy, paralleled in no other country, as a huge permanent constituent assembly, a collective sovereign, which claimed the right to decide in times of crisis the political destiny of the nation, as it had done in August 1792, July 1830 and February 1848 by dethroning three kings. A large part of its population over several generations had thus become aware of and actively involved in political life, often in its most dramatic forms: demonstrating, barricading streets, fighting the police and army, forcing their way into palaces and parliaments, chasing out or installing governments.

Who composed Paris's population? Nearly two-thirds worked in industry and commerce. In the 1860s there were over 450,000 male and female manual workers, 120,000 white-collar workers, 140,000 employers (mainly self-employed master-craftsmen and shopkeepers) and 100,000 servants. In all, more than one-fifth of all French workers were concentrated in Paris.[1] It was France's largest industrial centre, specializing in highly skilled craft manufacture (furniture, clothing, jewellery, printing, machine making), its largest permanent building site (which drew in locksmiths, masons, carpenters and labourers) and its largest commercial centre, employing an army of shopkeepers, clerks, merchants, brokers and transport workers. Economic

1. Statistics in Rougerie (1988), p. 12.

fluctuations therefore caused bankruptcy, unemployment, hardship and discontent on a huge scale. A relatively high proportion of these small businessmen, self-employed artisans, skilled journeymen and white-collar workers were literate and politically aware, solidly organized and determined to defend their craft interests and political rights, making probably the largest concentration of political activity anywhere in the world.

It seemed clear to contemporaries – and it has been broadly confirmed by historical research – who composed the active revolutionary force in Paris: ordinary working people. Although other groups tried to get involved, usually as would-be leaders – including politicians, journalists, intellectuals, even students – the great majority of those who fought, were killed or wounded, received medals in case of success or were prosecuted in case of failure were skilled male workers in their twenties and thirties, including white-collar workers and independent craftsmen or shopkeepers. As we shall see in detail in chapter 4, this was as true in 1871 as in 1848 or 1830.

However, agreement about who the revolutionaries were did not prevent disagreement, among contemporaries and historians, as to their motives. Sympathizers saw them as naturally virtuous and patriotic fighters for liberty, uncorrupted by 'bourgeois' vices. Conservatives saw them as the 'dangerous classes', idle, drunken and criminal, always on the lookout for an excuse to plunder. Many Marxists (though not Marx) have searched for signs that they were the embryo of a new 'proletariat' from the most modern and large-scale industries, fighting a class war against the capitalist bourgeoisie. Republicans of the time, and republican historians since, have seen them essentially as citizens fighting for political rights, the vanguard of a historic trend towards a Republic. Social historians have tended to stress poverty, unemployment, harsh living conditions and the decline of traditional craft industry leading to class consciousness. Recent urban sociologists have focused on the effects of the sweeping urban changes of the 1860s. Some feminist historians have seen the women who played a much-noticed part in revolt at certain moments as claiming an aggressive, new and consciously political role in a previously male preserve.

There have, then, been many hypotheses to explain the high level of politicization and radicalization of the Parisian people. Before considering them further, we should discard some of the simplest, seemingly common-sense, arguments. For example, if we assume that city life, with its relative freedom from constraint and openness to ideas, somehow naturally or inevitably creates radical and republican sympathies, we would face the question of why the inhabitants of all other great industrializing cities, whether in Europe then or in the developing world today, have not been equally rebellious. If we stress the hardship of Parisian workers as a cause of their militancy, we would face the problem that they were relatively well off by the standards of their own time or even by those of Third World cities today. We are, in short, attempting to explain a very unusual, probably unique, history.

It has often been suggested that a fundamental cause of Parisian radicalism was a long-drawn-out decline in the city's speciality, artisan industry: that capitalism, foreign competition, mechanization, commercialization and division of labour were causing a devaluation of craft skills, and a creeping 'proletarianization'. Christopher Johnson argued this in the case of tailoring: ready-made clothing using semi-skilled labour was undermining the prosperity and status of highly skilled bespoke tailors, hence their prominence in the socialist experiments of 1848.[2] However, this can be disputed as a general explanation of Parisian militancy. As Tony Judt and Lenard Berlanstein have pointed out, in few areas could machinery or unskilled labour replace the work of the Parisian worker elite. The traditional crafts continued to flourish, while industrialization opened up well-paid skilled occupations in new expanding industries such as engineering.[3]

Rather than simple decline and proletarianization, it seems likely that, within the traditional craft industries, there was an unremitting attempt to keep up with commercial competition by reorganizing, increasing productivity and cutting costs, and that this was a recurring cause of friction between large and small producers, between merchants and subcontractors, between employers and employees, and between men and women. This in its turn gave rise to tensions between the State and the various interest groups, which demanded assistance (such as wage guarantees or bans on machinery) or at least benevolent neutrality (especially by permitting workers' organizations and strikes). The inability of governments to control economic change and satisfy the often conflicting demands of discontented groups led many workers and small businessmen into opposition to a succession of regimes, seen as at best inadequate and at worst unjust and hostile to their needs.

The very high level of skill and literacy of many of these workers, and their craft *esprit de corps*, buttressed by strong family and corporate traditions, strengthened their defence of their status, economic

2. Johnson (1975).   3. Judt (1986); Berlanstein (1984).

independence and collective control over their craft. This often meant political demands for cheap credit and other forms of assistance for independent craftsmen, or alternatively (not necessarily very different in practice) inspired a concept of non-authoritarian decentralized socialist 'association', meaning independent producers' cooperatives regulated by workers themselves and protected by the State. This vision was most influentially expounded by Pierre-Joseph Proudhon in the 1840s and '50s, and his influence remained strong after his death in 1865. Briefly, during the Second Republic in 1848, an attempt had been made to introduce such a system. Skilled workers' strong sense of their own worth as citizens and 'producers', attachment to self-help, thirst for practical education and belief in social and scientific 'progress' also caused them to sympathize with democratic and, particularly from 1848 onwards, with anti-clerical and radical republican politics, which expounded those same values.

Parisian radicalism was certainly intensified by economic circumstances. Rising food prices were crucial in the 1790s. Former soldiers, probably many of them out of work, were active in 1815 and 1830. Printers, their jobs threatened by new press censorship, were the first to demonstrate in 1830. Severe economic crisis in the late 1840s, blamed on the 'bourgeois' government's encouragement of speculative investment, brought the overthrow of the July Monarchy in February 1848 and the proclamation of the Second Republic. Unemployed workers revolted in June 1848. These 'June Days', the biggest insurrection Paris had yet seen and in some ways similar (as contemporaries realized) to the Commune, broke out when the National Workshops – a large job-creation scheme with socialist overtones – were closed down by a suspicious and cash-strapped government. Thousands of workers fought, motivated by economic need and also by a sense of political betrayal. They were crushed by the army and the pro-government National Guard in the worst and bloodiest defeat of the Paris Left so far. Many hundreds were killed and 5,000 prisoners were transported to the colonies.

Economic grievances are not alone sufficient to explain popular revolt, however. None of these events were merely hunger riots. The participants were not the poorest and hungriest people. Economic grievances had to be seen as having political causes and political remedies, rather than being merely acts of God: otherwise, why blame a government for harvest failures or trade recessions? When mass revolt occurred, as in Paris in 1830 and 1848, and in Lyons in 1834 – it was always against governments seen as indifferent to the economic welfare of ordinary people, and in response to government actions seen as oppressive and unjust.

The State – its laws, its actions – was always the main catalyst of Parisian radicalism. The Revolution had abolished craft guilds and forbidden workers' associations in the name of liberty, equality and fraternity. William Sewell and Roger V. Gould have argued that corporate craft traditions nevertheless survived clandestinely, often masquerading as friendly societies. These were able to enforce closed shops, make collective agreements and organize strikes.[4] Governments often tolerated, or were unable to prevent, this activity. But in times of economic crisis, political instability or open labour militancy, successive governments, fearing sedition and revolution, repressed workers' organizations, arrested leaders, broke up meetings and protected strike-breakers. These repeated and often violent clashes with the State tended to push workers into opposition, and even towards revolutionary utopianism. This radicalization of workers is particularly clear in the 1830s and '40s, when disillusioned workers in Paris and other cities such as Lyons moved from support for the new 'citizen king' Louis-Philippe to republicanism, Bonapartism and socialism.

Yet these circumstances, paralleled in other cities and countries, seem inadequate fully to explain Paris's unique political history. There remains the cultural dimension: ideas, expectations, loyalties, resentments and patterns of behaviour learnt and transmitted within the Parisian population over several generations, which François Furet has summed up as 'a tremendous over-investment in politics'.[5] The repeated experience of revolution from 1789 onwards, far from invariably positive but on the contrary marked by frequent suffering, repression and disappointment, had nevertheless implanted the idea of the possibility of change through popular political action, and created a repertory of ideas, language, actions and symbols through which revolutionary aspirations could be expressed. No regime was regarded as legitimate or permanent. In short, Parisians knew that revolution was possible, and knew how to carry it out. Although not all Parisians, or even Parisian workers, were revolutionaries, there were always a few thousand who did support revolutionary groups, either secretly under government repression, or publicly when political life was freer, as in 1848 and the late 1860s.

Revolutionary action came to follow a familiar ritual, in the same places, with the same sequence of symbolic acts. Crowds would gather

4. Sewell (1980); Gould (1995).   5. Feher (1990), p. 176.

in the streets, with spontaneous speeches, marches and banners. Police and troops would sooner or later try to disperse them, often half-heartedly. Stones would be thrown, and then – often a fateful moment – shots fired. Then church bells would be tolled and drums beaten to call people to arms; bodies of victims might be paraded through the streets. There would be attacks on gunsmiths' shops and police posts to seize arms. Barricades, from 1830 onwards the unmistakable symbol of insurrection, would be hastily thrown up using paving stones, upturned carts, trees, old furniture, 'the people's castoffs', in Victor Hugo's words, 'that door! that grating! that awning! that doorframe! that broken stove! that cracked stewpot!' Barricades set the scene for serious conflict, as happened in 1827, 1830, 1832, 1834, 1839, 1848, 1849, 1851 – and of course 1871. The outcome would be decided by the reaction of the army and the Paris National Guard, a part-time citizens' militia recruited mostly among the middle classes, though expanded to include workers in times of crisis in 1814, 1830, 1848 and 1870. If the National Guard sided with the insurgents, the army and police would be unwilling, and perhaps unable, to deal with the uprising. Once the forces of order gave way, the revolutionary crowd would go on the offensive, attacking and occupying the centres and symbols of political power: the Château des Tuileries, the royal residence; the Palais Bourbon, the parliament building; and the Hôtel de Ville, seat of the Paris city government, where, at the heart of Parisian popular power, would-be leaders presented themselves for the revolutionary crowd's approval.

Those on the Left applauded the leading role of 'the sacred city', the 'beacon' of progress, 'the intellectual, moral and political centre of France' where 'the sovereign [i.e. the people] resides'. Conservatives, on the other hand, feared and even hated Paris as the political volcano, the lair of the mob, the usurper of national sovereignty: 'ten times in eighty years Paris has sent France governments ready made, by telegraph', protested an angry royalist deputy in 1871. Although the rest of the country usually followed Paris's lead, often joyfully, if Paris went too far the provinces might rebel. The 1790s had seen serious revolts in the west and the south. Within living memory the workers' uprising in June 1848 had caused a mass mobilization of National Guards in the provinces who had marched on the capital to crush 'the Reds'. June was followed by a long period of repression culminating in Louis-Napoleon Bonaparte's *coup d'état* of December 1851. Though this saw short but bloody fighting in the streets of Paris, and a sizeable uprising in the south of France, the coup was approved by a large majority of French voters. And a majority in the provinces consistently thereafter supported the authoritarian but populist Second Empire.

Revolutionary Paris, then, had been crushed militarily and defeated politically, losing control even of its own municipal government, placed in the hands of appointed prefects. From 1848 onwards there was an open gulf between Paris, mostly left-wing in sympathy, and small-town and rural France, in majority conservative. As one provincial newspaper wrote in 1848, 'Paris must finally realize that it is only one-thirty-sixth of France, and that the provinces, while they look to it for a lead, will not leave in its hands a tyrant's sceptre or a slave-driver's rod.'[6]

Did 1848–51, when the silent majority in the provinces defeated the Parisian Left, mark the real end of the capital's era of revolutions? Parisian rebels had managed to overturn unpopular and undemocratic monarchies in 1792, 1830 and 1848, but had failed to resist democratically elected governments in June 1848 and December 1851. Did this show that the political predominance of Paris had been ended by universal male suffrage, which favoured conservatives and buttressed the self-confidence of those in power? (As Louis-Philippe put it bluntly, republics could shoot people.) If so, the 1871 Commune must appear as an anachronism, an accident of circumstances. But several historians and sociologists have argued on the contrary that the startling reemergence in the 1860s of violent left-wing opposition to the Empire showed that another inevitable explosion of the Parisian volcano was on the way. And, moreover, that this revitalized radicalism was a symptom of a new urban society.

Paris, 'capital of the nineteenth century'

Between the revolutionary episode of 1848–51 and that of 1870–71, the city underwent an unprecedented transformation in its physical and social geography, its economic life and its population. This created the physical, social and political setting for the Commune. It created discontents and political demands that contributed to a revival of radical republicanism in the 1860s and influenced the Commune's programme. Was the Commune then a symptom of cultural and social modernity, one of the ways in which Paris was

6. Vidalenc (1948), p. 84.

showing itself to be, in the much-repeated phrase of the Marxist theorist Walter Benjamin, 'the capital of the nineteenth century'?

'HAUSSMANNIZATION' AND ITS EFFECTS

Louis-Napoleon Bonaparte, later Napoleon III, was a visionary, and one of his visions was a new Paris. He was influenced by the absolutist tradition of prestige building that has adorned or disfigured Paris from François I to François Mitterrand. The actions and projects of his uncle Napoleon I had stimulated his ambitions. He was also impressed by the projects of the Saint-Simonian socialists for state-led economic modernization and grandiose engineering projects, and he certainly wished to buttress his power by creating prosperity in the wake of the economic collapse of the late 1840s. His years of exile in London had contributed more down-to-earth ideas about sewerage, traffic and parks.

Old Paris, partly medieval and with its layout determined by a series of successively demolished city walls, was cramped, often stinking, undrained, unhealthy, short of water, labyrinthine and difficult to cross. The poor physical condition of the city had long seemed to require action, and there had been plans for sweeping change from the Revolution onwards. But no government had done more than tinker. Napoleon III had the vision and the dictatorial power to dare to undertake the wholesale remodelling of a huge and ancient city, an enterprise unequalled until the era of Mussolini and Stalin. His chosen agent was Georges Haussmann, a ruthless and ambitious official not overburdened by scruple and described by an appreciative contemporary as 'like a large feline'. He ran Paris as Prefect of the Seine from 1853 to 1869.

The plan, Jeanne Gaillard tells us, was essentially political, not merely an 'innocent enterprise' of public health, urban renovation, job creation or profit. It was intended, above all, 'to make an ungovernable city governable'.[7] It aimed to extinguish Paris's insurgent embers as part of Napoleon III's broader ambition of ending the era of revolutions: to make it penetrable, controllable, healthier and more prosperous. The swarming bazaar-like city centre, so prone to turbulence and whose narrow streets facilitated barricade building, was physically pushed back from the government buildings which

---

7. Gaillard (1977), p. 2. The question of the political and strategic elements in Napoleon's thinking has long been debated. I have followed Gaillard's view; Pinkney (1958), however, argues that the main intention was more benign.

had proved so vulnerable to crowd invasion. Broad new streets such
as the Rue de Rivoli and the Boulevard de Sébastopol were driven
through. Slums were levelled, including practically the whole of the
Ile de la Cité, and their population dispersed. Much of the centre of
the city became an administrative enclave: the Tuileries, the Louvre,
the Hôtel de Ville, the Palais de Justice and the Prefecture of Police
were surrounded by open spaces, easily reached by reinforcements,
as military experts had advised as early as the 1830s. Massive barracks
were built at sensitive points. Trouble spots such as the Faubourg
Saint-Antoine, a centre of revolt from 1789 to 1848, were surrounded
by new straight avenues to facilitate the movement and deployment
of troops. The aim was (in the words of the 1858 law) 'to assure wide,
direct and multiple communications between the main parts of the
capital and the military bases destined to protect them'.[8] The revolutionary conflicts of 1848 had shown that the problem concerned
the whole city and its suburbs, and so in 1860 the suburban villages
inside the city's military defences were annexed, and the enlarged
Paris divided into 20 administrative *arrondissements* (Figure 1.1).

Napoleon and Haussmann were following a strategy that was
also social and economic. They wanted to reduce the population of
the city centre. So the central markets were moved north, and local
markets set up further out. Railway stations, unlike in London, were
deliberately built away from the centre. A road system – 485 miles
of new or widened roads – was built to encourage the movement
of business and settlement to the less developed outskirts. Large
industry was encouraged to move out of the city, and in the late
1860s Haussmann introduced tax changes to penalize those who
failed to take the point.

The pill was sugared in several ways. The city did need renovation as its population and industry grew. Better communications,
wider streets, parks, sewerage and more and cleaner water were easy
to justify, especially as here Paris lagged behind London. Moreover,
the aesthetic of Haussmannization was impressive, if banal: the long
wide avenues, the regular lines of buildings, the broad squares, the
carefully calculated vistas, the grandiose monuments. As a symbol
of a powerful, brutally modern regime, its impact was undeniable.
A few malcontents – romantics, antiquarians, poets – criticized its
'Americanized' flashiness. As Baudelaire lamented: 'Le vieux Paris
n'est plus (la forme d'une ville change plus vite, hélas! que le coeur
d'un mortel).'

8. Gaillard (1977), p. 38.

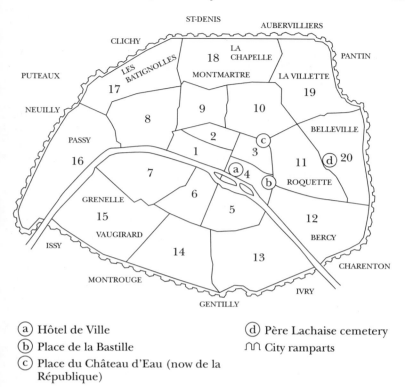

ST-DENIS

AUBERVILLIERS

CLICHY

LA
18   CHAPELLE

PANTIN

PUTEAUX

LES
BATIGNOLLES

MONTMARTRE   LA VILLETTE

17

NEUILLY

8

9   10

19

PASSY

2

BELLEVILLE

1

3

16

7

4

11   20

ROQUETTE

GRENELLE

6

5

15

12

VAUGIRARD

BERCY

ISSY

14

13

CHARENTON

MONTROUGE

IVRY

GENTILLY

ⓐ Hôtel de Ville   ⓓ Père Lachaise cemetery
ⓑ Place de la Bastille   ⌒⌒ City ramparts
ⓒ Place du Château d'Eau (now de la
   République)

Figure 1.1   *Paris after 1860 (showing the 20 arrondissements)*

The economic consequences of Haussmannization were two-edged: there were benefits but also costs. It created a huge number of jobs: by the 1860s, 20 per cent of Paris workers were to some extent involved. It provided big profits to landowners, developers, speculators and investors. Commerce and craft industry also grew, and wages rose. Chronic pauperism was reduced. Families may have become a little more stable. Health improved because of better water supply and a less polluting sewerage system. Some physical conditions improved, with public parks opened in working-class districts, and new housing which could not fail to be an improvement on the delapidated medieval slums that had been demolished. But rents and prices shot up. There was more food available than ever, but at higher prices, as subsidized bread was phased out and cheap street traders were regulated. Eventually, Haussmannization had to be paid for: the total cost of 2.5 billion francs (45 times the city's total annual spending in mid-century) had to be covered through higher land values, rents and taxes. The *octroi*, a municipal excise duty on goods entering the city, was extended to coal and raw materials, which hit small as well as large firms, and their workers. In the late 1860s, its abolition became a major opposition demand. Pressure for wages to keep up with prices led to a sharp increase in strikes. When some of the secrets of Haussmann's creative accountancy began to be discovered, leading to his removal in 1869, the result was a slowdown in public works which caused its own problems for the greatly expanded building industry. What all the grievances boiled down to in political terms, and what all the opposition groups could agree on, was a demand for democratic control of municipal city government, with the prefect, the emperor's agent, being replaced by an elected city council. As Gaillard summarizes it, there was resentment of the authoritarian nature of the Empire's treatment of Paris, and a feeling of dispossession, when people were forced out of a city that was no longer theirs, and in which rights of citizenship had been lost. This is certainly one of the reasons why opposition to the Empire reemerged in the new Paris of the 1860s. It also explains in part why the radical Left, who were later to lead the Commune, made municipal self-government such a prominent part of their programme. Haussmann, as Gaillard sums it up, had transformed the city in order to transform its people, but had ended up by rejuvenating republicanism.[9]

A feature of the new Paris was the mushrooming of peripheral districts for people who had left or been forced out of the old city centre, or had immigrated from the provinces and abroad drawn by jobs and high wages: more than half the population had been born outside the city. On the western side, these districts could be quiet and suburban, such as Passy and Auteuil, or metropolitan and opulent, such as the districts round the Place de l'Etoile, the new Parc Monceau or the refurbished 'grands boulevards', perfect for the ostentatious display of wealth and status. At the other extreme were industrial and working-class districts round the eastern, northern and southern fringes of the city, with cheap housing, workshops, railway yards, docks, warehouses and factories: these were districts such as Montmartre, La Chapelle, La Villette, Belleville, Charonne and Grenelle, annexed to the city in 1860 and forming the 12th to 15th and the 18th to 20th *arrondissements*. They bore the usual marks

9. Ibid., p. 334.

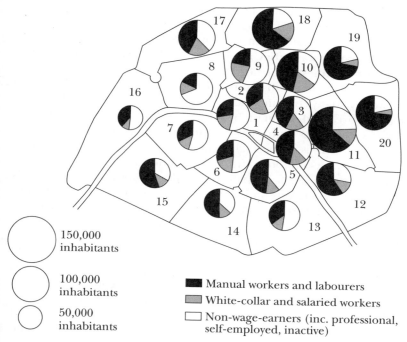

150,000 inhabitants

100,000 inhabitants

50,000 inhabitants

■ Manual workers and labourers

▨ White-collar and salaried workers

☐ Non-wage-earners (inc. professional, self-employed, inactive)

Figure 1.2   *Social geography of Haussmann's Paris*
Source: Rougerie (1971), p. 18

of urban poverty: high rates of tuberculosis, pauperism, illiteracy and illegitimacy. (See Figure 1.2.)

The new Paris was thus more socially segregated than the old, where it had been common for different social classes to occupy different floors of the same building – the richest on the first floor, the poorest in the garrets. A good deal of mixing did still survive, especially in the centre (where it could still be seen until very recently), because Haussmann's new streets and buildings were often façades imperfectly concealing an older and denser urban fabric of alleys and courtyards still containing workshops and cheap lodgings. Even in the outer districts suburban 'villages' such as Belleville, Ménilmontant and Charonne remained, their gardens and lanes hemmed in by the new expanses of brick and plaster. Nevertheless, the change was great. In much of western Paris the only workers were servants or others in service trades. In the eastern and northern *arrondissements* there was practically no bourgeoisie: there were fewer than 1,000 dwellings renting at over 1,000 francs per year (roughly the cost of a five-roomed flat) among a population of several hundred thousand.[10]

What was the consequence of embodying class divisions in bricks and mortar? It was surely not unique to Paris, being more marked in industrial cities in the north and east of France, and, indeed, was a feature of nineteenth-century urban growth from San Francisco to Sydney. Many contemporaries and later historians have described it as a source of discontent, being perceived as enforced exile from the city centre to drab, poorly equipped 'Siberias', short of basic amenities such as schools, churches and piped water, and a cause of long journeys on foot to work. After annexation in 1860, the cost of living in these outer districts rose, as the *octroi* was now levied. This was especially onerous on basic necessities such as food, drink and fuel, which increased by some 20 per cent, and this removed the main advantage of living in the peripheral districts. Yet we should not exaggerate the extent of this upheaval. The population of the old central districts had fallen only by about 30,000 by 1861. Those who did move did not move far, and if they continued to work in the central districts where craft manufacture was concentrated they can in most cases only have been a fairly short walk away.

Exile from the centre to the periphery was not the main social effect of Haussmannization. A more important consequence was the arrival of immigrants, mainly from northern France, who constituted most of the inhabitants of the outer *arrondissements*. Most Communards – as many as 70 per cent overall – were immigrants, and we must take account of this as a fundamental element of their experience. Allner's sample of 'Jacobin' Communards shows that 80 per cent were immigrants, typically arriving in their late twenties in the second half of the 1850s, skilled workers attracted by the economic expansion of the city, but also subject to its high cost of living and, during the late 1860s, bearing the brunt of economic slowdown, bankruptcy and unemployment – which was blamed on the Empire. They also brought with them their own political traditions: in Louis Chevalier's view, the Parisian revolutionary tradition was fuelled during the 1850s and '60s by political ideas exported from Paris generations earlier and brought back again by worker and peasant immigrants. Workers at the Cail engineering works – one of the city's few large factories – were overwhelmingly immigrants, with few connections with traditional Paris radicalism and more aware of struggles in the provinces.[11]

10. Ibid., p. 84.
11. Allner (1978), p. 232; Chevalier (1950), p. 15; Gaillard (1960–61), p. 37.

Geographical segregation conditioned political activity and organization. When in the 1860s the Empire became less restrictive, and began to permit open political activity, it found that it had very few supporters or intermediaries in huge areas of the city, which proved to be fertile soil for left-wing opposition politics. As we shall see below, it was in Belleville and La Villette that large and turbulent public meetings became a feature of popular politics in 1868–69, and where serious riots accompanied the elections of 1869 and 1870. Segregation also affected the imagination: political and social conflict was seen in spatial terms. In the 1840s writers such as Eugène Suë and Victor Hugo had imagined a secret and threatening life existing within or below the visible city, in garrets, cellars and sewers; and Alexis de Tocqueville in 1848 had imagined that 'the spirit of insurrection . . . had penetrated into our houses, around, above, below us'. During the 1860s, the threat seemed to be outside, surrounding the city on the high ground of Montmartre, Belleville and Ménilmontant, from where it might 'descend' to assault the cleaned, modernized and policed city below.

AN URBAN REVOLUTION?

How do we fit Haussmannization into the history of the Commune? The answer is not obvious. We might conclude that it must have failed in its main purpose of making Paris 'governable', because the Commune happened. Or we might conclude, on the contrary, that Haussmann had succeeded in making it more difficult for revolt to break out or to succeed, because the Commune was defeated. But either conclusion would leave unanswered the more precise question of exactly what political effects Haussmannization produced, and how these might have contributed to the Commune. Three urban sociologists, Manuel Castells, David Harvey and Roger V. Gould, have attempted to theorize this question with a view to explaining the Commune as essentially an urban revolution of a new type: 'The largest urban revolution in modern history occurred on the heels of the first experiment with urban planning in an industrial city.'[12] But while all place Haussmannization and the specific conditions of the transformed city at the forefront of their analysis of the Commune – unlike historians, who typically regard it as merely one of several causes, and not the most important – they adopt very different approaches and reach contrasting conclusions.

12. Gould (1995), p. 9.

Harvey attempts to reconcile a Marxist approach with urban theory, combining the concepts of class and of community: he calls the Commune 'the greatest class-based communal uprising in capitalist history'.[13] He argues that the Empire, 'a form of national socialism', had fundamentally economic motives in undertaking the transformation of Paris. It aimed to solve the economic crisis caused by 'overaccumulation' of capital by 'primitive Keynesianism' to absorb surplus capital and labour. The principal effect of Haussmannization was therefore to 'make [Paris] a city in which the circulation of capital became the real imperial power'.[14] He stresses class conflict as the key consequence of Haussmann's undermining of 'traditional notions of community' and craft industry by favouring finance capital and big business over small commerce and industry. Paris workers had become 'a rather more conventional sort of proletariat' engaged in direct confrontation with bosses, and the outcome was 'the fierce class struggles fought out in Paris between 1868 and 1871'.[15]

Very different is Castells's interpretation, influenced by the sociologist Henri Lefebvre, who saw the Commune as the recapture of Haussmann's city by its own dispossessed people.[16] For Castells, class conflict is not the issue: indeed, 'most social movements are not class struggles'. The Commune was essentially an *urban* revolution, that is, the revolt of the population of a city, sharing a 'particular political culture'.[17] The Communards, men and women, identified themselves first as Parisians, not proletarians. They fought to defend the rights of the city against external attackers and to defend their interests against everyday urban antagonists – not capitalists, but landlords, policemen, priests. In short, the Commune was the struggle of the inhabitants of Paris to determine its 'urban meaning':[18] would the city – including the physical forms of its buildings and streets – be shaped to work in their interests (for example, with cheap, conveniently placed housing) or those of speculators, landlords and the State (expensive housing and shops, spaces for bourgeois display, prestige monuments)? For Castells, the crucial issues at stake were those of everyday urban life. Some of this fits the evidence, as we shall see. But as a total explanation it leads to absurdly reductionist conclusions: that the Commune was 'the most repressed rent strike in history', and its defeat left Paris with 'the most permanent housing crisis of all Western capitals'.[19]

13. Harvey (1985), p. 154.   14. Ibid., pp. 67, 77, 76.   15. Ibid., pp. 161–2.
16. Lefebvre (1965).   17. Castells (1983), pp. 26, 25.
18. Ibid., pp. 302, 333.   19. Ibid., pp. 23, 26.

Gould's book is the most ambitious and iconoclastic interpretation, and moreover seeks to make its case by detailed research, unlike Castells and Harvey, who simply reinterpret, occasionally in slightly garbled form, data provided by Rougerie and Gaillard. Gould's most challenging assertions specifically contest both what he calls the 'humanist' view (held by Lefebvre, Castells and also to some extent by Rougerie and Gaillard) that 'Haussmannization' was a cause of the Commune because it dispossessed the ordinary people of their city and exiled them to a bleak and alienating periphery, and also the Marxist view (held by Harvey and in some form by many historians) that Haussmannization increased class identity and class tension, leading to the Commune understood fundamentally as a class conflict.

Arguing against the 'humanist' view, Gould contends that the new peripheral districts were neither lacking in community, nor were they working-class ghettos. He argues that a study of marriage records in the 19th and 20th *arrondissements* shows (in summary) that, compared with the old city-centre districts, marriages between neighbours were common, and that marriage witnesses were also frequently neighbours from different social classes: three-quarters of working-class couples had 'middle-class' or 'bourgeois' witnesses to their marriages. In the older Paris, social life was more restricted to people in the same trade and social status. He concludes that 'life on the periphery was not characterized by a loss of community, but by a substitution of neighbourhood bonds for communities based on the world of work'.[20] He also argues that class conflict was not evidently increasing as a consequence of the economic modernization of Paris: labour militancy was strongest not in new industries but in the traditional skilled crafts, especially when these were concentrated in old central Paris. Furthermore, labour militancy did not represent itself as class conflict, but rather as the defence of corporate interest and solidarity within a single trade.

The evidence presented in support of these challenging suggestions is arguably not strong enough to prove the case,[21] but they are certainly stimulating hypotheses. The main implications are important: that the new communities of the peripheral districts, less fragmented by old divisions of class and craft, were 'available for a different kind of radical activity . . . framed by a different collective identity'.[22] This local community solidarity and Parisian identity

20. Gould (1995), p. 90.   21. For a discussion, see Tombs (1997).
22. Gould (1995), p. 121.

Gould sees as the social and political foundation for opposition to the Empire in the late 1860s, and for participation in a Commune insurrection. Class consciousness, which he argues was weaker by 1871 than it had been in 1848, was relatively unimportant.

These sociological interpretations contain many ideas that empirical historians would accept, and indeed have put forward. Rougerie and Gaillard, for example, have diagnosed a sense of dispossession and exile caused by Haussmannization, and point to acts of symbolic reconquest after the fall of the Empire. The importance of local urban issues and the strong sense of 'Parisian' identity among Communards is one that several historians have emphasized, and which we shall examine later. However, where the sociologists differ from the historians is that their interest in urban theory and focus on recent urban change lead them to play down or even ignore two elements that probably all historians stress. The first element is ideology and political culture, in shorthand terms the 'revolutionary tradition' of Paris that has been discussed above. Gaillard warns against forgetting that the Commune was part of a longer history, and so confusing 'explanation of the revolutionary phenomenon with explanation of the urban phenomenon'.[23] If we agree with her in seeing the Commune as part of a long series of Parisian revolts, then clearly the effects of Haussmannization can only be of contributory importance. The second element is the momentous events that were unconnected with 'the urban phenomenon' of the Haussmann years: the war against Germany, the siege of Paris, and the chronic political tension between republican Paris (and some other cities) and the mainly conservative provinces that came to a head immediately after the end of the war. These events gave the Commune dimensions that went far beyond purely urban concerns.

Paris against the Second Empire

It is possible to portray the 1850s and '60s as a period of growing opposition to the Second Empire, of radicalization and class consciousness, building up inexorably to the overthrow of the Empire in 1870 and the Commune in 1871. Indeed, this is one of the conventionally accepted accounts, put forward by many contemporaries soon after the event, and accepted by historians of varying political sympathies. But is it a convincing story? Let us look at what happened.

23. Gaillard (1977), p. 569.

Louis-Napoleon Bonaparte's campaign for the presidency of the Republic in 1848 won strong support in working-class Paris. However, from the time of the December 1851 *coup d'état* onwards, voting results showed that Paris had become the main centre of opposition. In the plebiscite called to approve the *coup d'état*, 42 per cent of the popular vote in Paris was negative, compared to 7 per cent in the country as a whole; nearly a third of all the country's No votes came from Paris. From the 1863 parliamentary elections onwards, all the Paris seats were won by the opposition. There is no doubt, then, that the position of the regime in its capital deteriorated. The crisis of 1848, which had brought Louis-Napoleon Bonaparte to power as a saviour, was a fading memory. Some of the most characteristic Bonapartist initiatives – economic expansion, free trade, urbanism, war – created opposition as well as support. If rebuilding Paris created jobs and profits, it also raised rents, taxes and food prices. If winning wars made crowds cheer, it annoyed taxpayers, conscripts and their families. Reforms to strengthen the army by extending conscription after Prussia's victory over Austria in 1866 were deeply unpopular and caused riots in Paris. If free trade lowered consumer prices, it was also blamed for bankruptcy, job losses, pay cuts and strikes, especially after the world economy began to slow in 1867 after nearly two decades of expansion. All this could plausibly be blamed on misjudgements by the emperor himself: criticism of 'personal government' led to calls for a more liberal political system to control the regime's activities. Moreover, he was in increasingly poor health, and there was speculation that the regime would collapse when he died.

Yet the Empire was not always or uniformly unpopular with workers generally, even those in the capital. The war in 1859 to liberate Italy from Austrian domination had brought out cheering crowds in the working-class districts of Paris to escort the emperor on his departure for the front – a 'truly disgusting' display, according to the future Commune member Gustave Lefrançais: 'So everything is forgotten! The throttling of the Republic, transportations, massacres . . . all over and done with! Long live the emperor!'[24] Napoleon followed this with important concessions to workers. With the support of his Left-leaning cousin Prince Jerome he aimed to encourage non-political trade unions to wean workers away from republicanism. In 1862 the authorities subsidized the sending of a delegation of workers to the London Exhibition, following which

24. Lefrançais (1972), p. 208.

the International Working Men's Association – the famous 'International' – was set up. The famous 1864 'Manifesto of the Sixty' by labour leaders urging the election of workers to parliament was published in Prince Jerome's newspaper. The emperor legalized strikes in 1864, a measure 'greeted with stupor by the judiciary and anger by employers'.[25]

Yet for Parisian workers as a whole, these concessions did not stem alienation from the imperial regime. Kulstein suggests that the propaganda effort was not sufficiently sustained or consistent: different government agencies did not always follow the same policy, and no government-subsidized workers' press was set up. There were probably more fundamental reasons for Bonapartism's failure. It was based on a vision of charismatic paternalist government that would unite all classes in harmony and prosperity. This had proved attractive to Parisian workers amid economic crisis in 1848, but it aroused extravagant hopes that could never in practice be fulfilled. Economic fluctuations and industrial conflict made it difficult for the regime to act out its paternalist role consistently: the need to retain the support of conservatives and business interests meant that, like its predecessors, it often repressed workers' activities, sometimes violently. Similarly, its political need to maintain relations with the Catholic Church angered the Left, including many anticlerical workers, for whom Catholicism was a barrier to progress, especially through its power over schools. Finally, Bonapartism wished to embody the powerful, visible, active and benevolent State, creator of unity and wealth, embodiment of national power and glory; the other side of the coin was that it equally embodied the oppressive, expensive and parasitical State, the tax-gatherer, policeman and strike-breaker. Especially for Proudhonian socialists, the State was a root cause of poverty and oppression. As one speaker put it at a public meeting in 1869, 'The primary cause of unemployment is the power employers have over the labourers. They say ". . . if you attack us, look out: there is a legal system to defend us".'[26]

Furthermore, the regime's concessions to workers, and its more general liberalization measures, far from defusing opposition and conflict, enabled its more open expression, which the authorities then found themselves vainly trying to control and even repress. Legalizing strikes led to an explosion of industrial conflict in 1864–65, with demands for shorter hours and pay increases, most of which were successful. This probably did buttress the emperor's popularity

25. Dalotel et al. (1981), p. 16.   26. Gould (1995), p. 125.

among many workers in the provinces, but it had no visible effect on opposition in the capital. The economic downturn in 1867–68 changed the climate. A noticeable proportion of Communards were small masters who had gone bankrupt at this time. Employers attempted to reduce costs, increase productivity and cut wages, which led to defensive strikes. At the same time, rising food prices caused riots in the provinces. An unprecedented strike wave took place in 1869–70, with some of the biggest strikes of the century in the major mining and industrial centres, including Paris, with demands for higher wages and shorter hours in an attempt to win back the ground lost to rising prices over the previous two years. The International made attempts to involve itself in the strikes and provide political leadership. Although some imperial authorities urged concessions and moderation, military intervention to move coal stocks led to a serious clash on 12 June 1869 between strikers and troops at La Ricamarie in the Saint-Etienne coalfield, in which 10 strikers were killed, and again in October at Aubin, in the southern Aveyron coalfield, when 14 were killed. For many workers, especially those already inclined to republicanism, this showed the empire in its true colours.

Relaxation of press controls in May 1868 immediately hatched in Paris a provocative opposition press which was vehemently republican, bitterly hostile to the empire, and often revolutionary in its language. The circulation of the most popular papers, such as *La Marseillaise*, reached well over 100,000, which meant (allowing for multiple readership) that a large part of the city population saw them. Their contributors included illustrious republican names from the past, such as Victor Hugo (in exile since 1851), and left-wingers from the 1848 generation, including Charles Delescluze and Félix Pyat; and a swarm of young writers, most famously Henri Rochefort, editor of the notoriously irreverent *La Lanterne* and later *La Marseillaise*. The influence of the press made these men politically important, and, as we shall see, several – including Rochefort, Delescluze, Pyat, Auguste Vermorel and Jules Vallès – were prominent after the fall of the Empire and during the Commune. Republicans were able now to embarrass the regime over the taboo subject of the *coup d'état* of 1851. In July 1868 a comprehensive history of the *coup* was published for the first time, and republican journalists and politicians organized a subscription to build a memorial to Baudin, a republican deputy killed on a barricade in the Faubourg Saint-Antoine. The organizers were prosecuted, but the defence barrister, the young and hitherto unknown Léon Gambetta, turned the trial into an indictment of the Empire with an outspoken attack heard in stupefied silence by the court.

The government gave permission in June 1868 for public meetings to debate non-political social and intellectual topics, in the hope of encouraging rational discussion and hence peaceful reform. These proved very popular: over 900 meetings were held in Paris between June 1868 and 1870, attracting thousands of listeners. They immediately turned towards often inflammatory discussion of political matters, with some open calls for revolution and class war. A *commissaire* of police had to be present on the platform to keep an eye on the debates and close the meeting if necessary; his presence almost certainly acted as a provocation, and indeed his confrontations with speakers proved a crowd-puller. Openly political meetings were also permitted during election campaigns.

Political agitation peaked in 1869 and 1870, marked by the national strike wave, tense parliamentary elections and a plebiscite. Both election campaigns caused great excitement in Paris, with over 400 public meetings being held. Some of the city's largest dance halls and music halls were used, especially in working-class districts such as Belleville and Montmartre, with audiences of several hundred or even some thousands. These were exciting and enjoyable occasions, with much rowdy heckling, not infrequent brawls with the police, and even serious riots. Should all this be regarded as a symptom of approaching revolution, or as a safety valve through which, after years of censorship and restrictions, people went to let off steam and enjoy the thrills of noisy opposition? It seems that the authorities did not take verbal opposition too seriously: although 121 meetings were closed by the police, only 55 speakers were prosecuted. However, meetings were forbidden after disturbances following the 1870 plebiscite.

The 1869 elections showed a further increase in support for the opposition parties. The main beneficiaries nationally, however, were not the republican and even less the revolutionary parties, but deputies who formed a law-abiding opposition, critical of the regime's errors, supporters of reform, but enemies of revolution. Even in Paris, though the opposition swept the board with 234,000 votes against 77,000 for government sympathizers, the mainstream republican leaders tacitly or openly opposed revolution. They were bitterly denounced by revolutionaries – an eclectic mixture of neo-Jacobins, Blanquists, Proudhonists, a few Bakuninists, many of them affiliated loosely to the International. But the real balance of force was shown at the ballot box: extreme-Left candidates were all beaten, the strongest receiving only some 15,000 votes. Concluded one frustrated revolutionary, 'the best elections are rifle shots'.[27] When the results were announced, there followed several days of serious rioting in Paris, from 7 to 11 June, the biggest popular mobilization for twenty years.

The most left-wing of the successful candidates, elected in the working-class north-eastern constituency, was Gambetta, and when he opted to sit for Marseilles instead, the journalist Rochefort was elected in his place. Both had accepted a manifesto drawn up at public meetings by their supporters, the famous Belleville Programme, which supported radical reforms to destroy the authoritarian State, including abolition of the police and standing army, replacement of the centralized bureaucracy with locally elected officials, and disestablishment of the Church – very similar to the programme later followed by the Commune (see below p. 79). But in private Gambetta opposed revolution, hoping that the Empire would last a few more years and permit a peaceful transition to a republic.

Faced with these opposition gains, the emperor introduced further liberalization of the regime to increase the powers of parliament at the expense of his own prerogative. A new government, led by a convert from republicanism, Emile Ollivier, took office in January 1870, beginning the episode known as the 'liberal empire'. There immediately occurred a bizarrely unpredictable incident which kept Paris on the boil. A young radical journalist, Victor Noir, was shot dead in a quarrel by a disreputable cousin of the emperor, Prince Pierre Bonaparte. Noir's funeral on 12 January 1870 at Neuilly, a leafy western suburb, attracted huge crowds, estimated at 80–100,000 – over a third of all Parisian republican voters – wishing to demonstrate their disgust at the Empire. The most determined revolutionary leaders, particularly a swashbuckling anthropologist, Gustave Flourens, wished to use the occasion to start an insurrection by leading a mass march on the centre of Paris carrying Noir's body – a familiar revolutionary ritual. However, in the face of forces ostentatiously mustered by Ollivier in the Champs Elysées – six regiments of cavalry with artillery – cooler heads prevailed and the crowd dispersed.

In May 1870, Napoleon called a plebiscite to approve his liberal reforms and strengthen his own position: a Yes vote would be a vote for liberalization but also for a continuation of the Empire. This divided the opposition groups. Republicans disagreed over whether

---

27. Dalotel et al. (1981), p. 327.

to call for a No vote or to boycott the ballot: most moderates preferred the former, revolutionaries the latter. The campaign aroused great excitement, with hundreds of public meetings and vehement calls for a boycott. However, the national vote showed overwhelming support for the new system: 7.4 million Yeses to 1.5 million Noes. Although Parisians voted No by 184,000 to 138,000, this meant that some 60,000 republican voters had voted Yes. Few indeed had obeyed the revolutionary groups' boycott call: Girard estimates them at only about 6,000.[28] The Left had fallen into the emperor's trap, causing most French voters to interpret the plebiscite just as he had hoped: 'The adversaries of our institutions posed a choice between revolution and the Empire. The country has chosen.'[29] Paris – along with Marseilles – was out of step. And even in Paris, outright revolutionaries were shown to be a tiny minority. They reacted by denouncing ignorant peasant voters and even calling for 'free cities' – an idea that would return in 1871.

The announcement of the result of the plebiscite caused several nights of violence in Paris, as in 1869. Thousands of demonstrators battled with police and troops, smashed windows and built a few barricades. Two or three were killed, an unknown number wounded, and several hundred arrested. A few rioters and their supposed leaders, including journalists and militants of the International, were put on trial, and several received stiff jail sentences. Others escaped to Belgium. 'The leading militants were now imprisoned, on trial or dispersed into exile.'[30]

Was Paris on the brink of revolution? It seems a familiar and ominous pattern: economic problems, government scandals, tumultuous meetings, violent speeches, hostile election results, riots and barricades. It proves that most Parisians opposed Napoleon III; a considerable number undoubtedly wished to be rid of him by almost any means. This has often been taken to show that a 'revolutionary situation' was in existence; that 'the Commune was born under the empire'.[31] Of course, a revolution did occur in September 1870, and the Commune in 1871, and so 1868–70 is literally a 'prevolutionary' period, or, in La Gorce's words, 'the preface to the Commune'.[32] If by this we understand that part of the Parisian population had developed radical political aspirations, that several thousand took part in violent demonstrations which some would have liked to turn

28. Girard (1960), p. 407.   29. La Gorce (1930), vol. 6, p. 118.
30. Dalotel et al. (1981), p. 365.   31. Ibid., p. 32.
32. La Gorce (1930), vol. 5, p. 375.

into insurrection, and that political campaigning had brought to local and even national prominence journalists, politicians and labour leaders some of whom were to play a role during the Commune, there is no reason to dissent.

But such claims generally imply more than mere chronological anticipation; they suggest that the causes of revolution were already present, and that the first stages of a revolutionary process had actually begun, like the first pebbles of a landslide. There are reasons to be cautious here. First, in theory, the concept of a 'revolutionary situation' is imprecise, and probably purely metaphorical. Efforts were made by political scientists in the 1960s and '70s to formulate models of revolution, but no satisfactory or generally accepted version emerged. Hence there is no set of criteria by which we can identify a 'revolutionary situation' – except the obvious but tautological fact that a revolution subsequently occurred. Second, in practice, there were formidable obstacles in the path of revolution. The republican party was divided: mainstream 'bourgeois' republicans – and even some supposed revolutionaries – had tacitly discarded the idea of revolution, at least in the immediate future. They even went so far as to condemn the riots of 1869 and 1870 as provocations organized by the police. In short, argues Girard, 'the liberal bourgeoisie quitted the united front of people and bourgeois, a coalition without which revolution was impossible in Paris'.[33] This does not seem wholly convincing: leading opposition politicians had been equally opposed to revolution in July 1830 and February 1848, which had not prevented it from happening. But certainly, as long as moderate republicans maintained their popularity and influence, they were an obstacle in the revolutionaries' path.

A more formidable practical obstacle was that not enough people, even among the tens of thousands who attended public meetings or turned out for Victor Noir's funeral, were ready to risk throwing themselves into armed insurrection as in 1830 and 1848, when hundreds of barricades were built spontaneously all over eastern Paris, and when crowds of men, with some women and children too, joined battle with troops and police. In the riots of 1869 and 1870, although some would-be insurgents went through the motions of the 'revolutionary passion play', as Richard Cobb aptly called it, only one or two barricades were built, and quickly demolished. It is impossible to be sure why this was so: plausible speculation would be that, on one hand, memory of the crushing repression of 1848

33. Girard (1960), p. 407.

and 1851 acted as a deterrent, while, on the other, the regime's liberal concessions made peaceful political methods seem a better option, as shown by the sizeable republican switch towards a Yes vote in the 1870 plebiscite.

The form taken by some of the riots – wrecking pubs, looting shops and attacking brothels – suggests antisocial frustration rather than purposeful politics. Dalotel argues that these acts were expressions of class anger, but Rougerie doubts that 'republican fervour' was the main element: the violence in Belleville in May 1869 began when a man was thrown out of a pub for refusing to pay for his drink, and came back later with a gang to smash it up.[34] Whatever the rioters' motives, Haussmann's demolitions of crowded areas of cheap accommodation in the centre of Paris had deliberately shifted much of the working population, and thus the focus of popular action, two or three miles away from the locations of power. Breaking windows in Belleville was a feeble substitute for storming the Tuileries Palace, and even vicious fighting between police and demonstrators had little impact on the rest of the city.

A third, and fundamental, reason to doubt that Paris was in a 'revolutionary situation' was the balance of physical force in the streets. However we explain the 'erosion' (in Gaillard's word) of 'the traditional revolutionary myth'[35] compared with 1830 or 1848, it was partly a function of the greater effectiveness of the government's forces. The uniformed police force had been increased from a mere 750 men to over 4,000, backed up by a picked military-police unit, the Garde de Paris (2,900 men) plus the army garrison. Unlike its predecessors in 1830 and February 1848, the imperial government showed no hesitation in putting down popular agitation by mass arrests, prosecutions and stern, even brutal, measures to clear the streets. It does not seem to have doubted that they could and would restore order. Far from being paralysed by uncertainty, as in earlier periods, they were bold to the point of provocativeness. Quite small police forces seem to have broken up meetings and charged rioters without hesitation. The popular hero Rochefort was arrested actually in the middle of a public meeting at La Villette on 7 February 1870 'under the noses of ten thousand workers'.[36] The accusation by republican politicians that the police organized the riots as a pretext for repression at least shows how effective that repression was. The writer Ludovic Halévy watched from a theatre balcony the

34. Dalotel et al. (1981), p. 332; Rougerie (1960), p. 32.
35. Gaillard (1977), p. 569.   36. Dalotel et al. (1981), p. 347.

'free show' of troops in action on the boulevard below: to the apt strains of Gounod's 'Soldier's Chorus' audible from on stage, they got 'stuck into the crowd like a fist into a tub of butter'.[37]

Did the forces of order find that popular resistance was less determined and less violent than in the past? It seems likely that many of those attending meetings and demonstrations were there in part out of curiosity or for the excitement, rather than being bent on revolution. Many middle-class people attended meetings and went to see the riots as a spectacle – very different from the social fear inspired by the June 1848 uprising. We cannot be sure of how the real rioters felt about the situation – they may well have been just as angry and determined as their parents and grandparents had been in earlier revolutions – but we can be sure of crucial differences in the balance of force. On one hand, there were now more troops and more police, and they were more reliable. On the other hand, the rioters had less access to weapons – the looting of a gunsmith's in 1869 produced only a handful of firearms and cartridges. A vital change was the running down of the National Guard, the citizen militia, and its replacement by a strengthened police force and military garrison. Until 1851, the National Guard had been an in-dispensable instrument for keeping order in Paris. Yet so unreliable had it been that Charles X disbanded it in 1827; it had turned against Louis-Philippe at the critical moment in February 1848; some of its companies had joined the rebels in June 1848; and it had often proved to be a source of weapons for insurgents. One novel and welcome consequence was the limited bloodshed: earlier *journées* had often ended in a bloodbath, with shooting on both sides and use of artillery. Very few, if any, shots seem to have been fired in 1869 and 1870. Rioters had to make do with sticks and iron bars, and seem to have given the police relatively little trouble. These events were much more like riots in any other city, and much less like the irresistible Paris *journées* of previous generations.

The reasons for not regarding Paris as in the first throes of revolution during the last days of the Second Empire are vividly encapsulated in the events of 14 August 1870, when Blanquist con-spirators deliberately attempted to spark off an insurrection. The Blanquists were the most determined exponents of armed revolution and – in their own minds at least – the most professional, disciplined and intellectual, who had thought out their tactics, and perfected their training and organization. But now they were divided about

37. Halévy (1935), vol. 1, pp. 212–16.

whether a 'revolutionary situation' really existed, being no clearer about this than twentieth-century political scientists. Blanqui himself was against the attempt. Furthermore, they could not decide what to attack – a clear sign of the disorientation of the old revolutionary arena brought about by Haussmann. They settled, incongruously, on a fire station, where they hoped to seize arms, out at La Villette, one of Haussmann's peripheral working-class districts which they were confident would prove a revolutionary tinder-box. But the attack went wrong. The firemen resisted, and one was killed, along with a policeman and a little girl of five. The sixty or so revolution-aries ran off, calling the population to arms. But, in the Blanquists' own words, 'in this revolutionary quarter ... the action did not attract a single recruit'.[38] On the contrary, bystanders were angry at what they regarded as a treacherous and unpatriotic attack. There could be few clearer proofs that Paris was not teetering on the brink of revolution in August 1870.

Yet, ironically, a bloodless revolution did take place three weeks later. The crucial change in the meantime was the stunning inter-vention of outside forces: the Germans overwhelmed the French at Sedan on 2 September, capturing Napoleon III and his army. Paris's last revolutionary period then began – thanks not to Blanqui but to Bismarck.

38. Paz (1984), p. 210.

CHAPTER TWO

From People's War to People's Revolution, June 1870–March 1871

All wars threaten the political stability of belligerents. They test the competence of governments. They demand sacrifices from citizens, which have to be justified and rewarded. They arouse extreme emotions. They disrupt economic and social life. Unless they can be limited in duration and intensity, the effects become acute, and the political consequences potentially revolutionary. These consequences are, of course, hugely aggravated by defeat. The Franco-German war of 1870–71, unlike the European wars fought over the previous two decades in the Crimea, Italy, Denmark and Germany, quickly overflowed the limits of diplomatic and political calculation. The expectations of the statesmen and generals who began it proved false, and the dynamic forces unleashed by the war – as they realized to their alarm – slipped out of their grasp. 'The war takes on an ever more hateful character,' wrote the Prussian General von Moltke on 27 October. 'It is bad enough that armies must slaughter each other; one must not lead whole peoples against each other.'[1]

At the centre of the maelstrom was Paris. To a degree rarely paralleled, the citizens of a single city forced themselves into a position in which they dominated the conduct and duration of an international war. In the process, their economic, social and political life was transformed. Paris was not a fortress like any other in France or Europe. The ramparts of other capital cities were relics of the past. The fortifications of Paris – a 30-mile bastioned rampart and 16 outlying forts – had been built only in 1840–41, when a European war seemed likely. The French calculated that modern war, on the pattern of the revolutionary wars, would have as its object the domination of the State and the nation, not merely the

---

1. Moltke (1922), vol. 2, p. 404.

seizure of frontier territory. Paris had become the essential target because of its unique political importance in post-revolutionary France, encapsulating the political life, and even the sovereignty, of the country:

> In the days of our forebears, its occupation had little influence on the rest of France; Charles VII, Henri III, Henri IV did not cease to be kings by ceasing to reign over Paris; [but] two recent examples have proved that this great capital . . . [now] takes with her the destiny of all our provinces. . . . Because of this importance of Paris we have to defend her.[2]

War and revolution, July–September

From the beginning of the crisis with Prussia over the candidature of a Hohenzollern prince to the Spanish throne in July, Parisians were a crucial element. Jingoistic street demonstrations played a part in the government's disastrous decision to take a tough line, not only demanding the withdrawal of the candidature but insisting that the King of Prussia personally should promise never to renew it. When this demand was rebuffed, war was declared, which sparked more popular patriotic fervour. This was a familiar Parisian emotion. In the 1790s, mustering volunteers and the punishing of traitors had roused their energies. In 1814–15, the 1830s, 1840, 1848–49, 1859 and 1863, the reality or the prospect of war had brought bellicose crowds into the streets. The links between war and revolution were evident to all. On one hand, mobilizing the people for all-out war demanded potentially revolutionary measures and was usually expected sooner or later to bring a revolutionary government to power, as the Jacobin dictatorship had emerged to deal with national emergency in 1793. On the other hand, a revolution seemed likely to lead to war against reactionary foreign powers both to defend the revolution within France and to spread it among the other nations, as had happened in 1792 and had been widely expected in 1830 and 1848. Generally, therefore, the Left had been bellicose as well as revolutionary; the Right, pacific as well as conservative. However, Napoleon III had successfully used war in the Crimea in 1854 and Italy in 1859 to strengthen his prestige and power, and this had caused leaders of the Left to alter their views and espouse a more pacific, internationalist and antimilitary position.

2. Gen. Lamarque in Chamber of Deputies, 13 April 1831.

Some opposed war in 1870 because they feared that another victory would revive the Empire's popularity, and there were some small antiwar demonstrations in Paris. This had little effect on the genuinely popular outbursts of patriotism, which, as after the plebiscite riots in May, the Left tried to blame on police *agents provocateurs*. Once the war was under way, and especially after it began to go badly for the emperor's armies, the Left in Paris and other cities demanded an expansion of the National Guard (the citizen militia) and the arming of the population with an eye to taking political power as well as strengthening national defence.

The catastrophe at Sedan, when Napoleon and his army were captured, changed the meaning of the war: it could no longer be regarded as merely a dynastic quarrel. The imperial government and its agents simply melted away in France's only bloodless revolution. As the news of Sedan reached Lyons, Bordeaux and Marseilles, republicans took over. In Paris on 4 September, a crowd gathered peacefully at the Palais Bourbon, where the deputies of the Corps Législatif proclaimed the downfall of the empire. The republican deputies for Paris, elected in 1869, then went to the Hôtel de Ville, symbol of popular Parisian power. In a rather decorous reenactment of a revolutionary *journée*, they proclaimed a republic and installed themselves as the Government of National Defence, acting deliberately to forestall the possibility that the revolutionary Left might try to seize power. This tension between moderate and revolutionary republicans, already bitter in 1848 (and many figures from that generation were still active), had reemerged in the late 1860s. It was to continue throughout the war, and finally explode with the Commune insurrection. The leading figures in the new government were the moderate republicans Jules Favre, Jules Simon, Jules Ferry and Ernest Picard and the radicals Léon Gambetta (who installed himself as Minister of the Interior by getting to the ministry first in a cab) and Henri Rochefort the journalist. They chose as president a popular general, the conservative but anti-Bonapartist Jules Trochu.

It seemed to many republicans, including those in the government, that the war could now end. They had no quarrel with the German people and blamed the war on Napoleon III. So they intimated to the advancing Germans that they could now go home. To their surprise and indignation, Bismarck, the Prussian minister-president, replied by demanding a large indemnity and – far worse – the cession of France's eastern border provinces, Alsace and much of Lorraine, with the fortress cities of Strasbourg and Metz. This proved unmistakably that the war had changed its meaning: no longer the emperor's war, it now became a war to defend the very substance of the nation; and because a republican government was willy-nilly in control, it necessarily became a war to defend the Republic, whose prestige and very survival now seemed to depend on victory, or at least on mounting a gallant defence leading to peace with honour.

So the whole Left, from moderate republicans to revolutionary socialists, threw themselves into the battle of the nation against the German princes. 'I sense at this moment that I love my country passionately,' wrote the young socialist Benoît Malon.[3] The example of the 1790s was constantly invoked: then (so went the myth) patriotic fervour and revolutionary audacity had thrown back the invading monarchist troops. For the older leaders, such as the socialist Louis Blanc, Victor Hugo and Auguste Blanqui, the revolutionary struggle they had expected and even advocated in 1830 and 1848 had begun at last, and their deep-seated nationalism could be given free rein. 'How I hate this people,' Blanqui wrote of the Germans. 'They are a people of brutes!'[4] The republican war effort gave the Blanquists a wonderful opportunity 'to restore their battered prestige and raise their sunken morale' after their fiasco at La Villette.[5] Blanqui founded a newspaper entitled *La Patrie en Danger*. Left-wing activists held meetings to organize vigilance committees in each *arrondissement* and set up a central committee of delegates. These began to function as early as 11 September. In the working-class *arrondissements* they included many of the labour and political spokesmen who had made themselves known through the public meetings described in chapter 1. Six months later, they would provide many of the leaders of the Commune, including Eugène Varlin, Jules Vallès, Benoît Malon, Charles Longuet, Edouard Vaillant and Gabriel Ranvier. From the early weeks of the war, then, the future revolutionaries were organizing. But as we shall see, their efforts had little immediate consequence: they were never able to attract a large enough following to constitute a serious revolutionary force as long as war continued.

As early as 5 September vigilance committee activists called for an elected 'Paris municipality' and a couple of weeks later for a 'Commune'. Their ideas, summarized on 15 September in a 'red poster' (*affiche rouge*) drawn up by the Central Committee of the Twenty Arrondissements, did not greatly change over the next few months. Complete democratization combined with fervent patriotism inspired a programme to prosecute the war which would at the same time

3. Vincent (1992), p. 23.   4. Bernstein (1971), p. 323.   5. Ibid., p. 319.

transform the political, social and economic systems permanently: abolition of the police and bureaucracy, election of all officials, the National Guard to be responsible for public order, expropriation of all foodstuffs, equal rationing, distribution of weapons, and total mobilization of the population, 'Republican Paris being resolved, rather than surrender, to bury itself beneath its ruins'.[6]

Victory, they believed, required this *levée en masse* of all the people of Paris and the provinces, as in the 1790s. Even women and children could fight, as the *affiche rouge* urged. The arming of the people also meant that internal opposition would be neutralized. As ever, the revolutionaries were very much aware of the presence of traitors and backsliders – 'the foreigner on one side, reaction on the other'. Power now and in the future must remain in the hands of the armed people and their leaders. At stake was national victory and also the survival of a revolution that during and after the war would create the long-awaited democratic and social republic. Expropriating private food supplies as a wartime measure would be the first step towards 'abolishing poverty' afterwards; requisitioning factories for arms manufacture would lead after the war to their handover to workers' associations. Defeat of the Prussian monarchy might even lead to that old dream of a 'universal republic', a United States of Europe.[7]

The mobilization of Paris, September–October

The new government, not without misgivings, agreed on 6 September further to increase the size of the Paris National Guard by 90,000 men. Social pressure to join up was great: noted one young Parisian, 'Any young and healthy men encountered in the street in civilian clothes are vilified.'[8] On 12 September it was decided to pay them a daily 'indemnity' of 1.50 francs – '30 sous' – to which was later added 75 centimes for wives and 25 for each child. As the Paris economy was soon to come under siege, this meant that National Guard membership became not only a patriotic duty but also an indispensable means of subsistence for most families. The government's manpower target was greatly exceeded as men of all ages clamoured to join: within a week, 78 new battalions had been formed, and 194 by the end of the month. Irregular units of *francs-tireurs*

6. Text in Dautry and Scheler (1960), pp. 32–5.
7. Ibid., pp. 58–9, 104–5, 113.   8. Clayson (1998), p. 389.

also formed, often with romantic names and glamorous uniforms. A suggestion was made to raise a women's regiment of 'Amazons of the Seine'. National Guard uniform, or at least some vestige of it – a kepi, silver buttons on the overcoat, a red stripe sewn on to the trousers – became standard male attire, whether on or off duty, even for those, such as Victor Hugo, too old to serve.

The Paris National Guard thus became a popular army – or at least an armed horde – of over 340,000 men, with 280,000 rifles, many of them modern breech-loaders, and eventually with artillery too, partly paid for by public donations. It was, however, a very unusual army. It was raised and organized locally. Battalions and companies consisted of neighbours: a company would typically be raised from two or three adjoining streets, with several men from each building. Given the greater social, occupational and political homogeneity of the districts of Haussmann's Paris, seen in the previous chapter, National Guard units obviously took on the social and political colouring of their neighbourhoods. As everyone knew, battalions from Montmartre or Belleville (especially those recently raised) were very different from those from the residential districts of western Paris. This was often visible in the quality of their uniforms, as well as the numbers on their kepis (new battalions had higher numbers), and it was no less clear from their political loyalties. It became common to refer to 'good' and 'bad' or (depending on one's sympathies) 'reactionary' and 'republican' battalions.

These differences were reflected in the elections by the rank-and-file of NCOs and company officers, who in turn elected battalion commanders. Only the high command was appointed by the government. The men elected were usually well-known local figures, often with military experience or social standing. Not infrequently they were also men with a political reputation, as had long been a tradition in the National Guard. Consequently, some revolutionary leaders were elected commanders by newly raised battalions from the working-class *arrondissements*, among them Blanqui, by the 169th battalion of Montmartre, three of his leading disciples, Eudes, Granger and Sapia, by battalions from the industrial 11th, 14th and 20th *arrondissements*, and the International members Eugène Varlin and Charles Longuet, by units from the Left Bank.[9] Gustave Flourens, one of the firebrands of the late 1860s, was elected by 10 battalions from Belleville, and appointed himself colonel. Thus, the war created local, democratic, armed organizations on an unprecedented scale.

9. Serman (1986), p. 122.

However, repeated efforts by the revolutionaries in late September and early October to put pressure on the government by demonstrations had no effect: members of the Government of National Defence received delegations, usually politely, and fobbed them off. It did not intend to coexist with, and even less to make way for, a Commune. The various revolutionary tendencies – Blanquists, neo-Jacobins, socialists – found that they had in reality a limited following. Suggestions as early as October that a federation of battalions should be formed came to nothing. Blanqui was booed at a demonstration on 8 October and his battalion demanded his replacement. Even more humiliating was the experience of Sapia, who, when he tried to march on the Hôtel de Ville on 9 October, was arrested by his own men, tied up and handed over to the authorities.

Change in the political climate depended on the military situation. The Germans had defeated the French regular army in six weeks, and on 19 September surrounded Paris, cutting off all land communications and supplies. Parisians, including the military commanders, expected that they would try to storm the city. This had been prepared for: the permanent fortifications had been strengthened by earthworks and reinforced by armoured trains and even a flotilla of gunboats; barricades were built inside the city. Available regular soldiers, sailors and marines had been summoned, as had Gardes Mobiles (reserve troops) from the provinces. With the 340,000 National Guards, this made a motley garrison of some 500,000 – more than double the number of Germans outside the walls when the siege began. Patriotic Parisians rightly decided that their city was unassailable; but the Germans had no intention of assailing it. They began to dig themselves into siege lines 50 miles long encircling the city and its suburbs, with the intention of starving the 2.2 million inhabitants into submission.

What could the French do? General Trochu and his commanders were convinced that most of their vast forces were unfit for action, being untrained and poorly disciplined. Skirmishes with the besiegers in September, when French troops had been routed, and the reluctance of National Guardsmen to volunteer for active service outside the city walls, confirmed their prejudices. Their only hope was that new armies could be raised in the provinces to march to their relief. They would then mount a sortie to break through the siege lines, join up with the relief forces and, with luck, force the Germans to raise the siege. Parisian patriots, however, inspired by selective memories of revolutionary victories of 1792, took a far more optimistic view of the situation. They believed that patriotic Frenchmen, imbued with revolutionary zeal, could defeat the half-hearted soldiers of monarchy by will-power and self-sacrifice. Besides, there were so many of them: how could they be penned inside Paris by a smaller number of Germans? A *levée en masse*, directed into a *sortie torrentielle*, would overwhelm the besiegers.

Such contradictory views were bound to lead to mutual suspicion, recrimination and contempt. Revolutionaries accused the government of at best incompetence and cowardice, at worst treachery. Ministers and generals accused the revolutionaries of at best loudmouthed recklessness, at worst of pretending patriotism to foment revolution. Neither side was wholly wrong. The government and the generals were fatalistic, indecisive and sometimes incompetent; they were excessively dismissive of citizen-soldiers; they could have done more to harry the Germans and make it more difficult to blockade Paris. But there is no reason to imagine that this could have won the war. The revolutionaries, for their part, were carelessly ignorant of military realities. Their panacea of a *sortie torrentielle* was terrifyingly impractical. Was it to be in all directions at once? If in one direction, it would take many hours for hundreds of thousands of men to squeeze through the rampart gates and across the drawbridges – plenty of time for the Germans to get ready to slaughter them. Even if a large number did break through the siege lines, what then? What was their objective? How could they be supplied and fed? Could they stand up to the battle-hardened Germans in the open field? Military daydreams were a recipe for carnage, yet the revolutionaries preferred to accuse cautious generals of cowardice or treason.

The first serious clash came on 31 October. Simultanously, news reached Paris of the capitulation of the fortified city of Metz and with it the remaining 150,000 men of the regular imperial army; of an abortive attempt by the conservative elder statesman Adolphe Thiers to negotiate an armistice with Bismarck; and of the capture by the Germans of the village of Le Bourget, north of Paris. For the revolutionary patriots, women as well as men, all this proved their suspicions of a sell-out. A crowd of several thousand civilians and National Guards gathered outside the Hôtel de Ville, demanding more energetic military measures and denouncing negotiations. The gates were forced, and hundreds of National Guards swarmed in. Flourens and a group of his Belleville men burst into a meeting of the government, who became in practice prisoners. Blanqui and others arrived later, and began signing decrees and nominating new ministers in what had turned into an improvised revolution. Flourens, booted and spurred, paced up and down on the cabinet table at which the ministers stubbornly sat tight. Gardes Mobiles came into the building through a tunnel (Haussmann had taken precautions) and confronted the rebels. Some of the ministers escaped and later returned with a force of loyal National Guards, who were less than enthusiastic about the government's record, but were alarmed at the prospect of revolution. After hours of noisy, sweaty, dangerous, but nevertheless rather ludicrous confusion, the revolutionaries left with promises of new elections and no reprisals. These were swiftly repudiated: 22 left-wing leaders were arrested and 16 National Guard commanders were dismissed. There was no bloodshed, however: patriotism and prudence meant that nearly everyone wanted to avoid an open clash.

To strengthen its authority after this lucky escape, early in November the government called a plebiscite and municipal elections in the 20 Paris *arrondissements*. The plebiscite yielded a big pro-government majority: 221,374 to 53,585 among civilians and 236,623 to 9,053 in the army. The revolutionaries, then, mustered some 60,000 voters. Although this was several times their following in the 1870 plebiscite, they clearly remained a minority even of workers. However, in the northern and eastern *arrondissements* that minority was sizeable: over 20 per cent in Montmartre and La Villette (18th and 19th *arrondissements*), over 30 per cent in Popincourt (11th), 50 per cent in Belleville (20th).[10] In the municipal elections, moreover, unambiguously revolutionary candidates were elected as mayors in two *arrondissements* (the 19th and 20th) and as assistant mayors in nine (the 3rd, 11th, 13th, 14th, 15th, 17th, 18th, 19th and 20th). If the electors of the working-class districts were not ready to overturn the government in the face of the enemy, they clearly wanted 'reds' in charge of local affairs, which included food supply, housing and organization of the National Guard.[11] Nevertheless, it was a defeat for the revolutionaries, and it sapped their strength. Blanqui's newspaper was soon to close for lack of readers, and the Central Committee sank into inactivity. As Rougerie sums it up, 'the revolutionary groups vegetated, popular meetings languished, everywhere the 31 October fiasco was cruelly felt'.[12]

The siege routine went on. The National Guard, unimpressed by measures to turn it into something more like a conventional army

---

10. Estimates in Rials (1985), p. 171.
11. Election details in Dautry and Scheler (1960), pp. 126–7.
12. Rougerie (1971), p. 59.

by forming combat companies of the younger men, remained firmly local in recruitment and activity: it drilled, paraded with bands and colours, stood guard in its own *arrondissement*, and did spells of guard duty at the nearest stretch of ramparts, which for all the battalions of the outer districts meant home ground. Elections of officers and delegates to its *conseils de famille* (officially to look after the welfare of dependants, but tending to act as quasi-shop stewards) meant constant political activity. The almost universal nature of its functions – as substitute workplace, provider of family income, political club, source of neighbourhood status, recreation organization, expression of patriotism and channel for 'male bonding' lubricated by convivial drinking – made it the centre of urban life and an unprecedented instrument for local social integration in a mobile, rather impersonal and largely immigrant city where it was notorious for neighbours never to meet. 'Everyone stays in his own *quartier*; you talk to anybody you run into,' wrote the painter and National Guard Edouard Manet.[13] The attraction of playing at soldiers was powerful: for Frenchmen of Right and Left, military virtues were honoured. The Right had its legends of chivalry, the Left its saga of 'the volunteers of the Year II'; none were averse to dressing up in dashing uniforms. Now they were playing the part in deadly serious, under the eyes of their neighbours, and with their families exposed to the sufferings of war.

However, enthusiasm turned to disillusion, for the military high command never trusted the National Guard or regarded it as a serious military force. This was a self-fulfilling prophecy, as they made no significant effort to train it or give it useful employment. Its indiscipline, insubordination and tendency to panic if ever placed in situations of real or imagined danger was therefore never remedied, and indeed probably worsened by enforced inactivity, drunkenness and the often undisguised hostility and contempt shown to it by the regular army. It therefore became dangerously disaffected: 36 battalion commanders, 185 company captains and more than 270 lieutenants were cashiered by the high command.[14]

Privation and frustration, October–December

The dying imperial government had brought food stocks into the city as a precaution – including large numbers of sheep and cattle

13. Clayson (1998), p. 391.   14. Rougerie (1955), p. 212.

which grazed in the Bois de Boulogne and the Champs Elysées. It was assumed that two months' supply would be ample, because Paris would necessarily have been relieved by then or the war would be over. The siege of such a vast city was unprecedented, and the very idea that Paris, centre of civilization, could become a military target, subject to all the privations of war, was difficult to conceive. Hugo professed indignant incredulity: 'Is the nineteenth century to witness this frightful phenomenon? . . . Can you give this spectacle to the world? Can you, Germans, become Vandals again; personify barbarism decapitating civilization?'[15] The answer was yes, and with gusto: the 'New Babylon' would be chastised, with German troops as the willing agents of divine wrath.

So besieged it was, cut off from news except by balloon and carrier pigeon, and forced to rely on the food stocks in public and private hands, supplemented by risky market gardening in the devastated suburban no-man's-land. Stocks began to dwindle detectably in October. The government favoured economic freedom in principle and was reluctant to cause public alarm or provoke the disappearance of food stocks underground into a black market. So it introduced a bare minimum of requisitioning and rationing. Policy was incoherent and less than efficient. Requisitions and controls were brought in piecemeal, often too late. They were incompletely applied. Horsemeat (sometimes replaced by salt cod) was distributed from the end of October at controlled prices but rapidly diminishing quantities (by late November only 35 grammes per day); most other sources of meat were exhausted by mid-November. Bread, the main staple, had its price controlled on 23 September but was not rationed. This meant a good deal of waste, with allegations of cheap bread being fed to animals, for example. Its quantity and quality deteriorated, until it appeared to be made from 'old panama hats picked out of the gutter': wheat-flour was eked out with rice, peas, barley, bran and even straw. 'Luxury' bread was forbidden on 12 January, and belatedly rationing was introduced on the 18th, at 300 grammes a day per adult. Other foodstuffs were freely traded, and hence rationed by their steeply increasing price. Rice, however, remained plentiful. Domestic pets (whose keeping was frowned on as unpatriotic), zoo animals, wild birds, Seine fish and urban fauna (a market in rats and mice grew up outside the Hôtel de Ville) provided an intriguing but minor supplement to the main source of protein, the city's horses, two-thirds of which were eventually

15. Horne (1965), p. 73.

consumed at a rate of 500–600 per day. Wine (of which there were huge stocks at Bercy, the centre of the trade) remained plentiful, as, reportedly, did Colman's mustard. Many people lived mainly on bread, wine and coffee.

In these circumstances, local power and local administration, that of the mayors and assistant mayors of the *arrondissements*, became crucial. Haussmann had already decentralized some functions, such as poor relief. His road building, Gaillard and Gould have argued, tended to slice the outer districts of Paris into chunks; and these chunks may already have developed a rudimentary sense of community. Life under siege hugely accelerated and deepened these trends: *arrondissements*, previously impersonal bureaucratic divisions, now became the focus of everyday existence. The administration of the National Guard, on which most families depended for their livelihood, was in the hands of the mayors, who had to arrange for clothing, equipment and armament, which meant work for thousands of unemployed seamstresses, among others. The lodging of thousands of refugees was also the mayors' responsibility. So was poor relief, and as food and fuel prices rose, more and more people resorted to it – 477,000 by December. So was food distribution, which became probably the greatest preoccupation of all but the wealthiest Parisians. The mayors set up controlled municipal butchers' shops, supplied ration cards, and distributed flour to bakeries. As other foodstuffs, and fuel for cooking, rose to unprecedented prices, municipal canteens supplied 190,000 meals per day, 25,000 in the 18th *arrondissement* alone.[16] Much of the cost was met by charitable donations.

Political activity was therefore focused on the *arrondissements*. Republican mayors, appointed by the government, began to secularize local schools; they set up cooperatives and employment exchanges; they called on women to form committees to organize care of the wounded – all activities that would be taken up later by the Commune. The vigilance committees set up soon after the 4 September revolution involved themselves in organizing – or criticizing the official organization of – arms, uniforms and food. In left-wing districts, they coexisted with, merged with, or in one case (the 13th *arrondissement*) practically replaced the mayoral administration. Political clubs, meeting in dancehalls and other meeting rooms, probably attracted a mainly local audience, as before the war, and local politicians and activists used them to try to win support or

16. Serman (1986), p. 149.

explain their actions to their constituents. Attendance, however, was fairly small (usually a hundred or two), and probably usually the same people. Those political activists who were elected as National Guard commanders also found their time and energy absorbed in organizational details and petty rivalries.[17] This localization of activity, which may have helped Parisians stand the strains of the Prussian siege and later the civil war, was probably also one reason why the revolutionary activists found it hard to organize on a city-wide basis, even as living conditions and the military situation went from depressing to desperate.

There has been a long literary tradition from 1870 onwards of jaunty descriptions of the siege as experienced by middle-class men, which stress its incongruous and amusing aspects, illustrated with unlikely menus and recipes for braised elephant's trunk or fricasseed cat. That Parisians were reduced to eating rats has undoubtedly always been the most widely known fact about the war of 1870 (and it is often wrongly assumed to have been so during the Commune too). But the siege was a gruelling, tedious, claustrophobic and debilitating ordeal for poorer Parisians, which largely explains the resentments that developed during and after it. The daily burden, which fell almost entirely on women, began with long waits on dark and icy mornings outside butchers' and bakers' for scraps of meat and bread: the word *queue* now became familiar in English via journalists' descriptions. The writer Edmond de Goncourt, not always very sensitive to the sufferings of his poorer neighbours, noted in his diary on 12 December that a girl had offered to sleep with him for a crust of bread, and on 18 January wrote, 'Imagine that there are people condemned to live on so little! Women were weeping in the line at the Auteuil bakery.'[18] Milk for babies was short, and often adulterated; mothers who breastfed were themselves existing on a more than usually inadequate diet. Victorine Brocher recalled her desperate, and finally unsuccessful, struggle to keep her baby alive: 'until then he'd been quite happy, but he took on such a twisted, sad little face'.[19] Haussmann's newly created water supply was cut off by the besiegers, leaving the city dependent on dirty water from the Seine. The temperature fell regularly below zero towards the end of December. There was little fuel for heating and cooking, and at very high prices. Accommodation, cramped at the best of times, bore the extra burden of refugees from the suburbs

17. Lefrançais (1972), p. 322.
18. Goncourt (1969), pp. 171, 199.   19. Brocher (1977), p. 112.

and in January from the Left Bank, which the Germans began to shell. Struggles for food, fuel and shelter inevitably involved and politicized women, as so often in the past. They were a strong presence in political clubs, criticizing the failings of the government and often goading men in general into greater activity: as Hollis Clayson puts it, 'a beleaguered and disempowered masculinity co-existed and contrasted sharply with a masculinized and empowered femininity'.[20] The mobilization of women in a struggle of the whole community would carry over into the postwar months, and give a distinctive shape to the Commune.

The consequences of deteriorating conditions were grimly predictable: sharp increases in pneumonia, tuberculosis, smallpox and typhoid. By the end of the siege, the death rate was four times its peacetime level. Nearly 42,000 more people, especially babies and the elderly, died during the siege than in the corresponding months of 1869–70.[21] Goncourt noted on 7 January: 'The sufferings of Paris during the siege? A joke for two months. In the third month the joke went sour. Now nobody finds it funny any more, and we are moving fast towards starvation.'[22]

Privation was not equally shared. Those who had had the means to lay in tinned and dried food or even their own livestock, or who could afford to pay the market prices for meat and vegetables, did not need to go hungry, even if they had to vary their diet with dubious meat and were deprived of crisp white bread. For the poor and even the moderately well off it was a different matter. Remember that the daily pay of a National Guard was 1.50 francs: by Christmas, a rat cost 50–75 centimes; an egg 2 francs; a cabbage, 5 francs; a rabbit, 40 francs. Boulevard restaurants and wealthy private households, however, managed festive Christmas and New Year dinners. A fashionable intellectual dining club had a medal struck to thank their favourite boulevard restaurateur for having ensured throughout that 'they never once noticed that they were dining in a city of two million besieged souls'. In short, the siege, far from creating the socio-economic levelling effect of twentieth-century wars (in which conditions were often far worse), produced a gross caricature of peacetime social inequality, with differences in basic living standards between the rich and the rest not seen since the eighteenth century. Moreover, the government's vacillating policy

20. Clayson (1998), p. 397.
21. *Enquête sur les actes du gouvernement de la défense nationale* [*EGDN*], vol. 21, pp. 464–5. See also Vacher (1871).
22. Goncourt (1978), p. 181.

caused many to believe that their sufferings could be alleviated by fairer and more determined action.

Nevertheless, the privations seem to have been borne with remarkable forbearance, though we know too little to be sure. Perhaps the full extent of the differences in living standards was not generally known, though there were persistent and well-founded suspicions of hoarding and speculation. There were often minor troubles at the central market: grumbling, shouts of 'Down with the profiteers', sometimes food being snatched, and occasionally National Guards either helping themselves or forcing stallholders to sell at lower prices. A bakery in the Rue Montmartre was attacked when it persisted in baking white bread for its richer customers – seen as particularly provocative. During the late December cold spell, firewood was seized from building sites and woodyards by sizeable crowds of men, women and children in many of the poorer districts; fences and trees were also chopped down. But there was seemingly little open revolt or violence. When a property-owner shot a would-be thief (probably with his National Guard rifle) the police regarded this as a shocking isolated incident.[23] The calm was perhaps testimony to the relative effectiveness of the mayors' administration and the labours of the municipal canteens.

In any case, the struggle for food and fuel was not seen in conventional class terms: on the contrary, it made peacetime conflicts between employers and employees obsolete. Moroever, some observers thought that the lower-middle class suffered the most from shortages and high prices. Significantly, the only popular member of the government, whom the revolutionaries hoped to win over to their side, was Dorian, a wealthy iron-master who had been the target of serious strikes in the late 1860s. Far from being seen now as a capitalist exploiter, as minister of armaments he was both a patriot and a provider of jobs. Popular resentment was concentrated on a minority (partly imaginary, or at least remote) – the well-fed, hoarders and profiteers. A speaker in a Belleville club complained that 'in the rich quarters the bread is white'. The wives of (former) workers and (former) employers must have waited in the same queues and shared the same grievances, just as their husbands in the National Guard shivered together on the ramparts and grumbled about their commanders. In the words of a speaker in a club in the working-class 11th *arrondissement*, 'three-quarters of Paris is suffering the most frightful misery, while the other quarter is getting rich

23. Police reports in *EGDN*, vol. 25, pp. 557–64.

by speculation'; in other words, profiteers were the enemy.[24] Shared
privation explains the reiterated demands made in clubs in the
popular districts and in the left-wing press for requisition of food
stocks and general rationing: this was a constant element in demands
for a Commune.

The livelihood of most Parisians had become extremely precarious in what amounted to a mass pauperization of the lower-middle-
and working-class population, reliant on palliative wartime measures
taken by the government. Up to 900,000 people were dependent
on the pay and allowances given by the National Guard. This had
become the main or sole income for those dependent on industries
that the siege had closed down, including the luxury-goods industry,
which employed a large number of wage earners and self-employed
craftsmen. Women formerly employed in the huge Paris clothing
industry were given work, sometimes in cooperatives, making uniforms
or (more excitingly) balloons; this became the 'training ground'
for women activists, says Schulkind.[25] Engineering firms large and
small went over to arms manufacture. Foundries cast cannons and
shells. Builders worked on ramparts and barricades. Because these
were means of subsistence only, the imperial government had suspended the payment of commercial bills on 16 August; the republican government halted payment of rents for the duration of the
war on 30 September, and instructed the municipal pawnshop, the
Mont de Piété, to allow the reclaim without repayment of items up
to 15 francs. These were not unprecedented measures: similar steps
were taken by municipal authorities in other French cities, as they
had been in other countries at war. Taken as a whole, they meant
that the Parisian economy, and most of its population, had become
dependent on the war for a livelihood, and that transition to peace
would be a delicate operation.

Defeat and disillusion, November–January

Peace, however, was a taboo subject. Parisians knew little of the
situation beyond the German lines. News via pigeon and the occasional smuggled newspaper was irregular, and so optimistic rumours
were frequent almost to the end. The great hope was that new
armies in the provinces, raised by Gambetta, Minister of War and

---

24. *EGDN*, vol. 25, p. 579. See also comments in Gould (1995), pp. 138–52.
25. Schulkind (1985), p. 135.

the Interior, who had left Paris by balloon on 7 October to galvanize the war effort, would march to their aid. In November, the new Army of the Loire pushed the Germans out of Orleans. This was hailed as a triumph, not least because of the parallel with Joan of Arc; in reality it was a minor and precarious advance. But when the news reached Paris, a sortie was hastily organized to join up with the supposedly advancing relief force. On 30 November, in freezing weather, 60,000 men tried to break out on the south-eastern side of Paris. They showed stubborn courage, suffered 10,000 casualties, but could not pierce the German lines. The temperature fell to minus 14 degrees, and after three nights in the open, their commander ordered a retreat. Ironically, the Army of the Loire was simultaneously being defeated, and so the sortie, unknown to the combatants, was in any case doomed. From this time on, there was really no hope for Paris: it could only hold out as long as its food stocks did.

This was probably not the view of most Parisians, and certainly not of the Left. There ensued a long struggle between invincible discourse and material impotence. Since September, Parisian patriots, led by the revolutionary leaders and National Guard commanders, had been expressing practically daily in speeches, poems, pamphlets, posters and articles their utter determination to pursue *la résistance à outrance*, to die rather than surrender, to mount a *sortie torrentielle* to trample the Germans underfoot, and if necessary (in a commonly used flourish) 'to bury themselves beneath the ruins of Paris' rather than surrender. The Government of National Defence and the generals had felt obliged to promise the same. It was now extremely difficult to retract. The authorities made statements and followed policies which they regarded as undesirable but necessary to appease public opinion. The revolutionary patriots had the easier task of publicly blaming all failures and sufferings on the weakness or treason of the government: patriotic fervour and political ambition went hand in hand. Hence, a constant theme of the clubs and the left-wing press was to demand more vigorous and revolutionary measures to sweep away the obstacles to victory, as 'our forefathers' had done in 1792–93. All this was encapsulated in the word 'Commune', the revolutionary embodiment of the people of Paris, which would surmount all difficulties. A speaker at the Club de la Reine Blanche on 10 January explained how a Commune would save Paris:

first it will easily ensure the resistance of the population for two months by decreeing general requisition of food, and carrying out the necessary searches in convents and the houses of the rich bourgeois who have piled up a year's supplies and stuff themselves while the people starve (*applause*); the Commune will then get rid of military dictatorship; it will divide the command between several generals, with a Commissar of the Republic behind each of them ready to blow his brains out in case of treason (*expressions of agreement*); and finally the Commune will do justice to cowards and traitors.[26]

The people of Paris had become the principal determinant of the continuation of the war. As winter dragged on and repeated military failure, occupation, requisitions and reprisals sapped the will to resist of a growing proportion of people outside Paris, the war became increasingly a battle of wills between Germans and Parisians: 'the Republican dictators in Paris do not dare to consult the country', noted Moltke on 12 October.[27] Jules Favre understood perfectly that the defence of Paris was a political imperative, to which purely military considerations had to give way:

> the generals should remember that they are not merely the defenders of a citadel, they are also and above all the champions of a great city, which encloses a large population, whose passions and political and social movements impose their own requirements. The city of Paris wants to be defended *à outrance*.[28]

This situation was probably unique in modern history. A very high level of mobilization for war of the civilian population, with arming of most men, was being carried out in a framework of liberal democracy, with broad freedom of speech, assembly and the press, and reluctance to use extreme measures of repression against political insurrection or military insubordination. Only one death sentence was carried out throughout the siege: of a soldier caught deserting to the enemy. The French and Prussian governments faced the same problem: how could the Parisians be induced to accept defeat?

Bismarck insisted that 'five or six days' bombardment would do the trick, by frightening 'the sovereign Paris mob . . . which has the final word' into surrender.[29] On 5 January shelling of the city began. It continued with varying intensity for three weeks, averaging a shell every two or three minutes. The effect was much less than expected in casualties (about 400 in all) or material damage. The place hit most heavily was Montparnasse cemetery. Watching the bombardment became a popular spectacle, and small boys set up a trade in shell fragments. If anything, determination to resist may have been

---

26. Molinari (1871), pp. 222–3.   27. Moltke (1922), vol. 2, p. 400.
28. Speech to council of war, 31 December, *EGDN*, vol. 21, p. 314.
29. Busch (1898), vol. 1, p. 333; Howard (1967), p. 357 n.1.

strengthened, though there was eventually a sizeable migration from the Left Bank, the area within range of the guns.

The beginning of the bombardment had political consequences. A second *affiche rouge* appeared on 6 January. It reiterated criticism of the government for its military failures ('We are 500,000 combatants and 200,000 Prussians surround us!'), and warned Parisians that defeat would mean 'famine, ruin and shame', with the destruction of the city's economy and the National Guard dragged off as prisoners to Germany. Its remedies were now familiar: 'General requisitioning. Free rations. Mass attack. . . . Make way for the People! Make way for the Commune!'[30] General Trochu's response was a poster of his own promising no surrender. He also planned another sortie, involving for the first time the combat units of the National Guard, as the Left had long demanded. As military planners knew, this was a morally dubious enterprise: it had virtually no chance of success. But it would prove to the National Guard and the Left that there was no military panacea. As one general put it bluntly, 'These National Guard clowns want to get their heads blown off. We'll give them the opportunity.' Ordinary Parisians, National Guards and Gardes Mobiles persisted in believing that victory was still possible. One wrote home as late as 16 January, 'The population is enduring admirably the sufferings inflicted on us by the besiegers. We shall hang on, no one thinks of surrender.'[31] This made the sudden collapse of their hopes all the more devastating, and their anger with the government all the greater.

The sortie on 19 January was the first time since 1814 that the National Guard had faced a foreign enemy. The attack was aimed towards the German headquarters at Versailles, 10 miles south-west of Paris, defended by a thick belt of trenches, fortified buildings, batteries and obstacles. The 90,000 French, including 42,000 National Guards, were soon brought to a standstill. Some National Guard units panicked, fired in all directions causing casualties on their own side, and scattered; others, determined to prove themselves, suffered heavy casualties in frontal assaults on strong German positions. After a day's fighting, counter-attacks pushed them all back to their starting point. Some 4,000 men were killed or wounded, 1,500 of them National Guards. The Germans lost only 600.

Many must now have realized that surrender was inevitable. Only a few hundred protesters, including a few National Guard

---

30. Dautry and Scheler (1960), pp. 146–7.
31. Audoin-Rouzeau (1989), pp. 276–7.

units mainly from the 13th and 14th *arrondissements* where Blanquists were active, gathered once again at the Hôtel de Ville. As before, revolutionary leaders waited on events in the vicinity. Shooting started, and five people were killed, including the Blanquist Sapia, one of the leaders of the forlorn enterprise. Activists were angry that electrifying speeches in clubs had not translated into acts. One reproached a club in Belleville, 'For two days we've been calling you to arms. . . . How many came this morning to the Hôtel de Ville? I'll tell you, because I was there. There weren't even forty of us.'[32] The police reported apathy in the working-class districts: 'Agitation not expected in Belleville.'[33] But few of the conservative National Guard units turned out to support the government either. Despair and disgust had become widespread.

The government now openly sought an armistice. It was accorded on 28 January for 21 days, during which general elections would be called for a National Assembly to approve peace terms. This marked the end of the war: the government was determined not to allow Gambetta to try to continue resistance in the provinces; and few provincials indeed (except left-wingers in some of the cities) wanted to try. Food would be allowed into Paris, but first, the forts dominating the city would be surrendered to the Germans. The Paris garrison would not become prisoners of war. The regular troops would be disarmed except for 12,000 men to keep order; but the National Guard would keep its weapons – there seemed no way of disarming it.

There was general dismay and deep frustration at the news of the armistice. The press was full of protests. One drafted by five National Guard battalions was typical in its expression of impotent humiliation: 'In 1792 our forefathers defeated all Europe, without bread, without clothes, without shoes; in 1871 we are surrendering with only Prussia against us, when our arsenals are full of arms and munitions.'[34] But there was no revolt. Thirty-five National Guard battalion commanders tried to organize resistance, but the ringleaders were simply arrested. Paris had held out for four hard and dispiriting months; perhaps the hopelessness of its situation had become undeniable. Some felt a shamefaced relief that it was over: like relatives at a rich man's funeral, said one British resident, they were not quite so sad as they looked. Trainloads of food and coal began to arrive, and thousands queued for relief supplies, including

32. Molinari (1871), p. 265.
33. Audoin-Rouzeau (1989), p. 281.   34. Rougerie (1971), p. 82.

large quantities sent by British donors. As soon as they could, tens, perhaps hundreds, of thousands of people made for the countryside, many of them middle-class National Guards.

If acquiescent, Parisians were bitter. People of all parties blamed the government for their defeat, and for the hunger, cold, disease and bombardment they had suffered in vain. In the words of one National Guard (a non-revolutionary English volunteer)

> Gave my resignation to the Captain, feeling heartily disgusted with the whole affair. . . . I pity the people, but scorn the chiefs . . . having endured a bloodless campaign of 40 days' duration without hardly seeing the enemy or firing a shot. And for such services they talk of giving everyone a medal. Why I should be ashamed to wear it![35]

Yet there was no revolt and no civil war, in spite of the genuine emotion, the patriotic and revolutionary rhetoric, and the vast armed force potentially available. If we compare the situation of Paris with that of Petrograd in 1917 or Berlin in 1918, where revolution also emerged from the sufferings and failures of war, we see obvious differences as well as similarities. The similarities include material privations (more severe during the First World War), frustrated patriotism, discredited regimes, and weakened forces of repression. But in 1917 and 1918 revolutionaries aimed to stop wars that governments were attempting to pursue at the cost of intensifying the sufferings of the population; in Paris, protests had aimed to continue the war *à outrance* – perhaps inherently less appealing, and certainly less plausible as the military and food situation deteriorated. Also, the immediate political prospect after the armistice was for free elections – something that was bound to distract from revolutionary projects.

The road to revolution, February–March

Much more was needed to bring about revolution. The first step was the election of a National Assembly on 8 February. The primary issue was war or peace. Conservatives, supported by most rural voters, had campaigned for peace. The Left, centred on the cities, stressed patriotism and republicanism and urged continuation of the war: a Blanquist manifesto promised impeachment of the government and renewal of hostilities. But republicans also looked beyond the issue of war and peace to that of the postwar future. In the words of the

35. Horne (1965), pp. 241–2.

radical paper *Le Rappel* (8 February 1871) (main support of the Parisian republican candidates): 'It is no longer an army you are facing . . . it is no longer Germany. . . . It is more. It is monarchy, it is despotism.' Its editor, Lockroy, urged readers to vote for 'secularists to fight Catholicism, republicans to fight monarchy, socialists to fight proletarianization'. Republicans pledged that 'they would not permit the rural majority to call the Republic into question'.[36]

But over 400 royalists were returned to 150 republicans. Republicans derided this '*majorité rurale*': 'universal suffrage', proclaimed *Le Rappel*, 'is worse than ignorant, it is stupid'. The old-established division between rural and urban France had been greatly deepened by the war. 'There are two Frances,' wrote François-Victor Hugo,

> one whose capital is Paris . . . industrial, commercial, educated, labouring . . . democratic, loving liberty and equality. . . . The other France has papal Rome as its centre . . . a feudal . . . clerical and Jesuit France, which can neither read nor write, an enemy of progress and science.[37]

Paris (which had 43 seats) returned nearly all pro-war radical republicans. Mostly of the older generation of the 1848 Revolution, they were led by the 60-year-old Louis Blanc, 69-year-old Victor Hugo, and 64-year-old Giuseppe Garibaldi, all elected with over 200,000 votes out of some 329,000 cast.

The defeat of the established moderate republican leadership who had formed the now detested Government of National Defence gives a measure of the degree of radicalization caused by the war: Favre was the only one of the former government to be elected in Paris, narrowly, with a mere 81,000 votes. That these men were reappointed to the new government headed by Adolphe Thiers, nominated Chief of the Executive Power by the new National Assembly (and the man whose earlier negotiations with Bismarck had helped to provoke the abortive insurrection of 31 October), was bound to render the new government suspect to Parisians.

It was not the revolutionary Left that had come to the fore, however. The International and other revolutionary groups had put forward a list of 43 *candidats socialistes révolutionnaires*, who were standing 'without compromise with the bourgeoisie'; but only five were elected, and three of those (including Garibaldi) because of their personal prestige and support of more moderate republican groups. Even the best known of the rest could only attract 10–20

---

36. Giard (1966–68), pp. 35–6. This election was on the list system, with electors casting multiple votes.
37. Huard (1996), p. 216.

per cent of the total vote, roughly the number they had had the previous November. Blanqui himself received only 52,000, for example, and Eugène Varlin, a well known International militant, only 58,000. This amounted to no more than a quarter of the vote even in the reddest working-class districts, the 11th, 13th, 19th and 20th *arrondissements*.[38]

Paris's deputies were firmly opposed to the two ideas most clearly embodied by the National Assembly majority: peace and monarchy. A preliminary peace treaty was negotiated with Bismarck by Thiers. He had for months accepted as inevitable German annexation of Alsace and part of Lorraine, but the debate on this 'mutilation of the Fatherland' caused heart-rending scenes in the National Assembly on 1 March, in which Victor Hugo and other Parisian deputies played a prominent role. Thiers struck a deal with Bismarck by which France would keep the strategic fortress of Belfort (which had gallantly held out against a German siege throughout the war) in exchange for a German victory parade down the Champs Elysées – a blow to patriotic Parisians proud of having at least kept the Germans out of their city. The treaty was voted by the Assembly by 546 to 107. 'What shame, what dishonour, these royalists have brought upon the country!' wrote a National Guard to his family. 'The whole population has rage in its heart.'[39] Several leading republican deputies resigned their seats, including three of the four who had topped the poll in Paris – Hugo, Garibaldi and Gambetta.

The German parade, scheduled for 1 March, had grave unforeseen consequences. It was widely expected that fighting might break out when the Germans set foot inside the city walls, if it had not already done so when the original armistice expired on 26 February. So the Paris National Guard re-mobilized itself spontaneously and set up an autonomous political leadership, the Republican Federation of the National Guard of the Seine. In February, meetings of battalion delegates had been held to defend the '30 sous' pay, and to present candidates for the National Assembly elections on the grounds that the National Guard was now 'the natural framework for the political organization of the city' – a significant testimony to its importance.[40] The delegate meetings continued throughout February to coordinate action to defend the Republic, prepare for *guerre à outrance* and resist disarmament. At a series of mass meetings of delegates, said to represent some 200 battalions, statutes

38. Rougerie (1973), pp. 41–4.
39. Horne (1965), p. 261.   40. Clifford (1975), p. 81.

were drawn up for a Republican National Guard Federation (hence the name 'Fédérés' for its adherents – a name that also recalled the 1790s). A directing Central Committee was elected.

Big patriotic and republican demonstrations by National Guard battalions began on 24 February, the anniversary of the 1848 revolution, at the July Column (commemorating the 1830 revolution) in the Place de la Bastille. Tens of thousands took part, both women and men, and neighbourhoods across the city were involved in ceremonies which showed one of the highest levels of spontaneous mass activity of the whole period 1870–71. To take a single example, the 45th battalion from the mainly working-class 15th *arrondissement*, because its military prowess against the Germans had been criticized, 'considered it a question of honour to rehabilitate itself'. It did this by marching to place a wreath – 'a superb wreath, by the way' – at the July Column. 'The march from Grenelle to the Bastille was one big ovation.' On its return home, it found that a crowd of well-wishers had planted a Liberty Tree, decorated with both red flags and tricolours, in the Square du Commerce, in the middle of the *arrondissement*:

> This was another, entirely spontaneous, fête, and despite nightfall and the beginning of rain, the Grenellois came out *en masse* at the sound of the drums and bugles announcing the triumphant return of the regenerated 45th. All mingled together, citizens and militiamen, and despite the fatigue of the day, all stayed for quite a long while, singing patriotic songs and wishing this infant [tree] a longer life than its ancestors of 1848.[41]

Throughout that night, as the original armistice expired, thousands of National Guards assembled in arms to resist a possible Prussian attack. Every day, some 20 to 30 battalions were undertaking the patriotic pilgrimage to the Bastille. Not all was joyful festivity, however. On the day the 45th battalion laid their wreath, a plain-clothes policeman, Vincenzini, was caught there, beaten, thrown into the Seine and pushed under with boathooks until he drowned. Low-level violence became common throughout the working-class districts, which became 'no-go' areas from which police and regular troops had to be withdrawn.

Moreover, National Guard units were seizing arms, originally to safeguard them from capture by the Germans, but also in case of hostilities with the Germans or the government. Rifles and ammunition

---

41. Report of 45th bn, Service Historique de l'Armée de Terre, series Ly, carton 32 [SHA Ly 32].

were regularly seized from stores and arsenals before and after the German victory parade. Most important of all, 300–400 cannon – many of which had been paid for partly by public subscription during the siege and were therefore claimed as the National Guard's property – were removed from official gun parks by excited crowds. They were hauled away to Montmartre, Belleville and other parts of eastern Paris under the control of 'red' battalions. In short, the 300,000-man National Guard had escaped its official commanders: General d'Aurelle de Paladines, appointed by the government as its new general-in-chief, was regarded as a royalist defeatist, and his authority was not recognized. The government, for its part, had only 12,000 armed regular troops and a few thousand gendarmes and police. Paris was not yet in a state of insurrection, but neither was it under the government's control.

The Central Committee of the National Guard won credibility by seemingly deterring a (non-existent) German attack, while yet helping to avoid a dangerous clash by keeping its followers under control when on 1 March German troops did come for their parade, wandered around a cordoned-off area of western Paris, and went away again two days later without serious incident. At first, most of the Central Committee's members were unknown patriotic National Guards with no history of political militancy. But revolutionary activists – Blanquists, members of the International, club and vigilance-committee militants – began to infiltrate it from early March. A new Central Committee elected on 3 March saw an influx of revolutionary socialists: 11 out of 12 new members belonged to the International. It provided them with a far more popular and powerful organization than any they had managed to build for themselves. As Varlin urged his comrades:

> in two or three weeks the city will be controlled by socialist battalion commanders. . . . Another week and we shall be masters of 17 *arrondissements* out of 20 . . . the three others will do nothing to stop us. Then we shall chase the prefecture of police out of Paris, overthrow the government, and France will follow us.[42]

However, the Central Committee never 'controlled' the city or commanded the National Guard. Its importance was as a rallying point which encouraged widespread local self-mobilization in readiness to defend Paris and the Republic.

After the Germans left, tension relaxed. On 4 March, the Foreign Minister, Jules Favre, reported that 'the day has been calmer', and

42. Cordillot (1991), p. 207.

two days later advised Thiers to 'show trust in this great population and you will win it over without difficulty'. But then a series of measures taken by the Assembly, the government and the military authorities in Paris rekindled popular anger. On 10 March, the National Assembly, which had convened in Bordeaux, took two important decisions. First, it had to decide what to do when the wartime moratorium on commercial bills of exchange[43] expired on 13 March, and it resolved to phase in payments over three months. As many historians have mistakenly described this as making all debts payable overnight, it seems possible that Parisians too misunderstood. We know little about the precise effects of the law, but it was badly received by small businessmen in Paris – at least those who owed money. According to the minister Jules Simon, some 40,000 faced insolvency.[44] As they formed an influential part of the population, and especially of the conservative National Guard batallions, this was politically serious. Many Parisians believed that this measure was only a first step: that they would now be expected to pay the rent arrears that had been suspended during the siege, and that National Guard pay would be stopped. That would have reduced most Parisians to destitution, for as we have seen, they depended on these emergency wartime measures to make ends meet.

Second, the Assembly decided to move not to Paris, where conservatives feared they would be at the mercy of 'the cobblestones of the mob', but to Versailles. This Thiers regarded as a reasonable compromise (royalists had wanted to go much further away, to Orleans or Fontainebleau), but Parisians regarded 'decapitalization' as an insult, a blow to the city's prestige and economic prospects, and proof of the monarchists' sinister intentions. Louis Blanc, veteran socialist and Parisian deputy, warned presciently that this would cause 'formidable anger' among Parisians, cause them to give Paris 'a government of its own' and bring forth 'from the ashes of a cruel foreign war . . . a civil war more horrible still'. Fuel was added to the flames when the Paris military authorities announced the court martial sentences on the 31 October insurgents (including the Belleville hero Flourens, rescued from prison at gunpoint by his men) and banned six left-wing newspapers.

43. These were promises to pay at a future date (usually three months) for goods received, and thus resembled post-dated cheques; but the recipient could cash them before the maturity date at a discount at certain banks. Thus transactions could be financed on credit, very important for small Paris businesses.

44. Simon (1879), vol. 1, p. 207.

These developments, interpreted by Parisians as deliberately hostile acts by by a reactionary 'rural majority', reignited tension. Most importantly, they caused the failure of negotiations for a peaceful handover of the cannon seized earlier by groups of National Guards. These guns, held at several sites in northern and eastern Paris, most importantly Montmartre, La Villette and Belleville, had become a potent symbol of the independent power of the city and its people. That was why the Thiers government wanted them back. When negotiation failed, it tried surprise military action on 18 March, and, as we saw earlier, the outcome was an unplanned mass resistance that turned into insurrection.

The motives of the resisters can be explained in part in purely political terms: there was a community-wide determination to defend the Republic, seen as the only form of government friendly to popular needs. Motives were also economic: the need to defend the National Guard, source of subsistence for a pauperized population, and a concrete expression of the old revolutionary slogan 'Qui a du fer a du pain' (those who have weapons have bread). But there was surely too a refusal to submit to the final insult of forcible, unnegotiated disarmament by an unfriendly 'rural' government, following so closely behind the humiliation of capitulation to the Germans: an aspect of what Clayson diagnoses as a 'crisis of Parisian manhood' arising from their abject failure to fulfil the masculine function of defending hearth and home.[45] That the resistance was a spontaneous reaction of crowds of women and children as well as men shows how the National Guard, as a consequence of the war, had become central to the life of the community.

The conservative elements in the National Guard – such as those who had rather unenthusiastically rescued the Government of National Defence from the revolutionaries on 31 October – this time failed to appear. Many middle-class families had left Paris after the siege, weakening the anti-revolutionary forces by 50,000 men or more, and disorganizing their battalions. Those who remained ignored the government's belated call to arms on 18 March. The shared sufferings and emotions of the siege had blurred political and social antagonisms within the city: to applaud the discomfiture of the legal government by plebeian radicals was no longer unthinkable. The government and National Assembly had upset even moderate Parisians: accepting a humiliating peace, letting the Germans march into Paris, 'decapitalizing' it, damaging its economy and on

45. Clayson (1998), p. 402.

18 March attempting to disarm its citizen's militia in an act that many assumed to be the prelude to a monarchist *coup d'état* – these were seen as anti-Parisian acts, as well as unpatriotic and reactionary ones. The government's assumption that the middle classes would in the end support it against 'the mob' proved wrong. As the socialist songwriter Jean-Baptiste Clément had noted a few days earlier, 'bourgeois and workers, rich and poor, have been serving shoulder to shoulder in the same uniform for nearly six months'.[46]

Thiers and the generals retreated hastily to Versailles with their remaining troops. Paris had not so much revolted as been abandoned. The strategy of evacuating a rebellious city – which, recalled Thiers, had worked for Windischgraetz, the Austrian general who crushed the Viennese revolt in 1848 – had been studied in the past, but there is no evidence that it had been seriously considered, let alone planned, on this occasion. All the evidence suggests hasty improvisation by a government trying to catch up with events.[47] The Central Committee of the National Guard, barely aware of what was happening and rather alarmed, found itself in charge of the city, and, hours after the government had left, gingerly occupied empty public buildings and established its headquarters – where else? – at the Hôtel de Ville, seat of the Paris Commune of 1792.

The unprecedented flight of the government made civil war likely but not – at least in the opinion of those involved – inevitable. There followed several days of tense and rather confused negotiations between the mayors of the 20 *arrondissements* and the Paris deputies (representing legal authority and maintaining contacts with the government in Versailles), and the Central Committee, which showed little desire to keep the power that had dropped into its lap. The government in Versailles, militarily vulnerable, discreetly encouraged these negotiations; significantly, it strongly discouraged any aggressive action by several thousand conservative National Guards who had belatedly organized in opposition to the insurgents. A demonstration by 'The Friends of Order' to National Guard headquarters on 22 March was fired on by Fédérés, killing a dozen marchers, and seemingly deterring any further open opposition. The Versailles government's position was weakened by pro-Parisian insurrections in Lyons on 22 March, Marseilles on the 24th, Saint-Etienne on the 25th and Le Creusot on the 26th.

---

46. Lefebvre (1965), p. 230.
47. This question is discussed in Tombs (1981), pp. 40–3, 51–2 and Rougerie (1971), pp. 102, 106.

The Paris press, most of the National Guards and probably most Parisians wanted a peaceful outcome. The left-wing deputy Charles Delescluze – later one of the Commune's leading figures – appealed for 'conciliation', and well-known revolutionary leaders warned against a repetition of the terrible June Days of 1848. They demanded recognition of the 'rights of Paris' (which meant a high degree of autonomy for the city), and a guarantee that the National Assembly would recognize the Republic as the only legitimate form of government. Support for these demands was fairly wide, so when a meeting between the mayors, the deputies and the Central Committee agreed on 25 March to call elections to a city council for the following day, this was greeted in Paris as a peaceful way out of the crisis. Delescluze urged voting for 'republican' candidates as a way of 'putting out the fire that . . . may blaze up at any moment'.[48]

It proved not to be. The Versailles government would not overtly endorse the Parisian elections, which meant that many conservative and moderate voters boycotted them, while others had left the city. The resulting majority for revolutionary candidates made civil war more, not less, likely. In all, 229,167 men voted, compared with some 300,000 in the general elections of 8 February. Rougerie notes that the large number of abstentions proved that Paris was far from united.[49] On the other hand, despite lack of time for preparation – some of the propaganda was only hand-written – the turnout was almost the same as the total opposition vote in the 1869 elections (234,000). This indicates broad republican support for some form of autonomous Parisian government.

Many local committees and groups had put forward candidates, but most voters plumped for the lists supported by the Central Committee of the 20 Arrondissements (which had been in existence since the early days of the siege) or by the International. They phrased their appeals in the traditional language of republicanism as well as of socialism: 'The republic is in peril: to save it we must have scrupulous economy in finance, unceasing activity, and sacrifice unto death. Thus, in a similar predicament, did our forefathers of '93 pull France back from the abyss.'[50] By any measure, the election result showed a huge increase in support for the revolutionary Left. As we saw earlier, they had been able to count on as few as 6,000 obedient voters in the last year of the Empire. At the November

48. *Les Murailles politiques françaises*, vol. 2, p. 92.
49. Figures in Rougerie (1971), p. 145; the total number on the electoral register was 484, 569.
50. Rougerie (1955), p. 33.

1870 plebiscite and the 8 February Assembly elections, due to their championing of *la guerre à outrance*, their electoral following had risen to some 60,000. Now, due to extraordinary developments since the armistice and their stance as the most stalwart defenders of the Republic and Paris, it had reached 190,000. Only 40,000 votes on 26 March had gone to anti-revolutionary republicans, usually the existing *arrondissement* mayors, of whom only 19 were elected; they had hoped to use the elections to defeat the revolutionary party and reach a compromise with Versailles, and, this tactic having failed, they resigned. Consequently, the 66-strong Commune[51] which took power on 29 March was an unequivocally revolutionary body: a rare instance of a democratically elected revolution directed against a democratically elected government. The first fighting broke out only four days later.

The problem with explaining this Parisian revolution is that it has too many causes. If we recall discontents in Haussmann's Paris, agitation in the late 1860s, emotions and sufferings during the siege, disappointment at defeat, anger with the Government of National Defence and its successor, indignation at the peace terms, suspicion of the National Assembly, and resentment of its measures we have more than enough cause for popular feelings of outrage. If we recall the reemergence of a revolutionary Left under the Empire, the development of strong left-wing political culture in the working-class districts before and during the war, with clubs, newspapers and well-known leaders, we see the creation of a revolutionary leadership eager to act. The tremendous impact of war and siege disrupted everyday life and transformed politics. The raising of a mass National Guard with elected officers, the politicization and growing solidarity of its battalions rooted in local communities, its ample armament and its autonomous Central Committee constituted an unprecedentedly powerful revolutionary instrument. A measure of the change is the force commanded by the Blanquists, the most persistant would-be revolutionaries. In August 1870, they mustered about 60 combatants; by October, Blanquist officers controlled several battalions of National Guards; by late March 1871 the three generals commanding the insurgent National Guard were Blanquists. We can surely conclude that without the unique circumstances created by the 'people's war' against Germany the Commune is inconceivable.

---

51. There were 92 seats, but due to several men being chosen in more than one *arrondissement*, only 85 were elected, of whom the 19 moderates soon resigned.

The paradox is that it took so long for revolution to result. Neither opposition to the Empire and Haussmann, nor wartime privations, nor defeat had been able to bring about an effective revolt. In retrospect, we can see that the hesitation of Parisians to throw themselves into a revolutionary adventure was a poor augury for its success. Only when the ingrained political divisions between the 'two Frances' had created a stand-off did revolution occur – one can hardly say 'break out'. And even then it was a defensive response (as in July 1830 and February and June 1848) to an aggressive and inept government action.

CHAPTER THREE

'The Political Form At Last Discovered'? The Commune as Government

According to its first and most influential analyst, Karl Marx, who wrote as events were unfolding, the Commune was a historic turning point above all as 'the political form at last discovered' for the emancipation of the working class. Unlike previous revolutions, it had abolished oppressive and expensive class institutions – army, police, bureaucracy, Church – and power was exercised by the citizens themselves 'at workmen's wages'. This alone, he declared, was epoch-making: 'The great social measure of the Commune was its own working existence.' Its legislation, in the short time available, could only 'betoken the tendency of a government of the people by the people', suggesting what it might have done had it lasted – a claim also made by several Commune leaders after the event.[1]

There have been many discussions as to what this 'tendency' was, and particularly as to how socialist it was; or more subtly, what socialism meant to Parisians in 1871. Recently, there has been interest in broader questions of the Commune's cultural modernity, presumably on the assumption that a revolution ought to be revolutionary across the board, including in its attitudes towards education, gender, the family and the arts. This chapter will look at the term 'Commune', and at how an official meaning was defined. It will examine the Commune's use of power to see whether it constituted the newly discovered emancipating 'form' discerned by Marx, and assess its various reforms and their context. Finally, it will discuss evidence of cultural innovation, including in the broad sense of changing the experience of living.

1. Marx (1966), pp. 72, 68, 78.

Meanings of 'the Commune'

The term 'Commune' began to be used as a slogan as early as September 1870. For Parisian radicals it encapsulated the revolutionary nationalism produced by the war and the fall of Napoleon III, and also the Parisian patriotism heightened by the siege. Crucial was historical evocation of the first Paris Commune, the city government during the French Revolution, and more precisely of the 'revolutionary Commune' which seized power in the city in August 1792 and was prominent in overthrowing the monarchy, radicalizing national defence, and fomenting the September Massacres of suspected enemies of the Revolution – an example of unmistakable relevance in 1870–71, underlined by the Communards' constant reference to 'our forefathers of 1792' and use of the revolutionary calendar, which placed them in Germinal Year 79. This history gave the term far greater intensity of meaning than the ordinary sense of *commune* – the basic unit of local government – even if this was included within it. As one club speaker put it:

> the Versailles commune, the Rouen commune, the Marseilles commune, they worry nobody. But the Paris Commune! That's quite different. Why? Because there's blood on that word.[2]

As Rougerie notes, there were communes with a small c, but only one with a capital C. But in both cases, it meant local democracy. The socialist thinker Pierre-Joseph Proudhon (1809–65), whose ideas had durable influence on the working-class elite, had stressed the commune as the fundamental unit of democratic sovereignty. For Paris, this meant an assertion of its 'rights' to self-government. These had been abolished as too dangerous by the Second Empire, and to demand their recovery was one expression of opposition to Bonapartism and its centralization of power. The precedent of 1792, and the decisive role played by Paris in the 1870 war, also signified its unique prerogative as leader of the nation, heart of the Revolution, and bulwark of national defence. Rougerie sums up the meaning of Commune as it developed during the siege: 'direct popular government of a city, and, because that city is Paris, because Paris is the Revolution, quasi-government of France'.[3]

As the German siege intensified, the call for a Commune became, as we saw in the last chapter, a panacea for the Paris Left, conveying many meanings. Some saw it as a legally elected city government

2. Rougerie (1971), p. 39.   3. Ibid., p. 42.

that would support and galvanize the Government of National Defence; others, as a revolutionary movement that would replace it. But the vision was never precise, and the word had a talismanic power going beyond any programme:

> I bet that even here, at the Club Favié [in Belleville], three-quarters of the audience don't know what the Commune means. . . .
> (*Shouts*) Tell us what it is then!
> The Commune means the people's rights, it means equal rationing, it means the *levée en masse* and the punishment of traitors, and the Commune, in short . . . means the Commune![4]

For the same reasons that it excited revolutionaries, it alarmed conservatives and moderates, and must have helped to rally support for the Government of National Defence as a lesser evil.

Because of the potency of the word, when the Central Committee of the National Guard found itself in power after the events of 18 March, it did not immediately proclaim the Commune. Indeed, the word was remarkably little used during the next few days. It was not clear to all Central Committee members, or to the elected deputies and mayors of Paris, that the unplanned insurrection should or could become a revolution, as the name 'Commune' would imply. As Georges Clemenceau, radical mayor of Montmartre, posed the issue, 'What exactly are your demands? Are you limiting your mandate to asking the Assembly [at Versailles] for a municipal council?' The socialist Eugène Varlin answered, 'We want not only an elected municipal council, but major municipal liberties.' But another socialist, Benoît Malon, urged moderation in the hope of obtaining concessions. Most of the Central Committee wanted immediate elections in Paris to hand the decision to the people, but wanted the elections to be legally approved so as to encourage a large turnout. Some wanted to reassure public opinion in the provinces. But others declared that Paris had made its revolution, and rejected the authority of the Assembly and of the rest of France. The well-known socialist Jean-Baptiste Millière, a Paris deputy, warned that if they tried to make Paris independent of France, 'the government will throw all France against Paris, and I foresee inevitable June Days' – an allusion to the failed 1848 insurrection, crushed by troops and provincial National Guards, which was as potent a piece of history for the Parisian Left as the 1790s. Moreover, he warned, 'the hour for social revolution has not struck'.[5]

---

4. Molinari (1871), p. 213.   5. Lissagaray (1972), pp. 122–5.

As noted earlier, attempts to reach a compromise failed, as was clear after the 26 March elections. The election proclamation, however, had not mentioned a Paris Commune, and it was only at its first session, on a motion of the Blanquist Emile Eudes, that 'the new municipal council [took] the name Paris Commune'.[6] How difficult it had been for the Commune to be born, comments Rougerie, and how little did people know, or imagine, what it was going to be.[7]

For Parisian revolutionaries, it was a glorious victory after so many failures, and hence a justification in itself. The inauguration of the Commune on 28 March was a popular military festival at the Hôtel de Ville. National Guards with colours and bands assembled at the ancient centre of Paris, the Place de Grève, in what has often been seen as the repossession of Paris by a people evicted by Haussmann's clearances. Drums rattled, bugles brayed, cannon boomed, tens of thousands of voices sang the 'Marseillaise' and – during a brief lull – the Commune was proclaimed.

> What a day! That clear, warm sun that gilds the gun-muzzles, that scent of flowers, the flutter of flags, the murmur of the passing revolution, calm and lovely as a blue river. . . . O great Paris! . . . fatherland of honour, city of salvation, bivouac of the Revolution! Whatever may happen, if we are to be again vanquished and die tomorrow, our generation is consoled! We are repaid for twenty years of defeat and anxiety.[8]

The magical qualities that the siege had concentrated into the word 'Commune' could hardly be better expressed. But what did this victory promise? How was the Commune to be defined and put into practice?

The Commune defined, March–April

The new Commune Council (usually called simply the Commune) had to explain itself, and it had to govern – urgently. It took immediate action on the pressing problems that had helped bring the crisis to a head: rents, commercial bills and the National Guard. On 29 March came a series of decrees. One abolished conscription and (slightly paradoxically) proclaimed that all able-bodied citizens were part of the National Guard, the only military force allowed in

6. *Procès-verbaux de la Commune* [*PVC*], vol. 1, p. 42.   7. Rougerie (1971), p. 112.
8. Jules Vallès in his paper *Le Cri du Peuple*, 28 March.

Paris. Another cancelled rent arrears accrued since the beginning of the war, and suspended sales of objects pawned at the Mont de Piété. Another forbade public employees to obey orders from Versailles. Another proclaimed the separation of Church and State – for the whole of the Left one of the most fundamental and urgent of political reforms. On 1 April a maximum salary of 6,000 francs was decreed for public employees.

First thoughts on how the Commune ought to govern were outlined in a draft proclamation 'to the citizens of Paris', which proposed a street-politician's paradise, with constant party meetings, district meetings, meetings with elected representatives who could be criticized and summarily dismissed by their electors, and election of all officials. This showed one powerful democratic ideal, of abolishing alien bureaucracy and constantly involving citizens in government. This had emerged from Proudhonism, from the grassroots activism of the late 1860s and from the local politics of vigilance committees and clubs improvised during the siege. However, the draft was rejected by the Commune, which instead adopted a different proclamation, published on 30 March, of mainly Blanquist inspiration. This was more extreme in tone towards the Versailles government, stigmatized as criminals and monarchist conspirators, but it said nothing about reforming the system of government, and merely urged the population to support the new regime.

This was an early hint of a divergence of ideas that would emerge openly in May. On one hand, there was a Proudhonist aspiration to unleash a revolution from below, in which initiative would remain with the people and central power wither away. In the wishful words of the irrepressible Courbet,

> Paris is a true paradise! No police, no nonsense, no exaction of any kind, no arguments! Everything in Paris rolls along like clockwork. . . . All the government bodies are organized federally and run themselves. . . . The Paris Commune is more successful than any form of government has ever been.[9]

On the other, there was a more Jacobin and Blanquist tendency towards dynamic, inspiring and powerful revolutionary authority. However, this distinction is clearer in retrospect than it was at the time. Commune activists were very eclectic in their political ideas (see below p. 118): respect for the 'Jacobin' revolutionary tradition coexisted with Proudhonist anti-authoritarianism. Always more

9. Courbet (1992), pp. 416–17.

urgent than ideological consistency was the need to find a way for the Commune to govern effectively in adverse circumstances.

By far the most important of these circumstances was the outbreak of civil war. The first skirmishes occurred on 2 April in the western suburbs, the no-man's-land between Paris and Versailles. This put an end to dwindling hopes that some peaceful outcome might emerge. Before it had broken out, the Commune had already defined the conflict as a defence of Paris against a royalist conspiracy supported by a motley band of former papal soldiers, policemen and primitive peasants from the reactionary western provinces – Chouans, Vendéens, Bretons, 'who have risen against the revolution in 1871 as their forefathers did against that of 1793, and who will have the same fate today as the latter did eighty years ago'.[10] The Fédérés responded by mounting an abortive mass attack on Versailles on 3 April, which began civil war in earnest.

The slogan of unity was 'Paris ville libre', which appears repeatedly in official documents and the press. It appealed to Parisian patriotism – not only that of the revolutionary Left – while attempting to reassure opinion outside the capital that this was not an attempt to impose a dictatorship on the country at large, or indeed to restart the war against Germany. The message was spelt out in a proclamation 'To the Departments' (6 April), which declared that the Commune only wanted the Republic and municipal liberties. However, it was never clear whether – in theory or in practice – the Commune assumed powers over all of France. It did not recognize the National Assembly (on the grounds, later taken up by more moderate republicans, that it had only been elected to make peace with the Germans). It immediately passed decrees with inescapably national implications: to exclude the national army from the capital, to disestablish the Churches and to impeach (*mettre en accusation*) the government.

It also adopted the red flag, symbol of revolution since the 1830s. Did this symbolize class consciousness, hostility to the 'bourgeois' republic, rejection of the national symbol in favour of a proletarian emblem? We must beware of reading back from later attitudes. The Communard newspaper *Père Duchêne* argued for adoption of the red flag on the grounds that the tricolour was not only the badge of 'shameful' moderate republics, but more important had been polluted by association with corrupt and repressive regimes, the July Monarchy (1830–48) and the Empire, and disgraced by the

10. *Journal Officiel* of the Commune [*JOC*], 1 April.

military disasters of 1870. For the popular writer and Commune member Félix Pyat, the red flag symbolized 'the people's France' as opposed to the France of the nobles (the white flag) or bourgeois France (the tricolour).[11] Hence, the red flag was far from incompatible with popular patriotism.

After three weeks' delay and much prodding from the press, the Commune produced its Declaration to the French People of 19 April – the closest to a summary of its programme. This had been drafted mainly by three journalists, the veteran Jacobin Charles Delescluze, the socialist journalist Jules Vallès and the Proudhonist Pierre Denis. It was accepted by the Commune with only one dissenting voice.

Much of the document (appendix 1) is an attack on the Versailles government (which had just begun siege operations), and an assurance to the provinces that Paris was fighting for them too, combined with a plea for their support. The rest outlined the demands and programme of 'Paris' (not of 'the revolution' or 'the proletariat'). The first demand was for the 'recognition and consolidation of the Republic' as the only legitimate form of government, and, second, the 'absolute autonomy of the Commune extended to all localities in France'. Communal autonomy was then defined: complete control over its economy, administration, security and education. Every commune had equal rights, and there was brief reference to a free federation of communes.

It is easy to point out breathtakingly utopian elements in the declaration, as contemporaries and later historians have not failed to do.[12] We cannot know how far those who voted it really agreed with it or believed it feasible. Key concepts were not elaborated. Were all France's 36,000 communes, even the tiniest, autonomous and equal? What sort of federation was supposed to link them, and how was it to be set up? But the document was, we should remember, political propaganda, not a treatise on government or a draft constitution. It aimed to be widely acceptable and, where necessary, reassuring, especially to possible well-wishers alarmed at the dictatorial and ultra-revolutionary overtones of a 'Paris Commune'. This does not mean that it is meaningless: like all such documents it responded to what its drafters thought their constituents wanted. As such, it does summarize basic themes of radical and socialist republicanism. Moreover, it contains the main steps that the Commune actually took, or tried to take.

11. Girardet (1984), p. 23. 12. See discussion in Rihs (1973), pp. 167–74.

The Declaration has several significant characteristics. It is overwhelmingly political in emphasis, a synthesis of the main themes of an existing radical consensus to which Blanquists and Proudonists also subscribed. This synthesis had recently been formulated in the 1869 Belleville Programme (see above p. 35), and some of its demands had already been put into practice during the German siege. The Commune's declaration promised 'the permanent intervention of the citizens in communal affairs' through election, accountability and popular dismissal of 'magistrates and communal officials of every grade', and by giving responsibility for order and security to the National Guard alone, replacing army and police. 'Liberty of conscience' (a code phrase meaning disestablishment of the Church, already decreed on 2 April) was declared, for secularism was one of the principal themes of Communard beliefs and actions. This political revolution, by sweeping away injustice, superstition and oppression, would have fundamental effects on society: 'It is the end of the old governmental, priest-ridden world, of militarism, of bureaucracy (*fonctionnarisme*), exploitation, market-rigging (*agiotage*), monopolies, privileges, to which the proletariat owes its serfdom.' Political injustice, in short, was the source of economic and social injustice. The victory of Paris would accomplish a 'modern revolution, the most wide-ranging and fruitful of all those that have illustrated history'.

The Declaration is remarkable for the vagueness of its social and economic content. One brief paragraph refers to the use of the Commune's autonomy to 'carry out as it sees fit' administrative and economic reforms aiming to 'develop and propagate education, production, exchange and credit; [and] to universalize power and property'. However, no actions are specified; these are left to 'the necessities of the moment, the wish of those concerned, and the data provided by experience'. As we shall see, the economic reforms carried out by the Commune confirmed the cautiousness of these words, being far less clear and radical than its politics. This suggests that the Declaration was not consciously hiding more ambitious intentions.

There are several probable reasons for this prudence in social matters. Since the failures and divisions of 1848–51 which led to the triumph of Bonapartism and the overthrow of the Second Republic, much of the Left had consciously rejected social utopianism in favour of political realism. As Gambetta had put it in his acceptance of the Belleville Programme, the 'sequence and order of priority' was that 'political reforms' come first; achievement of social reforms 'depends absolutely on the political regime . . . the form involves and determines the substance'.[13] Moroever, though French socialism covered a range of views, most agreed that the State should not play a dominant economic role, but rather facilitate workers' control by voluntary 'association' in cooperatives. As the Commune member Eugène Pottier put it in his song 'L'Internationale', one of the pithiest summaries of Communard beliefs, 'There are no supreme saviours . . . Producers, let's save ourselves!' (appendix 2). Finally, the circumstances of 1870–71 – war with Germany and now civil war against Versailles – brought politics and military combat to the fore. The Paris economy was at a partial standstill, which made peacetime industrial issues almost irrelevant. The experiences of the siege and the armistice period, especially mass participation in the National Guard, had attenuated or at least redrawn class divisions. And the onset of civil war made the greatest possible unity within Paris indispensable.

The Commune as government

CENTRAL AUTHORITY

The Commune was not, its members insisted, a 'parliament', merely debating and legislating separately from the executive. Like the revolutionary bodies of the 1790s, it was to combine tasks: to discuss, decree and execute. Executive power could only be delegated; the Commune itself would take final decisions. However, this created a never-resolved tension between decision and democratic accountability. If the Commune was not a debating chamber but a revolutionary 'council of war', as Jacobin and Blanquist members insisted, then its proceedings should not be published; and although its debates were usually published in the press without authorization until publicity was conceded on 18 April, it frequently went into secret session. It usually ignored the political clubs (which regarded themselves as the voice of the people), and banned opposition newspapers. Freedom would have to await victory.

On 29 March the Commune created a seven-man Executive Commission, composed of Jacobins, Blanquists and members of the International, to 'execute decrees and orders'. It also set up nine commissions to preside over administration: War; Finance; Public Services (including post, telegraph, roads, public assistance, etc.);

13. Text in Thomson (1968), p. 84.

Supply; General Security (police); Justice; Education; Labour, Industry and Exchange (which was to consider social and economic reform); and External Relations (to deal with the Prussians, other foreign powers, and the rest of France).

The Commune was opposed to anything like a ministerial cabinet, and it feared independence by the commissions. Hence there were no ministers (although the word was occasionally used): each commission was headed by a 'delegate' chosen by the Commune. The different political tendencies within the Commune – which were always uncoordinated if not faction-ridden – gravitated towards different commissions. Blanquists, fascinated by the seizure and use of power, dominated Security and Justice. Socialists moved towards Finance and Labour – nearly all the latter's members were affiliated to the International. Most of the Education Commission were teachers.

The delegates became the most powerful individuals within the administration, but active members of commissions, holders of certain offices (such as the public prosecutor) and forceful speakers in the Commune debates also wielded power or influenced policies. Gustave Cluseret, 47, War Delegate, a former regular soldier and revolutionary freebooter, was by far the most important figure during his tenure from 3 April to 1 May. François Jourde, 27, a clerk with little or no political history, and Eugène Varlin, 31, an autodidact bookbinder, labour organizer and leading Proudhonist member of the International, controlled the crucial Finance Delegation. Two young Blanquists, Raoul Rigault, 24, professional student and son of a Second Republic sub-prefect, and Théophile Ferré, 25, bookkeeper, were to build up unsavoury reputations for arbitrary action in Security. The Austrian Leo Fränkel, 27, a clockmaker, member of the International, influenced by Lasalle and close to Marx (one of the few Communards to be so), was active in the Labour Delegation. Educational reforms were pursued by Edouard Vaillant, 31, a philosophy graduate student of private means, and the struggling journalist Jules Vallès, 38. Gustave Courbet, the controversial realist painter, was in charge of arts and museums. However, there was no collective responsibility and certainly no chief minister.

This system had been improvised in three days. It lasted three weeks, until 20 April, when a new Executive Commission was appointed. This time it was made up of the delegates of each commission – hence, more like a conventional ministerial cabinet – in the hope that policy would be more effective if formulated by those responsible for carrying it out. That lasted only 11 days, until 1 May, when, after a debate that split the Commune, a Committee of Public Safety (Comité de Salut Public) was appointed, composed of five men, none of whom were commission delegates, with the opposite, though vain, hope that revolutionary dynamism would be generated by a body not bogged down in administrative detail. Some of the Commune's older members, mostly Jacobins, were active in these two committees. The most prominent were Charles Delescluze, 62, and the journalist and playwright Félix Pyat, 61, both in 1848 prefects and left-wing deputies; and one of the more forceful was Gabriel Ranvier, 43, a bankrupt master craftsman.

This system, with modifications, lasted until the dissolution of Commune authority when the army invaded Paris. Its last official meeting was on 21 May. Thereafter, dwindling groups of members met at the *mairies* (municipal offices) of the 11th and 20th *arrondissements*, and finally the last dozen gathered in a house in the Rue Haxo on 27 May. These lurches from one system to another were above all attempts to stem the deterioration of the Commune's military position, blamed on the incompetence or weakness of those in charge; but they were also influenced by factional and personal rivalry.

A further complication was the continuing existence of the Central Committee of the National Guard, which, having announced that it was making way for the Commune, decided to stay in being after all, and claimed special rights as representative of the National Guard. Cluseret seems to have tried fairly successfully to house-train it by keeping it busy with routine military administration. It seems to have been more a nuisance and an anomaly than a threat, as most of its members stopped attending and the rest quarrelled, though at times Commune members feared a National Guard *coup*, while the Committee feared the Commune would order its arrest.[14] The Central Committee was merely the most important of a wide range of would-be autonomous bodies whose zealousness aided or complicated Communal government.

The brief time-spans involved do not permit meaningful conventional analysis of the Commune's politics. Everything was improvised, carried out at frenetic pace amid the chaos and friction of revolution and civil war, and subject to disruption caused by outside events. The Commune certainly made its task more difficult by attempting to apply a revolutionary model of multiplying functions and keeping power in its own hands. Consequently, this small group of men – around 65 core members of the the Commune, not all dynamic,

14. See minutes of meetings and correspondence, SHA Ly 20 and 36.

competent or even regularly present at its 57 sessions – were trying
to exercise all political, legislative and administrative power in a great
city at war. Many were also active National Guard officers. At the same
time they oversaw the administration of their own *arrondissements*
and tried to keep contact with their electors, for example by attending meetings of clubs. There was simply never time:

> We were overcome with work, dead tired, not having a minute of
> respite to ourselves, or a moment for calm reflection. . . . We did not
> sleep. Personally I do not remember having undressed to sleep ten
> times in those two months. A chair or bench served as our bed, for a
> few often interrupted minutes.[15]

Debates in the Commune were constantly interrupted by the arrival
of some other urgent business, often caused by military crises. Powers
and reponsibilities were never properly defined. Its members were
used to opposition and oratory, not government; their reflex was to
'control' power rather than exercise it. As one exasperated member
put it, 'we're just a talkative little parliament'. The rapid succession
of two Executive Commissions and then the drastic step of creating
the Committee of Public Safety showed the continuing but vain
desire to create an effective authority able to cut through rivalries
and administrative delays and work a political and strategic miracle
by willpower and revolutionary fervour. None of these bodies ever
seems to have conceived any long-term direction: perhaps because
'calm reflection' was impossible, or because it was no one's responsibility, or simply because the Communard leaders could not collectively face the looming prospect of the defeat of their revolution.

The debate from 28 April to 1 May on the creation of a Committee of Public Safety,[16] provoked by alarm at the military situation
and mistrust of Cluseret and the Executive Commission, was the
the final attempt to define the nature of the Commune as government. It was also the occasion of the clearest political split in the
Commune's brief existence. The 'Majority', the 45 members who
voted to set up the committee, did so on the grounds that a united
dictatorial authority was needed to prevent defeat. The 'Minority'
of 23 who opposed argued that they had no right to hand over to an
unaccountable group power delegated to them by the people. This
has often been seen as the open manifestation of a divergence present
from the beginning between authoritarian 'Jacobin' and Blanquist
tendencies, and democratic, decentralist, 'Proudhonist' elements.

15. Arnould (1981), p. 156.   16. *PVC*, vol. 2, pp. 33–7.

Although these were not organized parties (even the Blanquists were uncoordinated), there were sufficient differences between them to make them recognizable if overlapping tendencies. Jacobins (not a name they used of themselves) were generally older, and included nearly all the best-known figures, with a background in professional revolutionary politics often going back to 1848 or even 1830, with records of prison or exile. They formed the mainstream of consciously traditional revolutionary republicanism, based round a network of newspapers, freemasonry, clubs and committees. Their leaders were often middle class, and involved in journalism, such as Delescluze and Pyat, mentioned earlier, and Ferdinand Gambon, 51, lawyer and landowner, like them a Montagnard deputy from 1848. Blanquists were younger – some very young – often with a student or intellectual-Bohemian background such as Rigault and the young barristers Eugène Protot and Gustave Tridon, with a leavening of working-class revolutionary activists. Jacobins and Blanquists looked back explicitly to great ancestors of the 1790s, about whom several had written books. But not to the same ones: the Jacobins revered Robespierre and the great Committee of Public Safety of 1793; the Blanquists admired the dissident Hébertists, the ultra-radical opposition within the first Paris Commune guillotined by Robespierre in 1794. Support for the Committee of Public Safety as an emergency dictatorship was for many of them straightforward: 'Given that the term Public Safety is absolutely from the same era as those of French Republic and Paris Commune, I vote for it.'

Those who were to oppose them as the 'Minority' were usually younger than the Jacobins and conscious of themselves as democrats and socialists involved in a modern nineteenth-century movement: 'I desire that all the titles and words belonging to the revolutions of '89 and '93 should only be applied to that period [and] cannot be used in this socialist republican movement. . . . Let us use the terms that our own revolution suggests.' Many were members of the International (itself an ideologically variegated organization), and were influenced by Proudhon's advocacy of autonomous economic organization and decentralized self-government; they feared a revolution that would merely change one oppressive regime for another. They included worker militants such as Varlin, Avrial and Malon, and middle-class activists belonging to radical, masonic and secularist circles, such as Vermorel, Vallès and Vaillant, all in their twenties or thirties.

Yet the debate was less ideologically clear-cut than may appear with hindsight. Members of the International took different sides, as did the Blanquists. Some of the Majority had always favoured authoritarian methods and relished the 1790s model, 'given that our situation is even more terrible than that in which our fathers of '93 found themselves'. Others voted for the committee in spite of misgivings, in the desperate hope of somehow shoring up their deteriorating military and political situation – 'the situation demanding energy and unity of action, in spite of its title I vote for'. Some even voted for it to preserve their revolutionary credentials, like Fränkel, 'not wishing to expose myself to insinuations concerning my revolutionary socialist opinions'.[17] Some of the Minority opposed the committee because they regarded its dictatorship as 'a real usurpation of the people's sovereignty'. Others because they had no faith in its effectiveness, like the Blanquist Tridon: 'it is only a word and the People have for too long been led astray by words'. Some had no confidence in the Jacobin members proposing it. Others again disliked the title as frightening and archaic: 'we are reestablishing to our detriment a terror which is no longer appropriate to our time'.

In any event, the Committee of Public Safety proved a forlorn hope. Its five members – all Jacobins or Blanquists – were far from being the most capable of the Communard leaders and were removed after a week. The committee was never able to use its theoretically unlimited powers to any effect, and merely added another complication to an already incoherent system. The bitter split between Majority and Minority did not heal. One Majority member told an opponent that 'the happiest day of my life will be the day I arrest you'.[18] The Majority excluded the Minority from discussions and from the commissions, and on 15 May the latter ceased to attend Commune meetings. They appealed to their constituents for support – which the Majority regarded as treason – but the answer they received at a public meeting was that they should go back to the Commune and support the majority view. This shows how little their scruples about democratic rights were shared by 'the people' themselves.

ADMINISTRATION

It was in the Commune's administration that Marx diagnosed its novelty as 'government of the people by the people'. The Commune

17. Ibid. Opinions of Andrieu, Tridon, Courbet, Oudet, Pottier, Fränkel.
18. Arnould (1981), p. 214.

abolished high official salaries, which it saw as a characteristic feature of an unjust, hierarchical and oppressive state. It voted on 1 April a maximum of 6,000 francs for Commune employees. This has often been described (most notably by Marx) as a worker's wage. This was not so. The average male Parisian wage was 4.98 francs per day – some 1,500 francs if he worked a full year.[19] Serman points out that 6,000 francs was the pay of an army colonel. Middling officials were paid about half the previous rates: for example, the director of the state tobacco factory was paid 4,000 per year, his assistant-inspector 2,800 – comparable with the earnings of the highest paid craft workers.[20] Junior National Guard officers were paid a modest wage – 2.50 francs per day when not in action. This was an expression of the radical aim of cheap government, but it was not an attempt to equalize wages. And – eternal wartime grievance – ordinary soldiers risked their necks for less pay than workers whose skills were in demand away from the firing line.

Administration was carried out in the *arrondissements* under the control of the elected members of the Commune acting as mayors. Their responsibilities included registering births, marriages and deaths, continuing the supply of cheap food to the needy that had begun during the Prussian siege, recruiting National Guards and providing general political leadership. *Arrondissements* enjoyed much autonomy, usually jealously guarded, even concerning police and defence. The National Guard was reorganized on a more local basis into 20 *arrondissement* legions, each with colonel and staff. Some enthusiastically 'red' *arrondissements*, such as Montmartre, insisted on having their own General Security Committee and their own Artillery Committee, aping those of the Commune. Relatively conservative *arrondissements*, such as the 16th, 8th, 9th or 2nd, tried to keep themselves as much as possible out of the fight. They resisted the disarmament of their 'reactionary' battalions or the roundup of National Guard deserters, tried to keep 'foreign' units off their territory (especially the dreaded 'Belleville' battalions, who, it was feared, would be drunk and disorderly), sometimes resisted secularization of their schools, hospitals and churches, and prevented requisitions from their shops. At the end of April, the *mairie* of the 9th *arrondissement* was still refusing to fly the red flag. Stranger was the very 'red' 13th, where the local authorities blocked attempts by the Commune police to arrest or expel priests, brothers and nuns.

19. For details, Duveau (1946), p. 319.
20. Details in SHA Ly 24 and 26, and in Archives de la Préfecture de Police [APP] Db 509.

Other city and state administrations – such as Public Assistance (which included hospitals), the city excise department (the *octroi*), the state tobacco monopoly, posts and telegraphs, roads, museums and libraries – carried on under the authority of the Commune's delegates. The change was often superficial, with a Commune nominee at the top of the organization – sometimes a very young junior employee (such as Pauvert, a 23-year-old clerk promoted to be head of the telegraph service), sometimes a reliable political veteran, such as Charles Beslay, at 76 the Commune's oldest member, delegate at the Bank of France. In politically sensitive areas, the pressure for a change of personnel was greater. But, generally, 'pre-revolutionary' staff carried on as usual, sometimes with promotion. As senior officials had been summoned to Versailles by the government, sometimes a show of compulsion (such as a threat of arrest) was used to give them an excuse for staying on duty in Paris. In non-sensitive departments there seems to have been business as usual. In the highways department, for example, many employees continued to work for the Commune 'in the general public interest', and none lost their jobs afterwards.[21] Some seem still to have received wages from Versailles.[22] The Commune had no desire to interfere, especially if it gained much-needed revenue. Hence, for example, the Finance Delegate ordered 100 tons of tobacco in May from Alsace to keep the state tobacco factory functioning.[23] At a lower level, two men caught trying to smuggle in a barrel of wine by rolling it along the bank of the Seine must have been surprised to find the *octroi* officials still vigilant despite the revolution.[24]

The Commune's delegates and nominated directors (sometimes former employees) seem to have done their best to get on with their subordinates, even though strict work discipline was often maintained: 'Singing, shouting, insubordination . . . defiance of regulations will be punished by suspension [or] dismissal.'[25] There is little evidence that the Commune's administration became more democratic (the telegraph office may have elected some of its managers; as a result, according to the Commune member Andrieu, it worked very badly[26]) or accountable to the public. There were accusations that the Commune was lax with public money and property, but surviving documents show determination to run a rigorous and economical

21. Archives de Paris [AP] VO (NC) 234.
22. Ibid., and Andrieu (1971), pp. 86–7.
23. Order of 3 May, SHA Ly 24.   24. Report (n.d.), ibid.
25. Order to women workers in tobacco factory, 30 April, ibid.
26. Andrieu (1971), p. 86.

organization, which led to obsessive centralized control of expenditure to prevent abuses: sums as small as 1 franc 50 were being authorized personally by the directors of military supply.[27] 'Cheap government' was a fundamental republican demand.

There was in practice no attempt to revolutionize the formal structures of government, as Marx supposed. There was apparently no will – and perhaps no time – to organize elections for all functionaries, as had been promised from the beginning and was to have been the keystone of an ultra-democratic system of rule by the citizens themselves. Administrators were hastily recruited *ad hoc*, often among the friends, relatives or political acquaintances of those in power, many of them members of the wartime vigilance committees. The clubs, which continued to organize meetings, were largely ignored: according to Allner, they were 'virtually excluded' from running the revolution, while even Johnson, who ascribes much greater importance to them, concludes that they had difficulty in finding a role.[28]

A different kind of administrative reform originated in spontaneous initiatives outside the governing hierarchy. Thanks to research by Gonzalez Sanchez, arts administration is one of the best known of such areas. When the Empire fell, the republican painter Courbet and others had set up a committee aiming to take over arts administration, and this was now reactivated. Their Artists' Federation of 300–400 members was keen to evict imperial officials and take over museums and exhibitions. The Commune agreed to hand arts administration over to it. As Sanchez points out, this was 'an initiative *under* the Commune, not *of* the Commune'; moreover, not all Federation members were Commune supporters.[29] It can arguably be taken as typical of grass-roots participation in the revolution; education and women's organizations probably being similar cases. As a key element of Communard ideas of democracy and socialism was 'association' – devolving power to autonomous organizations of citizens – existing pressure groups took the opportunity to further their agendas.

In the key area of public security the record was mixed. From the beginning, the Commune had proclaimed this to be the responsibility of the citizens themselves, who would elect and dismiss neighbourhood police officers, and participate directly as National Guards. But the practice never caught up with the theory. Legal

27. SHA Li 119.   28. Allner (1978), p. 506; Johnson (1996), pp. 158–9.
29. Sanchez (1994), p. 87.

reforms – including election of magistrates – were announced but not implemented. That unpopular and oppressive institution the Prefecture of Police was abolished. However, the Blanquists, long fascinated by the police as an instrument of power, took over the ministry of justice, the public prosecutor's office and the prefecture of police itself, with over 500 staff, which they renamed in pre-Orwellian style the 'ex-prefecture', but with little but the name and most of the personnel changed. The commissaires in each quarter were not elected but nominated by the ex-prefecture. They still wrote legal documents beginning with antique formality 'We, *commissaire* of police . . .'. Little is known about the details of the ex-prefecture's activities – one Commune member attacked it as 'a state within a state' – but those that attracted most notice were directed towards the harassment of priests, monks and nuns, a revolutionary activity with which the Blanquists were obsessed. They were very bad, however, at catching Versaillais spies, who seem to have had the run of the city.

Routine policing was in the hands of the local commissaires and the National Guard. This was a genuinely democratic body, the only one of the Commune's institutions that did indeed elect its officials – though this, ironically, long predated the Commune. Foreign observers remarked on the good order in the streets; defenders of the Commune even claimed that crime had ceased. It is impossible to tell in the absence of records, burnt in the last days of the Commune. There was some gang vandalism, petty theft and fraud, pervasive drunkenness, but no breakdown of law and order. There was much fairly minor intimidation and harassment by officious police and National Guards, often acting without authorization. As will be suggested later, this was an important element of grass-roots revolution. It was sometimes rather ludicrous, with mutual arrest and counter-arrest on grounds of political and personal rivalry. About 3,500 people were arrested in all, including 270 prostitutes. The Blanquist Justice Delegate, Protot, complained of utter confusion at the ex-prefecture, with unknown people making arrests, and jailers holding or releasing people as they saw fit: he had released 680 innocents in three weeks.[30] Self-policing also meant tedious guard duty at public buildings, and even more tedious night patrols to seize banned newspapers and repress street gambling, begging, prostitution, drunkenness and nocturnal baking (see p. 97). It became difficult to get National Guardsmen to turn up for these duties,

---

30. *PVC*, vol. 1, p. 471.

or to obey the commissaires. Some local units, indeed, obstructed the ex-prefecture's enthusiasm for anticlerical bullying or freelance vandalism. One battalion saved Notre Dame from being set on fire. This was arguably the most important single act of citizen self-government, Marx's prototype for the dictatorship of the proletariat.

The Commune as social revolution?

The Commune was not a government with leisure to reflect, consult and plan – though it did (to the impatience of some members) spend a good deal of time debating. Nor did it have freedom of action, in an embattled city with hostile Versaillais on one side and menacing Germans on the other. We need to bear this in mind in considering the Commune's policies: what it did, and what it would have liked to do. Also, to assess how revolutionary its measures were, we must place them in the context of acts already taken by less revolutionary regimes.

The legacy of war and the pressures of civil war are the thread linking most of the Commune's social and economic reforms. Its first acts, as we have seen, were consciously stop-gap extensions of the wartime policies of the Government of National Defence on rent arrears, bills and pawnshop sales. Later important measures were equally dictated by circumstances. On 10 April, following the outbreak of hostilities a week earlier, the Commune decreed that pensions should be paid to the families of National Guards killed, including common-law wives and their children. The much-debated decree of 6 May on the municipal pawnshop aimed to relieve the hardship of the civil war, and measures on workers' cooperatives, pay and conditions were connected with the production of munitions and uniforms.

As with any government, money, not oratory, shows the real priorities. The Commune spent some 42 million francs in all: 33 million went to the War Delegation (mainly for National Guard pay); the other 9 million to the Intendance (military supply), the *arrondissement* administrations, and all other services. The Justice and Education departments each received a few thousand francs. This shows vividly how civil war overshadowed the Commune's existence. Jourde, the Finance Delegate who aspired to cheap government, said that he would have liked to halve the *octroi*, reduce the total budget, and yet increase spending in certain areas. In fact, the *octroi* was strictly imposed and produced one-third of total revenue,

13 million. Other regular state and city revenues produced 4 or 5 million, about half coming from the tobacco monopoly. Several million came from seizure of reserves and bullion, including 6 million found at the Hôtel de Ville and 2.4 million minted from silver, some of it melted-down plate from churches and state residences. The remaining needs – 16 million – came from the Bank of France.[31]

The Commune's dealings with the Bank show both inhibition and principle. Jourde and Varlin went to seek funds, and at a courteous meeting with the deputy governor arranged to draw on the city of Paris's account, and then when that ran out to borrow from the Bank – a compromise that suited both sides. Only towards the very end of the Commune's life, on 22 May, did it threaten force to obtain 700,000 francs for the National Guard's pay. Even this seems to have been courteously managed, perhaps with the mutually understood intention of covering the Bank's officials against prosecution.[32] With hindsight, this moderation was often criticized as fatal weakness, and Jourde condemned as a timid clerk obsessed with honest book-keeping. At the time, however, these policies were unanimously accepted by the Commune. As Jourde explained, it was important to prevent a collapse in confidence in banknotes, not to antagonize the Prussians and provincial opinion, and not to give credence to conservative accusations (so damaging in 1848) that the revolutionaries were looters and a threat to everyone's property. It was indispensable to maintain the import of goods, especially food, into Paris, and hence not to frighten off commercial interests. Hence, Jourde protected all Paris's banks, reopened the stock exchange, and returned cash seized by the Blanquist police from the Paris Gas Company.[33]

This raises the question of general relations of the Commune with business, capitalism and the middle classes. Communards were not 'communists' – the term dating from the 1830s and meaning advocates of a utopian system of common property. Although Proudhon, the greatest intellectual influence on French socialism, had declared famously in 1840 that 'property is theft', he meant property as a source of income unearned by work, not possessions used productively. Business, especially small business involving manufacture, was not condemned by the Communards, and most Paris business was extremely small: 90 per cent of firms employed fewer

31. Serman (1986), pp. 350–2.
32. Minutes of meeting of Bank council, 25 May, SHA Ly 24. The recent work by Cavaterra (1998) supports this interpretation.
33. Note by Jourde (undated), SHA Ly 32.

than 10 workers. Many small businessmen were radical republicans or socialists, and were eager to cooperate with the new government, signing their business letters with the correct revolutionary formula 'Salut et fraternité'. Some even asked for requisitions to cover them against possible later prosecution. There are piquant examples of the compatibility of business with revolution. One of the Commune's most spectacular symbolic acts, the destruction of the Vendôme Column, was carried out by a private company on a fixed-price contract. The 250 red flags for Fédéré battalions were supplied by a large firm of upholsterers ('suppliers to the Hôtel de Ville and the civil service') at 65 francs for red banner and guidon with embroidered inscriptions. Although during the German siege, demands for rationing and greater intervention in food supply were important left-wing demands, the Commune showed no doctrinaire desire to regulate, relying largely on private businesses and the market. Many prominent Communards were themselves small businessmen, independent artisans or professionals, as we shall see in more detail in chapter 4. The prevalence of small business influenced the Commune's reforms. There was a consistent desire to reconcile the interests of workers and employers. No decree contested the general right of property, and the Commune explicitly refused measures of expropriation. They even punctiliously decided that they could not lower the price of the *Journal Officiel* so that ordinary National Guards could afford to read about Commune decrees because the paper was privately owned. The only attacks on property were political: churches were vandalized and looted, and Thiers's house was ceremonially demolished.

The desire to reconcile interests and respect existing rights can be seen in the Commune's treatment of the question of commercial bills of exchange, which had caused such problems for the Versaillais. This was one of the issues to which the Commune gave lengthiest consideration, consulting workers and business organizations and setting up a committee to report. The technical sophistication of the debates shows how familiar Commune members were with small business, for which this was a crucial issue. They agreed on a compromise on 14 April aimed at saving the solvency of debtors and the rights of creditors, with repayments being phased in over three years, as opposed to the Verailles law allowing three months.

The decree of 29 March cancelling rent arrears clearly was a contravention of property rights. Rent and accommodation were always among the most important issues for poor families. They had been aggravated by 'Haussmanization' and by the upheavals of war. The strong action the Commune took may partly be explained by widespread dislike of landlords, nicknamed *les vautours* (vultures), who epitomized the Proudhonist category of the unproductive, parasitic property-owner. Nevertheless, tenants of furnished property were specifically not given absolute security of tenure. The official justification of the decree was not socialism but patriotism: the need to spread the burden of sacrifice imposed by the war. Similarly patriotic appeals were made to landlords and lodging-house keepers to cooperate in housing those made homeless as a result of the civil war. But the Commune did not accept suggestions to requisition all empty apartments, deciding on 24 April only to requisition those abandoned since 18 March, which implied that their occupants had deserted the revolution. Here again, social action was channelled by political circumstances. Moreover, the thinking is similar to that of the Government of National Defence, which had imposed a heavy tax on owners of abandoned property.

On 16 April the Commune passed a decree – remarkably, without debate – that was described by the Jacobin paper *Le Vengeur* as 'the most serious claim of the Commune to the gratitude of working men',[34] and by Marx and Engels as a stride towards communism. It aimed to hand over closed-down workshops or factories to 'the cooperative association of the workers who were employed in them'. This indeed bore the mark of the French socialist tradition, which envisaged workers' cooperative *association*, not state ownership, as the solution to 'the social question'. Their advocates believed that the superiority of cooperatives under a supportive government would be such that they would displace capitalist industry. In the words of a Commune member, the Jacobin artist Billioray, the decree was 'the first serious step taken on the road to socialism'.[35]

Cooperatives, however, were neither new nor necessarily revolutionary. Over 50 existed in Paris during the late 1860s, patronized not only by republicans such as Victor Hugo and Georges Clemenceau, but also by the leading liberal economist Léon Say, chairman of the Caisse d'Escompte des Associations Populaires. The Government of National Defence had encouraged cooperatives to create employment and provide war materials: 35,000 people, mainly women, were employed making uniforms – a far larger operation than the Commune was able to establish. Under the Commune both political leaders and workers' leaders wanted to seize the opportunity to expand cooperatives through loans and large orders from the War

34. Edwards (1971), p. 259.   35. *PVC*, vol. 2, p. 355.

Delegation. 'To favour the development of existing associations', wrote a Commune official, 'is to bring about the formation of new ones, and thereby release labour from exploitation by capital, and simultaneously release workers from the influence of monarchist capitalists.'[36]

Yet the 16 April decree, like the Commune's other social measures, was carefully limited in scope and emerged from the political and military struggle. It was aimed not at employers or owners in general, but at 'deserters' guilty of 'cowardly abandon' of their businesses to 'escape their civic obligations'. Even so, they were to be paid compensation. The Commune turned down a later proposal to 'requisition all large factories of monopolists', even with compensation: most members opposed general expropriation. The express motives of the 16 April decree were to ensure jobs and 'essential works' of military importance.

The decree had little practical effect. Although various workers' groups held meetings with a view to establishing associations, the number of operating cooperatives may have fallen during the Commune. Only one group seems to have taken over closed-down factories, an Ironfounders' Cooperative making shells for the War Delegation. However, it preferred to pay rent for its two factories rather than go through the requisitioning procedure. It ran its affairs on business lines, with strict discipline for its members, and it enjoyed good relations with private firms in the industry. Oddly, it tried to remain in business after the defeat of the Commune, and only stopped when the police arrested its managers, who were subsequently given excellent character references by private businessmen – including the owner of the factory they had taken over. However revolutionary this initiative has looked to historians, it clearly did not seem very subversive to those involved.[37]

Several other cooperatives – not using abandoned factories – were set up to produce military supplies. Cooperatives of women making uniforms, at home or in workshops, became more ideologically ambitious under the Commune. The socialist-run Union des Femmes (see below p. 135) asked the Labour Commission to make it responsible for organizing women's work throughout Paris. It looked forward to creating eventually a network of socialist cooperatives throughout Europe. Wartime arms workshops were also reactivated as cooperatives during the Commune. In that at the Louvre, workers elected a managing delegate, foremen and a

36. Rougerie (1971), p. 179.   37. Tombs (1984); Rougerie (1971), p. 185.

representative council, under the supervision of the socialist Augustin
Avrial, a metalworkers' trade-union organizer who ran the Commune's
artillery production.

However, cooperatives gave rise to unforeseen dilemmas. Private
firms too were eager to supply the Commune, as noted earlier,
often for economic reasons, but also because many small manufac-
turers supported the Commune. The attitude of bigger companies,
which were important to the Commune's war effort, is well summed
up in the words of one large supplier: 'Citizens, we have remained
at the service of all Administrations, and have never had other than
good relations.'[38] Small and large firms produced cannon, machine-
guns, chassepôt rifles, ironclad barricades, ammunition, water bottles
and uniforms. One machine-maker eagerly offered his whole factory.
National Guard battalions wanted to sign their own contracts with
private suppliers to obtain quick delivery of uniforms and weapons;
perhaps too neighbourhood contacts were in play. For example,
the garrison of Fort Bicêtre bought engineering tools from a local
building contractor and had shell damage repaired by a neighbourhood glazier. The War and Finance delegations similarly wanted
speed and value for public money. Consequently, they put orders out
to tender, which put pressure on wages, and Varlin (the socialist
head of military supply) demanded reductions in prices charged
for uniforms.[39]

So the cooperatives found themselves being undercut. The
Ironfounders' Cooperative was paying its members well below the
usual rates, and women making uniforms also found their piece-
work rates falling. This led to indignant protests from workers in
several trades and an angry debate in the Commune on 12 May,
especially when it was realized with embarrassment that the Government of National Defence had done more to protect women's
wages than the Commune: 'it can be said that the social Republic
has done what those presently besieging us refused to do: cut wages'.
Fränkel, head of the Labour Delegation, burst out that 'the 18 March
revolution was made by the working class. If we do nothing for that
class, I don't see the purpose of the Commune.' Hardly surprisingly,
this was generally agreed, and future contracts were ordered to specify
minimum wage rates.[40] The decree also allowed existing contracts
to be revised, but Jourde, Varlin and even Fränkel were against
breaking agreements, and probably this was not done. Besides, not

38. Tombs (1984), p. 972; see documents in SHA Ly 29, 32 and 85.
39. Letter from Perrot-Jaluzeau, 7 May, SHA Ly 119.
40. *PVC*, vol. 2, pp. 348–67.

all socialist leaders were enamoured of the cooperatives' performance. Avrial and his subordinate who ran the Louvre cooperative
thought its workers lazy and greedy, and had no sympathy with
their demands for higher pay and danger money when National
Guards were fighting for 30 sous: socialism should mean no privileges
for workers either. 'Communism's a joke. Hard workers shouldn't
feed idlers.'[41] Jourde wanted to specify maximum as well as minimum wages. During the last days of the Commune, delivery was still
being taken of large quantities of uniforms from private manufac-
turers at prices officially recognized as being too low to permit a
living wage, while the Association pour l'Organization du Travail
des Femmes was barely getting off the ground.[42]

Also concerned with the welfare of families hit by war – 'we must
give a first satisfaction to the brave men who are going to fight' –
was a decree proposed on 25 April to resolve the knotty problem of
the municipal pawnshop. During the Prussian siege, tens of thousands of families had pawned household items and tools to make
ends meet. The Government of National Defence had allowed the
free restitution of household items worth up to 15 francs, and after
the armistice the Lord Mayor of London's relief fund (administered
among others by the Archbishop of Paris and the philanthropist Sir
Richard Wallace) agreed to pay for the redemption of tools up to
20 francs. The Commune on 29 March had suspended sales of
unredeemed items. Some members of the Commune urged giving
back goods worth up to 50 francs, and one urged it as a socialist
measure, 'a sort of social liquidation' redistributing wealth. But most
were more stringent, on grounds of cost or administrative practicality,
or with regard to the sort of goods that could be reclaimed – tools
and linen, but not jewellery and especially not wedding rings.
The Labour Commission wanted free restitution only to registered
paupers and to National Guards disabled by their wounds. There
were limits on what could be done in the short term. Only 'if the
Commune triumphs', argued Lefrançais, and 'a whole programme
of reforms' could be introduced, could they 'arrive at a system that
makes it possible to do away with Public Assistance in all its forms'.
Most weightily, Jourde objected that they could not afford to pay
compensation to shareholders, and to hand back property at their
expense would be unjust – 'an attack on property, something

41. Rossel (1960), p. 269.
42. See bills and payment authorizations, 20–1 May, SHA Ly 119. The women's
organization was due to receive its first payment of 998 francs, whereas private firms
simultaneously received over 17,000 francs.

we have never yet done'.[43] After lengthy consideration of practical problems it was decreed on 6 May (with only one dissenting voice) that the Commune would pay for a phased restitution of necessities – clothes, furniture, books, tools – worth up to 20 francs. By the end of the Commune, some 42,000 articles had been returned, worth 323,000 francs.[44] Charles Longuet (Karl Marx's future son-in-law) had warned against letting the heart rule the head: this level-headed revolution felt able to be 5 francs per item more generous than its predecessor – but no more than the Lord Mayor of London and the archbishop.

Only a few reforms had no connection with the war situation. Two responded to longstanding workers' grievances: forbidding employers to deduct fines from wages, and attempting to replace unpopular and expensive private job agencies by encouraging the *mairies* to set up municipal labour exchanges – a step already taken by several mayors during the war. However, the Executive Commission's order of 20 April banning night-work in bakeries – another longstanding demand – was the most notable, and noticed, of these measures, which is perhaps why Fränkel described it incongruously on 28 April as 'the only truly socialist decree that the Commune has passed'. Yet several Commune members, especially Jacobins, objected to 'these continuous regulations' that could not be enforced, and argued that it was not the business of the Commune to interfere 'in a question between bosses and workers' now that equality and democracy had been established: 'Let the workers themselves safeguard their interests.' Defenders of the ban replied that bakery workers were a special case because they were forbidden by law from striking. Moreover, it was a moral question: night-work was unsocial and prevented workers from educating themselves. Finally, the immediate reason for the ban seems to have been to head off threats of public disorder, also one of the reasons for the decision to protect women's wages in clothing contracts.[45]

These cautious reforms do not seem to have fallen far short of what supporters of the Commune wanted in the circumstances. Rougerie's survey of the main themes of the press and clubs shows that it was in the political field that more radical measures were demanded – against the clergy, deserters and Versailles supporters.[46] Though there were some familiar republican demands for reform of the *octroi* and for replacement of indirect taxes with a graduated

---

43. *PVC*, vol. 1, pp. 474–86. 44. Serman (1986), p. 363.
45. *PVC*, vol. 1, pp. 538–43. 46. Rougerie (1971), pp. 208–15.

income tax (issues that remained on the agenda for another fifty years), the Commune was not under pressure for more radical economic or social reform. It seems to have represented the views of its constituents, especially in the peculiar economic circumstances of the time. Although most Commune members would have described themselves as socialists, many did not turn up for the debates on social issues: 'When it's to quarrel everyone's here,' complained the International member Johannard, 'but when it's to vote for useful measures they go out and ride around on horseback.'[47]

The Commune as cultural revolution?

Fighting for survival left little money or time to spare. Yet the Commune gave freedom to those who wished to take their own initiatives, often with words of encouragement and even a little practical help. Much was begun in seven weeks. Did it amount to, or even point the way towards, anything truly revolutionary?

Education was an undoubted priority. All republicans shared the conviction that education – free, compulsory and secular – was the key to social and political progress. Although there had been a huge increase in primary schooling since the 1830s, since 1850 state schools had increasingly been placed in the hands of religious orders, seen by republicans as instruments of cultural and political reaction. Left-wing teachers, especially women, were limited to a small number of private schools. Secularization of schools was therefore a priority for all republicans. Socialists added to this a demand for technical education for the children of workers, both for immediate practical reasons and to prepare for the future society in which all would work, and workers would be found in every cultural and political domain. It was necessary, wrote *Le Vengeur*, 'that those who can handle tools can also write books'.[48] Jourde said that he would have liked to double spending on education had circumstances permitted; but by the end of April the Education Delegation had received a budget of only 1,000 francs.

So action clearly had to be left to the 20 *mairies* and to independent bodies, such as the *Education Nouvelle* group, founded during the war. After a slow start, a reshuffled Education Delegation, led by Vaillant and including Vallès and Courbet (one of the most distinguished such bodies France has ever had), encouraged experimental

47. *PVC*, vol. 2, p. 232.   48. Serman (1986), p. 388.

projects, coopting members of *Education Nouvelle* and appointing a committee including women to plan reform of girls' education. But time was short, money was short, and so were teachers and workers able to give technical instruction. Consequently, the practical results were minute, and less than enterprising mayors had undertaken during the German siege. One industrial art school for girls opened on 12 May; one for boys was about to open in a confiscated Jesuit school when the Commune fell. Some *mairies* carried out their own useful reforms, such as providing school meals and free equipment. The main effort, however, often orchestrated by Blanquists, went into enforced secularization.

Secularization was incontestably the Commune's outstanding cultural objective. Churches were occupied by clubs, and sometimes vandalized or ritually desecrated. Ceremonious secular funerals were held. Religious emblems were removed from courts, hospitals and schools. Most visibly, the arms were sawn off the cross on the dome of the Pantheon (for whose possession Catholics and secularists had tussled almost since it was built) and a red flag hoisted. Also removed, where possible, were religious personnel: nuns and brothers who taught children, nursed the sick and guarded prisoners. This sometimes involved harrassment, false accusations and arrest – some 200 priests were imprisoned – and it met resistance from parents, children and patients. Commune agents, especially Blanquists, and the Communard press invented a virulently anticlerical street-theatre. The were some deliberate parodies and profanations of religious rituals reminiscent of the 1790s. Drawing on an even older tradition of sexual accusation against the clergy, old bones found in several church crypts were publicly exposed as the remains of young girls raped and murdered by priests – a unique example of Communard agit-prop:

> Can you picture that horrible scene? These young women, these maidens, lured by promises of hope or pleasure, who awake here bound, sealed in, walled up alive ... choking, screaming, without anyone being able to hear. ... Credulous mothers, you who entrust to the priests the lives and honour of your children ... come and see what the old church of St-Laurent conceals in its hideous cellars.[49]

Similarly, instruments for sadistic torture and abortion were said to have been found in a convent in eastern Paris, and secret tunnels connecting monasteries and nunneries. Sizeable crowds were drawn to these spectacles.

49. *Le Cri du Peuple*, 12 May.

This was mainly the work of a determined minority, mainly Blanquist police such as the cartoonist Pilotell and the designer Le Moussu, attempting to provoke violent anticlericalism in a population suspicious of *les calotins* in general, but not necessarily of those they actually knew. Hence, it was churches in the centre, within easy reach of the Hôtel de Ville and the ex-prefecture, that suffered most. In outlying working-class districts, priests and nuns were familiar and sometimes respected figures, and local men and women sometimes took risks to protect them and church property. At St Marcel's, in traditionally 'red' south-eastern Paris, the *curé* publicly wore his soutane throughout, nuns carried on their charitable work and church services continued. The young police official Gaston Da Costa complained of lack of enthusiasm from the local authorities and National Guards, who refused to sack the nuns and released a *frère* he had arrested.[50] Grass-roots religion and anticlericalism (below p. 125) were more complex phenomena than adolescent Blanquist zealots realized.

State intervention in the arts had been an aspect of French life since the Old Regime, and had been continued by all subsequent governments, who exerted control though training (especially in the Beaux Arts school), grants, prizes, purchases and official Salon exhibitions. In the 1860s, Manet, Courbet and others had rebelled against the system, at least to the extent of holding exhibitions of works refused by the Salon. This is the context of the desire of the Artists' Federation (Fédération des Artistes) led by Courbet, who was elected to the Commune on 16 April, to free artists from State discipline and Beaux-Arts orthodoxy by taking collective control. The dramatist Félix Pyat, a Jacobin member of the Commune, was equally opposed to State intervention in the theatre. He condemned subsidies as 'antirepublican': 'there should no more be State literature or science than State religion'; furthermore, it was wrong for 'peasants in Berry to pay for ballerinas at the Opera'. The musician Salvator-Daniel, the Commune's director of the Conservatoire, took a similar view, as seemingly did Courbet, who wished to abolish the Ecole de Rome and Ecole des Beaux Arts, 'patronized and subsidized by the government'. The Commune passed a decree abolishing monopolies and subsidies, and announcing the intention of replacing exploitation by managers with 'association' – that is, democratic corporate control by artists. Vaillant announced that just as means

50. Report of 21 May, APP Ba 365–1. See also Marion (1981) and Lesmayoux (1871).

of production should be given to workers, so theatres should belong to federations of performers.[51]

Commune members and the Artists' Federation saw the arts as valuable educational tools, as sources of industrial design, moral improvement and political inspiration. They wanted to make practical artistic training part of the 'integral' education in their projected professional schools. The Federation also had a grandiose vision of commissioning uplifting allegorical frescos in railway stations and town halls as the central feature of a republican arts policy. However, budgetary stringency stalled their ambition of creating a subsidized corporate monopoly. So their immediate practical aim became reactivating artistic life, so that their members could earn a living. Courbet wanted to reopen museums and organize a major exhibition. Out-of-work actors and musicians were eager to stage charity concerts for National Guard wounded, widows and orphans, and these (organized by the theatrical Fédération Artistique) became some of the biggest cultural events during the Commune.

Did the Commune inspire 'proletarian' or avant-garde culture, either at the time or later, as some historians have suggested? Adrian Rifkin argues that 'the effect of the revolution on visual production was . . . profound', though seemingly confined to political cartoons; and he further suggests that it was the Commune's defeat that caused 'something like a revolutionary cultural movement' to develop in later years. But Sanchez points out the paradox that revolutionary political ideas now accompanied aesthetic conservatism: the Commune marked the end of a period, beginning with David in the 1780s, in which artistic and political progressivism went hand in hand. Although the Artists' Federation did not concern itself with style, its vision of easily understandable political art could no longer accommodate avant-garde experimentation. This would be seen during the 1880s and '90s, when the Third Republic adopted the Federation's artistic projects, and some of its leading personnel, to produce didactic official art widely regarded as kitsch. The militant artist Steinlen eventually got bored with doing drawings for 'comic pages'. The artistic avant-garde, including the Impressionists (who had kept clear of the Commune), copied some of the Federation's organizational ideas but not its political aesthetic. Pissarro saw himself as practising a progressive, scientific art that broadly served the cause, but it was never overtly political.[52]

51. Courbet (1992), p. 409; Johnson (1996), pp. 150–1.
52. Rifkin (1979), p. 216; Sanchez (1994). See also Varias (1997).

The most characteristic cultural events of the Commune were the numerous concerts organized by the theatrical artists' federation or by National Guard units – surely the most genuine expression of Fédéré taste. Some were very simple: bands playing in the streets to accompany collections for the wounded by the *cantinière* (canteen woman). Others were more elaborate, being given by professional performers from the leading music-halls in theatres or other places of entertainment. And there were huge concerts patronized by the Commune at the Tuileries Palace, attracting some 8,000 paying customers inside and as many more onlookers enjoying the illuminations in the gardens. Generally, the programmes were a middle-brow mixture of art, patriotic republicanism and sentimentality: arias by Gounod, Meyerbeer and Verdi, selections from the operetta *Frou-Frou*, poems by Hugo (whose venomous denunciation of Napoleon III in verse, *Les Châtiments*, had become almost obligatory), music-hall ballads ('Mon Vieux Grand'père' or 'Je ne t'aime plus') and political satire or instruction (songs called 'Libertés Municipales' and 'L'Internationale').[53] As the stated object of these concerts was to raise money for widows and orphans, broad audience satisfaction must have been prominent in the organizers' minds. A little more adventurously, a concert to have taken place at the Opera on 22 May (prevented by the Versaillais invasion) was to have featured stirring works by Gossec, revolutionary composer of the 1790s, and a contemporary piece entitled 'L'Alliance des Peuples' by the Communard musician Pugno.

It seems unlikely that many of the audience would have been surprised, let alone shocked, by these programmes, which resemble those of the popular Concerts Pasdeloup of the 1860s. Nor could workers in the audience have felt that this was somehow 'their' culture. Perhaps they would have been embarrassed if they had, for the Commune was dedicated to high-minded self-improvement. Many of its members were serious autodidacts who thought that the ignorant should be instructed and moralized. Observers were impressed by the decorous behaviour of the audience: 'in their Sunday best, these republicans have a fine appearance. . . . Their womenfolk are touchingly beautiful. . . . They leave to their monarchs the charms of [Offenbach]. No dance music or music-hall ditties. This, you see, is real art. . . . *C'est une fête*.' A more cynical witness thought that 'at the monotonous rattle of this already

---

53. From programme of concert given by 237th battalion held on 14 May. AP VD³ 14.

outdated romantic verse, which produces no echo in the minds or hearts of the crowd, they try to look serious and intelligent, but are visibly bored'.[54]

Much recent discussion of the Commune as cultural revolution has turned not on policies for education or art, however, but on whether the Commune showed, as Lefebvre sums it up, that 'total revolution' could happen by transforming broader cultural concepts and experiences such as those of gender, urban space and festival.[55] Gender provoked impassioned polemic in 1871 and arouses much interest today. The activities of women during the Commune are dealt with separately later (below p. 132). Here, the question is whether the Commune as a movement and a government manifested or promoted a changed understanding of gender in its treatment of women. Most French republicans and socialists traditionally believed that women were not citizens and not really workers, and that their natural and socially desirable role was as wives and mothers. As workers, women constituted cheap labour which depressed male wages; and they risked moral degradation away from the protection and authority of fathers, brothers and husbands. Their basic choice, as Proudhon had put it, was to be 'housewives or harlots'; and one of his aims for socialism was to 'restore the household' by returning women to 'the tranquillity of the domestic hearth'.[56]

However, attitudes among some socialists had begun to change in the 1860s, and the International demanded equal pay for work of equal value. Did the Commune go further in this direction, or did it reflect the misogynistic attitude which preceded it and survived it? It certainly differed strikingly from earlier republican regimes in permitting free political expression by women. The Revolution had briefly allowed women to have a political voice, but had banned women's clubs in 1793. The Second Republic had also for a time permitted women's political clubs and organizations, but had closed them on grounds of public order (they provoked male violence). The Commune always allowed women to speak out publicly. Political clubs had largely female audiences, and there were also specifically women's clubs, to the horrified fascination of conservative critics. A few female journalists and club speakers became fairly well known, though when André Léo (the male pseudonym of Léodile Champseix) wrote an interesting proclamation 'To the Workers of the Countryside', she addressed them only as 'Brothers'.

---

54. *La Commune*, 14 May; Barron (1889), p. 120.
55. Lefebvre (1965), p. 390.   56. Rendall (1985), p. 235.

The Commune's measures regarding women's work show a wish to improve opportunities, while accepting that they differed from those of men. In education, for the first time in France it decreed equal pay for teachers of both sexes. The Union des Femmes was noticeably active, and the Commune took belated steps, as seen above, to prevent cuts in women's wages. Cooperatives for women were encouraged by socialists such as Fränkel. But he wanted them to arrange for women to collect work 'so that they can stay in their homes'.[57] Similarly, the Russian activist of the Union des Femmes, Elisabeth Dmitrieff (Elisaveta Tomanovskaya), took it for granted that the cooperatives they were organizing would cover 'the trades essentially practised by women'.[58]

The significance of the Commune's 10 April decision to grant modest pensions (600 francs – reduced from an original suggestion of 1,000) to the wives 'married or not' and non-legitimized children of National Guards killed in battle has been much debated. It marked 'a radical break with patriarchy' in the opinion of Jones and Vergès.[59] It did indeed shock conservative commentators, and went against the reluctance of the Code Napoléon to recognize any rights of unmarried mothers and their children – though in principle it follows on from the 1869 decision by the Empire to allow unmarried mothers to receive public assistance, and therefore cannot be regarded as wholly new or revolutionary. In the Commune's decision there was surely a practical desire to encourage the combatants. Was it also intended as a blow against patriarchy? Perhaps rather against the 'old governmental and clerical world' of which official marriage was a part: Commune members recognized that many working-class families did not go through marriage ceremonies, partly on grounds of cost, and partly through anticlericalism. The latter was something they applauded, as shown by their priggish exclusion of wedding rings from the items that could be reclaimed free from the municipal pawnshop, because they were 'a sentimental Catholic notion'. Significantly, insistence on making no distinction between the married and unmarried came from a Jacobin, Grousset, whereas several socialists were reluctant to recognize equal rights for common-law wives, and there was also a proposal to take their children into care. Finally, Grousset's principle was accepted, though oddly the phrase 'married or not' was dropped from the published version of the decree. At the same time austere republican virtue was

---

57. *PVC*, vol. 2, p. 229.   58. Rougerie (1971), p. 182.
59. Jones and Vergès (1991), p. 731.

upheld: Delescluze suggested that a certificate should be required to prove the women's established relationship, and it was ordered that only when their status and 'morality' had been established by local committees of inquiry were common-law wives to receive a pension.[60] It was not, in short, theirs by right, but only when their quasi-marital relationship with a dead republican hero had been proved to the satisfaction of male officials. Moreover, National Guard *cantinières* were ordered to be married women only.

Discussion of this pension decree reflects disapproval of ephemeral sexual relationships and above all of prostitution, which political clubs frequently demanded measures to suppress. Rougerie has suggested that it was detested as a degrading exploitation of working-class women by the bourgeoisie. The honour of working-class men was obviously at stake here. During the Commune, popular and official attitudes seem to have been purely repressive, not unlike the conventional 'bourgeois' attitude; nothing was suggested to help the women concerned. On the contrary, in May the ex-prefecture ordered registered prostitutes once again to obey the old oppressive regulations, and reopened the resented dispensary (which they had to attend for medical inspections).[61] Under the Commune as before, women workers were extremely hostile to competition from other women workers in convents and prisons – often reformed or imprisoned prostitutes. However understandable, this is hardly evidence of new attitudes towards female victims of male exploitation.

Did the Commune, then, mark a revolution in gender attitudes? Much research remains to be done on the grass-roots activities of women, but my provisional answer (which differs from that of some recent scholars) is no. Moreover, the main Commune newspapers were much less aware of women's activities than historians have been: it is not evident that as an issue women's rights impinged much on Fédéré consciousness. After the fall of the Commune, exiles in London manifested conventional gender attitudes, expelling homosexuals from their groups, and regarding women's influence with suspicion.

Was the Commune a cultural revolution in behaviour and experience? An influential suggestion by Henri Lefebvre, taken up by several other historians and sociologists, is that 'the characteristic style of the Commune was that of Festival (*la Fête*)':

> an immense, grandiose festival, a festival that the people of Paris, essence and symbol of the French people and the people in general,

60. *PVC*, vol 1, p. 159; *JOC*, 11 April; order of Central Committee, SHA Ly 20.
61. APP Ba 365–6.

offered to itself and to the world. A Festival of springtime in the city, a festival of the disinherited and the proletarians, a revolutionary festival and a festival of the Revolution, a total festival, the greatest of modern times, which unfolds in magnificence and joy.[62]

Through such liberating festivity, the argument goes, the imaginative and physical constaints of everyday life were thrown off. Workers exiled from the centre of Paris by Haussmann's urbanism – which had deliberately created 'urban meaning' for the bourgeoisie to make money and 'urban space' to flaunt it – now returned to repossess the centre of the city, reconverting it into a cultural 'space' for the people, women and men.

Certainly, there were festive ceremonial occasions in which the Fédéré masses marched through the centre, particularly the huge parade on 28 March past the Hôtel de Ville. And thousands went to concerts in the Tuileries Palace. There were links here with familiar themes of the 'revolutionary tradition': the Hôtel de Ville had long been the focus of popular power, and triumphant revolutionaries-cum-sightseers had surged into the Tuileries in 1792, 1830 and 1848. The idea of the people of Montmartre and Belleville 'descending' on the city from their northern and eastern heights was commonly expressed. There is probably an echo here of the traditional 'descents' on the city by roistering crowds from the taverns of La Courtille, near Belleville, during the annual carnival. The 'descents' on Paris during the Commune appear to have been occasional excursions, and of course there is no way of knowing whether those involved in 1871 either felt themselves to be or really were returning exiles, as opposed to visiting sightseers. Most Fédérés would have been immigrants with little or no memory of pre-Haussmann Paris. Political activities and most of the public ceremonies that expressed them were based on the *arrondissement*, not the city. There was sometimes friction, fear and resentment when 'the Belleville people' made a 'descent' into the central districts. Even supporters of the Commune disliked interlopers on their territory, and complained about noisy drunken behaviour by National Guard 'outsiders'. This indicates that their presence was neither permanent, secure nor accepted: more a carnivalesque incursion than a 'repossession' of the city, whose central districts were relatively empty during the Commune, deserted by the rich and not inhabited by the poor (above pp. 4–5). But carnivals are, by their nature, an interruption of normal behaviour, not a transformation of it. As the most

62. Lefebvre (1965), pp. 20–1.

popular Communard paper, *Le Cri du Peuple* (30 March), put it rather depressingly:

> Tomorrow, citizen-soldiers . . . you must return, still proud, now free, to your places at the workshop and the counter. After the poetry of triumph, the prose of work. . . . Let us make it known everywhere . . . that the great Revolution is complete, that Paris is saved, and that her 500,000 fighters are ready to become once more 500,000 workers.

Several writers have suggested that the Commune, in a very broad cultural sense, transformed life by creating 'fantasy' and 'disorder', 'a dramatic upheaval in commonplace understandings of time and space, identity and language, work and leisure': 'while the cadres worry about food supplies, the people shoot at the clocks'.[63] These are beguiling notions, but evidence that people in 1871 thought and acted like this is at best slender. Cultural theorists seem reluctant to allow their imaginations to be restrained by lack of evidence – what Lefebvre grandly calls 'positivist banalities', and the inimitable Eagleton dismisses as 'empirical scholarly debate about whether [Rimbaud] actually leaned on a barricade on some particular Wednesday morning'.[64] But we must certainly beware of caricaturing the Commune as a non-stop street party – 'white nights and revolutionary days'.[65] To dismiss as irrelevant what living people at the time actually did and thought, and to overlook their labours, uncertainties and fears, is to treat them with the 'immense condescension of posterity'.

In so far as the Commune did represent a cultural revolution in a broad sense, it was in the rituals of politics and above all in relationships of power. The tradition of the political club in which members of the public could speak their mind, a feature of all revolutions since 1789, was no less present under the Commune. Yet there was a difference: the club movement had not this time been created by revolution, it had revived under the Second Empire, as was seen in chapter 1, and it had developed under the Government of National Defence. In this sense, it was not a revolutionary phenomenon, and certainly not specific to the Commune. But it had become an important aspect of popular political culture, whose participants were both actors and audience.

The real cultural revolution was the visible dissolution of relations of power and status. Martin Johnson has stressed the importance of forms of address: *Monsieur* and *Madame* were replaced by the

---

63. Eagleton (1988), pp. vi, ix, viii.   64. Ibid., p. x.   65. Ross (1988), p. 42.

republican *Citoyen* and *Citoyenne*.[66] Hierarchy was overturned when ladies and gentlemen could be questioned, ordered about and even arrested by armed citizens. Poor people found that many rules had ceased to apply, and that, in the eternal trench warfare against bosses, shopkeepers and landlords, power could be on their side and sometimes in their hands. Take two random examples, which could doubtless be multiplied by thousands. Constant Clerfayt, a young, sickly and illiterate orphan, found that he could now make a living as a flower-seller because nobody was insisting that he should have a licence. Nicholas Dugène, former petty criminal and now a Fédéré corporal, could help the girl next door when their landlady tried to evict her and seize her belongings for non-payment of rent and for having burnt the furniture as firewood: he turned up with a squad of Fédérés to show the landlady that the boot was now on the other foot. This must have been exhilarating: the world turned upside down. For those on the receiving end it was often frightening – many middle-class people were very frightened under the Commune – and always humiliating: 'You cannot imagine the suffering caused by the despotism exercised in the streets by the riffraff disguised as soldiers,' noted Goncourt on 15 May.[67] Many got their own back after the Commune's defeat by denouncing their tormenters to the Versaillais troops and police in a manner that even a military prosecutor considered 'excessive'. The Marquis de Forbin-Janson, for example, had several of his tenants arrested, one of whom was shot; the *curé* of St-Ambroise denounced 71 people. As for our examples, Clerfayt died in prison; Dugène was transported to New Caledonia.[68] Thus, at grass-roots level, social order was restored.

66. Johnson (1994), pp. 277–80.   67. Goncourt (1969), p. 289.
68. Clerfayt, SHA 15 CG 154; Dugène, 15 CG 188; police report on denunciations, APP Db 420.

CHAPTER FOUR

A New Revolutionary People?

Who the Communards[1] were has been taken as the acid test of what sort of revolution the Commune was. The question can be posed in several ways, each proceeding from different conceptual assumptions. If we think that revolutions are fundamentally class conflicts, we shall focus on the Communards' occupations to see whether they represented a more 'modern' working class. If we think that social and political solidarities are shaped by ideas, language and images, we shall wish to see how the Communards visualized and described themselves and their enemies. If we think that for interests and solidarities to be translated into acts social networks and formal organizations are crucial, then we need to look at what these were and how they operated. These different approaches are not all incompatible – people have multiple identities and motivations – but the following discussion will attempt to assess their value in explaining who the Communards were. Furthermore, interest in gender history has recently revived a problem that fascinated contemporaries: women during the Commune. Were they playing a new, separate and self-conscious role? To try to make the boundaries of Communard identity clearer, we shall also look at those – the majority of Parisians – who were lukewarm, noncommittal or hostile.

The map of the 26 March election results (Figure 4.1) shows that the 190,000 Communard voters were concentrated in the outer eastern, northern and, to a lesser extent, southern *arrondissements* – the newly built-up, mainly working-class 'red' districts that we

---

1. Supporters of the Commune were called by many names, including 'communists', '*communeux*', 'reds', 'insurgents', etc.; I am using 'Communard' simply as the most familiar, and 'Fédéré' when referring specifically to National Guards.

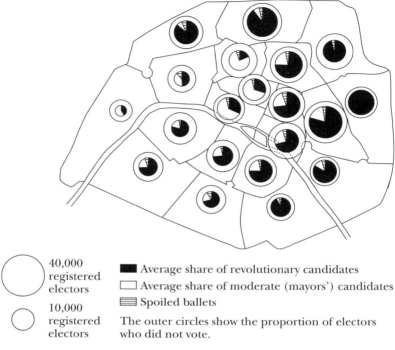

40,000 registered electors

10,000 registered electors

■ Average share of revolutionary candidates

☐ Average share of moderate (mayors') candidates

▤ Spoiled ballets

The outer circles show the proportion of electors who did not vote.

Figure 4.1 *Vote in Commune elections, 26 March*
Source: Rougerie (1971), p. 144

have already encountered so frequently. In some of the central *arrondissements*, especially the 1st and 2nd, a high proportion of voters supported more moderate republican candidates aiming for a peaceful solution to the crisis. In the generally opulent residential districts of western Paris, most electors had either left Paris or boycotted the elections as illegal; a high proportion of the minority who did vote supported Communard candidates. These results, when compared with Figure 1.2 (p. 25), might seem obviously explicable in class terms: the predominantly working-class outer districts were Communard; central districts, where middle-class, lower-middle, white-collar and working classes were mixed, saw a middle-of-the-road result; the bourgeois west – except for some working-class enclaves – was hostile. Why complicate a simple picture?

Complications and supplementary questions already lurk, however. Even if most Communards, male and female, were manual workers, which kinds of workers were most active or prominent? Why were many non-workers also involved, often as leaders? Why did Communards in their words and actions (including in their official declarations and legislation) not define the conflict as a class struggle? What made some people much more active than others of the same social and political profile? Why did some Communards carry on the struggle when most gave up?

Social categories: 'proletariat' or 'people'?

The assertion that the Communards represented, at least in embryonic form, a new, more proletarian working class was long a crucial part of the argument for its historic significance: it represented a further step towards history's final goal, a link between the 'bourgeois revolutions' of 1789, 1830 and 1848, and the 'proletarian revolution' to come. However, the pioneering research of Jacques Rougerie, based mainly on the statistics and court records of captured insurgents, demonstrated that the Communards were not a 'proletariat' – if we use that term to mean predominantly unskilled workers from relatively large-scale modern industries, rather than the much broader contemporary usage of 'proletariat' to mean those who worked for a living. Most Communards were skilled workers; they were fairly evenly spread over the age-range 20–40 (though some adolescents, children and older men were also involved); and they worked mostly in long-established and small-scale Paris craft industries. This made them very similar in profile to those (in some cases the same individuals) involved in the events of 1848–51, and recognizably similar to the combatants of July 1830 and even to the *sans-culottes* of the 1790s (Table 4.1).

The differences – notably the increase in the proportion of builders, labourers and metal workers – were caused by expansion of the building trade during Haussmann's transformation of the city and by a degree of industrial modernization. But an examination of the structures of Paris industry shows that even these changes cannot be seen as equivalent to proletarianization. The building industry was traditional in its organization, with many small subcontractors and partnerships. Metal working too was on a small scale, and mostly concerned with highly skilled finishing processes, not heavy industry. Rougerie suggests, moreover, that the prominence in the insurrection, and in left-wing politics, of metal workers might be because they had kept their habits and traditions, especially their dislike of

TABLE 4.1   *Participants in Parisian insurrections*

	July 1830[1]	June 1848[2]	May 1871[3]
Skilled workers (total) of whom:	73.3	60.0	54.4
wood	8.6	10.9	8.0
building	14.8	12.4	15.7
metals	19.2	14.8	11.9
leather	18.0	6.3	5.4
textiles/clothing	8.4	6.5	3.9
luxury goods	1.0	8.5	6.9
printing	3.3	0.6	2.7
Unskilled workers	4.2	13.4	14.9
White collar	3.1	6.7	8.0
Middle classes of whom:	2.0	7.3	7.6
small business	2.0	4.1	4.3
professional	0.0	3.2	3.3
Others (total) of whom:	17.2	12.6	6.0
servants	12.3	?	4.9
others	4.9	12.6	1.1

[1] 1830: % of casualties whose occupations are recorded
[2] 1848: % of those accused of insurrection
[3] 1871: % of those arrested during and after insurrection
Sources: Merriman (1975), pp. 33–4, Charle (1991), p. 134, Rougerie (1964), p. 127

modern work discipline.[2] Conversely, Paris's nearest equivalent to a 'modern proletariat', workers in the few large factories, such as the Cail engineering plant or the Say sugar refinery, were not prominent in the Commune.

Identifying those groups most actively involved in the insurrection – or at least those given the heavier sentence of transportation after the event by Versaillais courts martial[3] – again appears to show a somewhat higher level of involvement among building workers and metal workers, and a lower level among unskilled labourers (Table 4.2). This result is complicated by distortions imposed by the military judges' own prejudices about what sort of workers were most likely to be most guilty. It is further complicated by the fact that thousands – often those most actively involved – had been killed during the fighting or summarily executed immediately afterwards.

2. Rougerie (1964), p. 131.
3. For an excellent discussion of the problems of the sources, see Gould (1995), pp. 213–16; see also Maitron (1972).

TABLE 4.2   *Levels of active involvement (%)*

	Overall population	Arrested for insurgency	Transported to penal colony
Metals	8 ⎫	12 ⎫	12 ⎫
Construction	10 ⎬ 38	17 ⎬ 43	18 ⎬ 45
Labourers	20 ⎭	14 ⎭	15 ⎭
Textiles, clothing, footwear	8	9	9
Luxury goods, printing	10	10	9

Source: Rougerie (1964), p. 129

The conclusion that certain categories of workers were indeed more or less active than the average must therefore be tentative. There could, moreover, be reasons for such involvement that we know little about. Pre-existing levels of organization and militancy in certain trades could encourage political mobilization. Differing levels of unemployment could have affected the number of workers serving actively in the National Guard or other Commune organizations. Geographical distribution of certain industries and their workers could tend to involve them in political acts or in fighting. Their age profile could have had a similar effect. So obscurities remain.

The rank-and-file Communards were not disproportionately recruited among the poorest workers. On the other hand, two-thirds were semi-literate or illiterate, while only 2 per cent had a secondary education – revealing of their social status and of the low level of literacy even in skilled Paris trades. Nor were Communards disproportionately criminal, as their enemies alleged: Serman estimates that at most 10 per cent came from a genuinely criminal underclass.[4] Though unskilled labourers were, unsurprisingly, the poorest and most criminal group, metal workers were not relatively poor or criminal. Although taken as a whole, a fairly high proportion – some 20 per cent – had some criminal record, mostly these were for trivial misdemeanours (one with a conviction for 'public indecency' turns out to have danced the can-can) or for political offences such as being involved in a demonstration.

Just over 1,000 of the 36,000 people arrested after the Commune were women, 71 per cent of them workers, mainly in the various branches of the clothing trade or less skilled service industries

4. Rougerie (1964), pp. 132–4; Serman (1986), p. 283.

(laundrywomen, cleaners). Nearly half were 'living in concubinage' (common-law marriages), and a conspicuously high proportion – 24 per cent – were prostitutes.[5] While in part this reflects the genuinely dependent and vulnerable position of low-paid working-class women, it above all shows the prejudices of the authorities in making arrests.

At the top end of the Communard hierarchy there was no new proletarian leadership acting as the vanguard of revolution. The 79-man Commune Council[6] came from the lower-middle class and the working-class elite, mostly in four roughly equal groups: 25 'professionals', many of them full- or part-time journalists (which meant, in practice, professional politicians), with some teachers, doctors and permanent students; 21 wage-earning workers, nearly all from the highly skilled crafts such as porcelain-painting, jewellery, shoemaking, copper-moulding, hatmaking and boilermaking; 16 white-collar workers (including a salesman, a civil servant, a solicitor's clerk, a pharmacist's assistant, etc.); 14 self-employed artisans, shop-keepers or small businessmen; and three miscellaneous (two former officers and a *propriétaire*). It is noteworthy that among this hetero-geneous group there was not a single unskilled labourer.

Occupational categorization is somewhat arbitrary, as it was common to move from one status to another (for example, from employed to self-employed and from manual to non-manual work), or to combine several activities, such as a paid occupation, politics and part-time journalism. This was typical of the changing world of mid-century Paris, where more than a quarter of the working popu-lation were self-employed, and mobility, bankruptcy and uncertain status were common. Eugène Pottier, for example, best known as a political poet and songwriter, was by training a textile designer but was also part-owner of a public bath house, which places him simul-taneously in three different socio-economic categories. But precise class status is less significant than milieu and history. Commune leaders were drawn in large part from those who had been politically active since the late 1860s and sometimes earlier, in journalism, the labour movement, the cooperative movement or as speakers in public meetings and political clubs: 25 were freemasons (in practice a radical network) and 34 belonged to the International. Most had built up a following through wartime activity in the National Guard

5. Serman (1986), p. 287.
6. The total after the 16 April by-elections; Blanqui, an elected member, was in prison. For slightly varying statistics, see ibid., pp. 276–80, and Rougerie (1995), p. 34.

or in local vigilance committees: 43 were officers, and 12 former members of the Central Committee of the National Guard; 50 were members of various local committees.[7]

Leaders at a lower level came from the same social strata. National Guards mostly elected those who had the skills, and perhaps the social standing, to give orders, communicate with headquarters and do the book-keeping. In some battalions, this hierarchical element was plain: in the 42nd, from the mainly working-class 13th *arrondissement*, senior officers were mostly clerks or shopkeepers from the main streets of the district, and junior officers and NCOs were artisans, clerks or shopkeepers from the side streets. In companies recruited among workers from the Cail factory, they elected charge-hands and foremen, with a cashier (a former soldier) as commander. While a lower proportion of the *bourgeoisie populaire* and of the most highly skilled workers participated actively in the Commune than did manual workers, they provided a disproportionate part of the leadership. Only 7.3 per cent of building workers who served in the National Guard became officers or NCOs, and 16.9 per cent of metal workers; but 23.3 per cent of small businessmen, 31.9 per cent of print workers, and 36.8 per cent of white-collar workers held ranks.[8] One such activist described himself thus:

> I am the son of a good patriot of 1792. . . . Journeyman cabinetmaker at 18 years old . . . working during the day, studying at night, history, travels, political and social economy, making propaganda and taking part in all republican movements. . . . Arriving in Paris in 1854, two years later I set myself up as a furniture restorer. . . . I employed 1 to 3 workers, paying them 50 centimes per day above the official rate and propagandizing them too. . . . I practised association as much as I could. . . . In politics I want the broadest possible sovereignty of the People [and] all the Reforms our defective social and political organization demands.[9]

Women leaders, active in clubs, vigilance committees, occasionally in the National Guard, and in the Union des Femmes – activities we shall return to later – were a comparable mixture of skilled workers (a bookbinder, dressmakers, a gold polisher, milliners), and rather precarious members of the lower-middle class (teachers, journalists), including several prominent Russian and Polish *émigrées*.[10]

7. For details, see Maitron *et al.* (1967–71) *passim*; Winock and Azéma (1964); Johnson (1996), p. 104.

8. Rougerie (1964), p. 129. Figures based on arrests.

9. Rougerie (1971), p. 234.   10. Serman (1986), pp. 287–92.

As this brief analysis shows, it is clear, and no longer even controversial, that the Communards were 'the people' rather than 'the proletariat'. That most Communard combatants were workers was not new: it had been so in 1848, 1830 and the 1780s–90s. The significant differences were that in 1871 an unprecedented share of the political leadership went to skilled manual and white-collar workers, while established politicians and the commercial middle class largely kept aloof, rather than, as in past revolutions, attempting to take over the leadership. The proportion of working-class leaders – about half the Commune's membership – has probably never been equalled in any European revolutionary government.

If the Commune was a movement of 'the people', does this give greater weight to Castells's view, discussed in chapter 1, that the Commune should be conceptualized as an urban revolution? That is, were the Communards representative, not of a class, but of the urban population whose aims focused on changing the 'urban meaning' of Paris? It was argued in chapter 1 that his 'urban' hypothesis cannot explain the Commune because it overlooks its historical and ideological specificity and the extraordinary circumstances created by war; and it thus arrives at a reductionist view of its motives and meaning. On the other hand, we saw in the last chapter that many of the Commune's emergency social measures were indeed concerned with specifically Parisian rights and problems. So we need to pursue the Parisian dimension of the conflict, not only in terms of urban sociology, however, but also with regard to the city's history and political culture. This means approaching the identity of the Communards differently: not only by tracing their occupational profile, but also by examining how they themselves understood the struggle they were undertaking.

Subjective identities: the Communards and their enemies

There were several connecting themes in the way Communards consistently described themselves, the struggle they were engaged in, and their enemies. Communards were first and foremost republicans. And as republicans they were patriots, because France was the fatherland of the Revolution. They were also consciously Parisian, because Paris was the stronghold of republicanism and the patriotic leader of the nation in its struggle against invasion, treachery and reaction. All Parisians had the duty to take part in the struggle, but only the 'people' or 'proletariat' consistently heeded the call of duty. The 'democratic and social republic' would complete the progress towards liberty, equality and fraternity begun in 1789 in the interests of all humanity. So foreign allies were welcome to join the struggle. This way of understanding events was complex and yet coherent, and included elements of political, national, local and class identity. Let us look more closely at the component themes.

First, republicanism. This was always the first and irreducible demand, because all other benefits flowed from 'la République' (always with the definite article), synonym for democracy, liberty, secularism, equality and progress. Hence, 'the Republic' was the only legitimate form of government, which neither the National Assembly nor the majority of the electorate had the right to alter: it was 'above universal suffrage', and indeed could if necessary – at least while struggle continued – be dictatorial. The Republic was certainly non-negotiable, as was made absolutely clear immediately after 18 March in negotiations with the mayors: 'The Central Committee has received a regular, imperative mandate [which] forbids it to let the Assembly meddle with liberty, with the Republic.'[11] The Declaration to the French People was equally clear: 'What does [Paris] want? The recognition and consolidation of the Republic. . . .'

The Republic was not a mere constitutional formality, but the sole means towards progress, social equality and national recovery. A Fédéré officer told his company that 'Only the Republic can save and regenerate France.'[12] For socialists, the Revolution of 1789 had only emancipated the bourgeoisie; the final stage would bring the emancipation of the working class in a 'democratic and social republic'. Fränkel assured Marx that 'in the social domain there will be nothing more to ask for'.[13] Much of this would be a direct consequence of the abolition of the oppressive and expensive State. As Vallès had written a few years earlier, 'As long as there is one soldier, one executioner, one tax gatherer, one revenue man, one policeman believed on oath, one unaccountable official, one unsackable magistrate; as long as all this has to be paid for, People, you will be poor.'[14] We have seen how Commune policy reflected such thinking. There had developed over the previous thirty years a distinctly French variant of socialism, strongly influenced by Proudhon and to a lesser extent by the Russian anarchist Bakunin, which advocated destroying oppressive state structures by devolving

---

11. Rougerie (1971), p. 116. 12. Order of the day, 189th bn, SHA Ly 85.
13. Lefebvre (1965), p. 355. 14. Maitron *et al.* (1967–71), vol. 9, p. 264.

power to local democratic communities (federalism) and abolishing exploitation by decentralizing economic control to workers' cooperative associations. Proudhon's influence saturated Communard socialism – 'Its apostles are workers, its Christ was Proudhon,' proclaimed Courbet[15] – even though his dismissal of politics as irrelevant had been less congenial amid the anti-Empire campaigns of the late 1860s. But the ideas of the Parisian Left were eclectic, and one cannot define Communard social ideas too strictly. The International included Jacobins (who operated through conventional political action), Proudhonists (who stressed labour organization), Blanquists (who saw themselves as elite revolutionary shock-troops) and some more moderate republicans. Benoît Malon had written to a friend in 1869, 'I frequent all the parties, democratic, radical, Proudhonian, positivist, phalansterian, collectivist . . . Fourierist cooperatists etc. . . . I see everywhere men of good faith and that teaches me to be tolerant.'[16]

The Republic's enemies, consequently, were a coalition of all the enemies of progress, democracy and equality: monarchists, henchmen of former oppressive regimes, exploiters, parasites, the Church – the forces of counter-revolution since 1789. The newspaper *La Sociale* warned at the end of March

> The royalists of the Assembly are trying to raise armies in the provinces. . . . As yet they have only a gang of policemen . . . and the Pope's zouaves; as generals they have . . . Vinoy the Bonapartist, the Catholics Charette and Cathelineau, who have risen against the revolution in 1871 as did their forefathers against that of 1793, and who will have the same fate today as the latter had eighty years ago.

When fighting began on 2 April, the Commune announced it in almost identical terms (below p. 152). Repeated allusions to the struggles of the 1790s against the royalist peasant rebels of western France consciously – as in so many of the Communards' acts and words – placed the Year 79 in the context of the past and continuing Revolution.

The republican struggle was also a patriotic struggle. For all republicans, the great Revolution of 1789 had marked the birth of the free Nation, and made it the leader of world progress with a mission to enlighten less advanced peoples. The idea of the Republic had almost absorbed the idea of France and now embodied its greatness and its historic significance: 'Vive la République', never

---

15. Courbet (1992), p. 409.   16. Vincent (1992), p. 14.

'Vive la France', was their patriotic cry. As we have seen, this anim-
ated their resistance during the German war: the victory of France
and the Republic had become synonymous. As the future Commune
member Benoît Malon put it, 'I consider that those who are defending the capital of the Revolution against the Germans are performing a glorious act.'[17] Enemies of the Republic had, they believed,
betrayed the nation and made peace with the Prussian monarchists
as a way of restoring a monarch in France: just as in the 1790s, they
had become the allies of France's enemies. Republicans would continue to fight the traitors, 'the Prussians of Versailles', as they called
them. Even if it was necessary for the moment to avoid conflict with
Germany, for Communards the national struggle would continue
one day – perhaps soon – ideally ending with a republic in Berlin as
a step towards the final goal, cherished since the 1790s, of a Universal
Republic. This broad vision could accommodate many variations.
Blanquist intellectuals such as Tridon and Flourens (the Belleville
hero killed in the 3 April sortie) saw it as part of a millenary struggle
between Aryan culture, which was atheist, and Semitic culture, which
was mystical; Flourens taught that the intellectual, moral and physical
superiority of blond blue-eyed Aryans was destined to dominate or
displace inferior brown, yellow and black peoples.[18]

The struggle had become first and foremost a Parisian struggle,
even though aid from provincial cities was expected and welcomed.
Paris was – as Parisian deputies declared to a fuming National
Assembly in March – 'the sacred city' where 'the sovereign [i.e.
the people] resides, the intellectual, moral and political centre of
France'. Paris embodied those overlapping categories, Republic
and Fatherland; it was 'the salvation of the Gallic race' as well as
the unique centre of world revolutionary energy.[19] The epic of the
siege had confirmed this view, for the sufferings and efforts of *la
province* had not impinged on Parisians, who saw themselves as
having stood heroically alone. 'Paris spared France many disasters
by her sacrifices, but France did not rescue Paris,' wrote *Le Cri du
Peuple* (29 March).

This latest ordeal appeared part of a saga in which Paris had
repeatedly fought for progress and been defeated and punished by
foreign enemies and French reactionaries. Since male suffrage was
introduced in 1848, the instrument of Paris's subjugation had been
the voting power of benighted peasants manipulated by priests and

17. Ibid., p. 23.   18. Flourens (1863); and see also Hutton (1981), pp. 47–8.
19. *Annales de l'Assemblée Nationale* (1871), vol. 1, pp. 271–3, 277; declaration of
Central Committee of the 20 Arrondissements, in Dautry and Scheler (1960), p. 85.

nobles. The contrast had become stark since the 1860s. Wrote *Le Cri du Peuple* (24 March):

> Paris will always be crushed by [peasant] ignorance ... the brutal power of number! *Coups d'état* by the ballot box! Slaughter by the vote! ... Since Paris has been able to think, Paris has always condemned and fought its governments.... Three times in fifty years Paris has chased them from its walls ... and three times the peasants' votes have brought them back, under another cloak, into the enemy city.

The answer to this political impasse was to assert communal autonomy. This was both a principle and a tactic. It allowed Parisians to dismiss the votes of reactionary and backward masses who had no right to reject the Republic. Victor Hugo had said it in verse two decades earlier:

> They have voted!
> Behind the sacristan and the village Plod
> The frightened herd trails off to chew the cud ...
> Do you really think that France is you!
> That you are the People, you brutish beasts,
> And that you can rule us with your kings and priests?

In the words of *Le Père Duchêne* (15 Germinal), the most notoriously outspoken Communard paper, many peasants were 'animals who can't even read and write [and] don't even know how to keep themselves clean'. This conflict between the revolutionary city and the reactionary provinces was succinctly expressed by two terms already emerging at the time of the 1870 plebiscite (above pp. 35–6): *les ruraux*, the 'rurals' or 'yokels', used generally for Versailles supporters; and *Paris ville libre*, the independent city republic.[20]

The struggle involved all patriotic Parisians – even though more than half had been born outside the city. There was no contradiction here: Paris could be seen as the meeting place of the most progressive and energetic of France's people, who had risen out of rural reaction and stagnation. Consequently, class divisions in the 'free city' could be swept aside; indeed, the revolution had ended class conflict. According to *Le Père Duchêne* (19 Ventôse), it was the Second Empire that had fomented hatred between 'our brave proletarians and our good bourgeois', but under the Republic they could celebrate 'the people's wedding, let's marry the bourgeoisie and the proletariat'. *Le Cri du Peuple* (22 March) agreed that 'the working bourgeoisie, honest and robust' was 'the sister of the proletariat'

---

20. Huard (1996), p. 215.

– a sentiment shared by the tiny paper of the International, *La Révolution Politique et Sociale* (3 Floréal): 'the People and the hardworking bourgeoisie are one'. 'Proletarians' were conventionally all who worked for wages, and hence could include workers, teachers, clerks, journalists and gentlemanly left-wing intellectuals such as Blanqui, who spoke of 'proletarians like me'. Though this language had obvious political advantages in rallying broad support for 'Paris ville libre', it also accords with real political and social relations in an economy dominated by small industry and shifting economic status, and also with long-held socialist views of a society divided between 'producers' and 'idlers'.

But 'the People' did not include everyone, even within Paris. The others did not regard themselves as *citoyens* and *citoyennes* (above p. 107). One formidable Communarde complained to her club that near the stock exchange a snooty passer-by had told her that 'there were no "citizens" in that quarter, only ladies and gentlemen', and she urged that a few cannon should be sent 'to silence all those reactionaries'.[21] Ever since the 1790s, as republican patriots endlessly recalled, nobles had fought against the nation. The great republican historian Michelet had declared that not only nobles but also much of the bourgeoisie were not really part of the nation, because they excluded themselves by a selfish preoccupation with their own interests; only 'the People' were capable of disinterested patriotism, solidarity and self-sacrifice. Those who took advantage of unjust and corrupt political systems such as the Second Empire to exploit the people as speculators, overpaid officials and parasites of all kinds were very different from the 'hard-working bourgeoisie' praised in the Communard press, and were clearly not part of the People.

If not all those born in France were part of the French People in its full sense, foreigners who embraced the cause could become so. This had been a theme of the 1790s, corresponding to the cherished belief that the French Revolution was a liberating event for the whole human race. Even the most chauvinistic French republican patriotism – and it could be very chauvinistic, even racist – could ultimately be justified on the grounds that France stood for universal progress. These ideas had been brought up to date by events of the last generation: the pan-European 1848 revolutions, the Italian and Polish nationalist struggles of the 1850s and '60s, and the embryonic growth of an international workers' movement. Hence, the ultimate

21. Rougerie (1971), p. 211.

aim of the Commune was 'the universal republic'. Some believed that this might be brought about by restarting the war with Germany, and going on to spread revolution across the continent – a vision that brought political exiles and international revolutionaries into the fight. Several Polish men played an outstanding role as Fédéré commanders. Several women of upper-class Russian or Polish origin active in international revolutionary groups provided leadership in women's organizations. The best known among them are Elisaveta Tomanovskaya (known as Elisabeth Dmitrieff), 20, daughter of a Russian officer, sent to Paris by Marx in March; Paula Mekarska (known as Paule Mink or Minck), 31, daughter of an exiled Polish nobleman; and Anna Jaclard, née Korvin-Krukovskaya, 26, daughter of a Russian general married to a Blanquist medical student.

Communard leaders of diverse opinions were affiliated to the International, a loose and eclectic body. The idea of such affiliation clearly fitted with their view of the universal nature of their struggle, but it certainly did not mean that they countenanced outside direction: it was Paris, after all, that was the beacon of revolution. *La Révolution Politique et Sociale* (13 Germinal) scornfully rejected as a 'calumny' the suggestion that the International had a foreign president: 'Citizens of the International, have you ever heard of a citizen Karle [*sic*] Marx? No!' Marx, secretary of the International, indeed had neglible influence, although his son-in-law Paul Lafargue visited Paris, and he sent unhelpful advice to his associates Tomanovskaya, Fränkel and Serrailler (sent from London in September and elected to the Commune by the 2nd *arrondissement*), and he also wrote to Varlin. The significance of the International was not its foreign links, but its role as one of several coordinating bodies, and especially its value as a stamp of electoral approval.

Communard self-identification as simultaneously republican, revolutionary, patriotic, socialist, Parisian and international constituted a well-understood language which was reflected in the Commune's declarations, in its acts, in the press, and in many grass-roots pronouncements, even if these were not always rigorously coherent. For example, one Fédéré, a sign-painter named Yvonnet, taking his staff-officer's examination, answered the question 'What do you understand by social questions?' thus:

> I understand by socialism men uniting in a single policy, from the Unity point of view to make a country strong, from the material point of view uniting in cooperation, either collective or individual for everything connected with commerce, the sciences and the arts and establishing by that cooperation a cheap cost of living. As concerns

Justice, it should be established by Courts which will be accountable. As concerns war the standing army must be abolished, the citizen army alone to protect the honour of the fatherland and property. That, citizens, is a brief summary of my ideas.[22]

Communard views can be put to the test, as Rougerie suggested, by looking at the other side of the coin: whom in practice did they treat as the enemy? First, of course, the Versaillais, described as 'monarchists', 'Prussians of Versailles' and 'Chouans'. But Communards also identified enemies within: we have seen that important measures were specifically directed against those who had abandoned Paris in its hour of need – *les francs-fileurs* – and whose abandoned businesses or empty houses could be requisitioned. The only property-owners who suffered the equivalent of confiscation without compensation were residential landlords, whose arrears of rent were cancelled; but they were both the everyday enemy of poor Parisians (as many incidents during and after the Commune would illustrate) and also the epitome of 'property as theft' in its 'idle' (*oisif*) sense of extracting money merely by ownership. In popular language, they were *les vautours*, the vultures. Those who avoided National Guard service were also potentially enemies who could be disarmed, insulted, denied a livelihood or rounded up and forced to fight or at least build barricades. They might be thought of as a class stereotype – 'these dandies . . . strolling along the boulevards with monocles and walking canes, looking down their noses at the proletariat'[23] – but they were not a class.

Enemies so detested that their liberties or even lives were directly threatened were a much more circumscribed group. The men arrested as hostages were not class enemies in the socio-economic sense, but ideological and political delinquents. Gendarmes captured on 18 March were held. Priests, nicknamed scornfully *calotins* ('skull-cappers') or *corbeaux* ('crows'), were arrested, including the Archbishop of Paris, Georges Darboy. Few dared to wear clerical dress in public, but any clean-shaven man was suspect. Churches were occupied and vandalized; banks, remember, were untouched. Convents were searched for arms, and churches desecrated. Worshippers were sometimes mocked and bullied, and rituals parodied. A press campaign accused priests and nuns of sexual crimes, including murder. Women were rarely threatened physically, but policemen's

22. SHA Ly 36. The examiners were not impressed: 'Written paper, bad; oral, approximately nil; overall mark 2.' But he remained a staff lieutenant.
23. Rougerie (1971), p. 229.

wives and nuns were sacked from public employment and otherwise harassed. Even army officers were not so high on the list of enemies. Although two generals had been shot on 18 March and others roughed up, these were unplanned accidents, not policy. There was no attempt to round up members of the economic or social elite, nor even any suggestion of doing so. Though a dozen bourgeois demonstrators had been killed on 22 March, this was an unplanned and unrepeated incident. When in the last desperate days, 56 hostages were killed (below p. 178), they were again exclusively the enemies of the Republic and 'the People': nearly all priests or policemen, plus two other associates of the Empire (a banker and a judge).[24]

That priests were the only civilian group systematically targeted as hostages – 120 were arrested and 24 killed – reflects the centrality of anticlericalism in left-wing culture. There were several levels: ideological, political and social. Since the Enlightenment, and especially since the Revolution, Catholicism had been seen as an enemy of intellectual progress and a pillar of counter-revolution. This was why Proudhon abandoned Christian socialism in the 1840s and adopted a vehemently anti-religious position: 'For as long as men bow before altars, mankind will remain damned, the slave of kings and priests.'[25] In 1848 there had been a brief *rapprochement* between Catholics and republicans, both opponents of the July Monarchy. But the Church would not support social revolution. The death of Archbishop Affre, killed trying to mediate during the June Days, symbolized a new breach between Church and Revolution. The support of most of the clergy – like most Frenchmen – for Louis-Napoleon Bonaparte was regarded by republicans as a betrayal, the harnessing again of religion to reaction. It caused Blanqui to adopt an intransigent atheism: 'War on the supernatural, that is the enemy.'[26] The singing of a *Te Deum* at Notre Dame after the success of Louis-Napoleon's *coup d'état* provoked ferocious poetic denunciation in Victor Hugo's *Les Châtiments*, much repeated by Communards:

> Murder at your side reads the prayer divine
> Crying: Shoot the rabble dead!
> Satan holds the cruet, and that's not wine
> That stains your chalice red.

24. The banker, Jecker, was also shot, but because he was accused of plotting with the Empire to start the Mexican intervention of 1864. Both Archbishop Darboy and Abbé Deguerry, *curé* of the Madeleine, the two best-known clerical victims, had also been close to the imperial court.
25. Vincent (1984), p. 105.   26. Ibid., p. 110.

During the Empire, more disputes had rankled. The repeated electoral victories of Bonapartism among provincial voters, which so frustrated the Parisian Left, was blamed in large part on the influence of the clergy through the pulpit, the confessional and the school. Their support for Papal government in central Italy was a stumbling block to the Italian Risorgimento, which republicans enthusiastically supported. Materialistic ideas derived from science, notably Darwinism, affected younger left-wing intellectuals and their followers, and discredited the romantic religiosity of the older generation of republicans and Christian socialists. For many Blanquists, active in secularist societies, Catholicism was the prime enemy. To this may be added a less cerebral grass-roots resentment of clerical power and money, and traditional myths (not always wholly mythical) of sexual misconduct by priests and monks. Finally, many migrants to cities had abandoned religious practice, and attempts to 'moralize' the poor by preaching and charity were often counterproductive. This made a powerful mixture of resentments. Communards automatically accused the clergy of complicity with and spying for Versailles. Archbishop Darboy, once a prisoner, seems to have realized that he was to be a victim of history: 'I shall die wearing Mgr Affre's pectoral cross.' So he did, the third archbishop of Paris in succession to die violently.

But anticlericalism was not universal. It seems to have been strongest among the middle-class and skilled-worker elements of the Left, those most influenced by Proudhon, Blanqui and Science. Perhaps less educated workers, men and women, were less sure: very few people in the poorest parts of the city declared themselves 'without religion'. Religious funerals were held at the Madeleine for Fédérés who died at the nearby military hospital. Men of the bright-red 101st battalion sprinkled holy water on their dead comrades. Yet the same men could react violently to perceived betrayal, as shown by their massacre of a group of Dominicans, accused of spying, during the last days of the fighting (below p. 178).

Popular understanding of the Commune's struggle is perfectly summarized in by far the most famous of Communard texts, the 'Internationale' (appendix 2), written by a member of the Commune, Eugène Pottier. The universal and apocalyptic significance of the revolution for 'the human race' is plainly stated: 'Arise, the cursed of the earth! . . . It's the final struggle.' The revolutionary people are identified: 'producers', 'workers, peasants . . . the great party of those who labour'. The obstacles to 'salvation' are the oppressive State, the unjust law, kings, armies. The enemies are all there: 'Bandit, prince, exploiter or priest/ He who lives on man is a criminal'; there is no room on the planet for idlers (*les oisifs*). 'How many gorge on our flesh!/ But if the crows and vultures/ One morning disappear,/ The sun will always shine.'

Commitment and mobilization

So far we have seen two ways of analysing the Communards: by statistical occupational analysis, and by self-description. They create a broadly complementary stereotype: the Communards were, and considered themselves to be, the republican Parisian 'People'. But this is not a complete explanation of being a Communard. There are two questions worth further consideration. First, even among people of similar social, cultural and political background, the degree of practical commitment varied greatly. What distinguished between those who participated actively, even to the very end – a small minority – and those who stayed clear of the Commune or fell away early on in the struggle? Here we need to look at what mobilizes, encourages or constrains people to strenuous and dangerous action. Second, in spite of the inclusive republican, patriotic and Parisian language of Communard propaganda, it appealed in fact disproportionately to manual workers, as we saw above, while other social groups turned a relatively or entirely deaf ear. Why?

There were over 400,000 male wage-earners in Paris, plus over 60,000 self-employed artisans. Undoubtedly most were republican in sympathy. But only 230,000 men voted in the Commune elections in March, and only 190,000 (mostly workers) supported revolutionary candidates. Moreover, after the civil war had begun, support shrank drastically: in the 16 April Commune by-elections only between a quarter and a third of voters supported Communard candidates even in the 'reddest' *arrondissements*, the 18th and 20th.[27] Never more than about 170,000 (all classes combined) did some service in the Fédéré National Guard, and at a guess some 20,000 took part in the final combats. So only a dwindling proportion even of republican male workers participated in the revolutionary struggle. The proportion of female workers involved was far smaller.

What activated the activists? For some, the Commune was a liberation and opportunity. For the few hundred people who found themselves occupying important positions, it was a heavy responsibility

27. Giard (1966–68), pp. 38–45.

but could also be a euphoric experience. Some, though not all, had looked forward to a revolution for years; others, republicans but not necessarily revolutionary militants, found themselves unexpectedly in power because of opposition activity in the 1860s or patriotic exertions during the siege. For example, Courbet, a long-standing republican, mainly interested in reforming art administration, now discovered the unexpected delights of power. As he wrote artlessly to his family:

> Here I am, thanks to the people of Paris, up to my neck in politics, president of the Federation of Artists, member of the Commune, delegate at the *mairie*, delegate for Public Education, four of the most important offices in Paris. I get up, I eat breakfast and I sit and I preside twelve hours a day. My head is beginning to feel like a baked apple. But in spite of all this agitation in my head and in my understanding of social questions that I was not familiar with, I am in seventh heaven.[28]

Even after the disasters that followed, many must have looked back on it as the time of their lives: the artist André Gill (a better draughts-man than he was a poet) recalled running the Luxembourg Museum:

> Dear time now flown!
> When the gates were closed
> We wandered through the perfumed shade
> Lords of the lilacs, of the gentle hush.
> Only my voice hummed an ancient tune
> Do you recall? In the time of the Commune.[29]

We cannot understand the Commune without taking account of such feelings, which make the commitment of those riding the revolutionary wave so easy to understand. Their responses colour the 'collective memory' of the Commune as 'le temps des cerises' – a hopeful 'cherry time'. We have noted Lefebvre's influential characterization of the Commune as a 'festival' (above p. 105). But we must remember the fear, hardship and suffering that revolution and civil war also entailed. Some rank-and-file Communards did, as we shall see below, derive social status and self-fulfilment from revolutionary activity; but most in the nature of things received little tangible reward. We need to understand why thousands of them risked their lives none the less.

An obvious answer would be ideological commitment to revolution. But few Communards had been committed revolutionaries

28. 30 April, Courbet (1992), p. 416.
29. Sanchez (1994), p. 496. (My translation.)

before 1871, as earlier election results show; many who had little
or no previous record of political activism now risked their lives.
On the other hand, as Roger Gould observes, 'given the inherent
risks associated with serving in the National Guard . . . many Parisians
who sympathized with the insurgent cause remained passive in the
absence of further pressure to join in'.[30] We are not therefore looking merely for cerebral ideological commitment, but attempting to
identify the stimuli leading to action. As the Commune did not use
the high degree of compulsion generally exercised by revolutionary
states, we need to look at the social and organizational environment
of Fédéré activity. An indication of the importance of such factors
is that in some districts, far more men voted for the Commune
than fought for it; in others, more men seem to have borne arms
for it than voted for it. In the 2nd *arrondissement*, for example,
about 2,600 men voted solidly for the Commune, but 4,000–5,000
did some sort of National Guard duty. Some officers standing for
election openly negotiated an agreed level of service with their sub-
ordinates/electors: 'Timid but right-minded citizens, join our ranks
as *sédentaires*. . . . I shall force no one to serve at the ramparts.'[31]

Gould has argued that community ties were more important
than class. He supports this statistically by comparison with 1848.
After the June Days, he argues, the distribution of arrests by district
corresponded closely to the geographical distribution of workers:
'It would be difficult to find more persuasive evidence of the importance of class identity for the mobilization process' in 1848. In 1871,
by contrast, the pattern of arrests was much less closely linked with the
proportion of each district's population classified as wage-earners.[32]
This fits with Gould's argument (above p. 29) that the new outer
arrondissements such as Belleville had developed inter-class community
solidarity. This, he believes, explains their higher level of participation in the Commune, essentially a Parisian and community-based
movement, than the older central districts, where social ties were
more restricted to people in the same occupation and hence community solidarity weaker.

Gould has produced models combining sociological and organizational data to account for different rates of participation in various
districts. Are they convincing? I think not. Not only are the surviving
data irremediably distorted or incomplete, but so many contingent
factors are at work – including the administrative efficiency and

30. Gould (1995), p. 178.
31. *La Commune*, 24 April. *Sédentaires* served only inside the city.
32. Gould (1995), pp. 173–5.

political unity of Commune organizers, or proximity to the fighting – that building theoretical models of participation is extremely difficult; indeed several of Gould's results are highly implausible.[33] On the other hand, his stress on community is fruitful, and it is possible to illustrate, in a more empirical manner, a range of social situations that encouraged active engagement in the Commune.

We have seen how in the 1860s and especially during the Prussian siege and the period after the armistice, *mairies*, political clubs, committees and the National Guard focused local political activity. Shared sufferings, queuing for food, foraging for fuel, parades and patriotic ceremonies, even fighting together, intensified local solidarity for men and women. During the Commune many of these activities continued. Clubs still met, with high female participation. If food shortages were largely over, unemployment (80 per cent or more in many trades) kept most people dependent on the *mairie* or the National Guard for their subsistence, as even the somewhat better off were running down their savings accounts at the Caisse d'Epargne.

This explains two themes that constantly recur when, after their defeat, Fédérés explained to their captors why they had been involved in the Commune: economic need and community pressure. Of course, they had reason to play down any enthusiasm they may have had for the defeated revolution, but nevertheless, as Gould observes, the consistency of these claims across hundreds of cases suggests an element of truth. They were certainly believed by hard-bitten Versaillais police and army officers, who considered most Fédérés to be the victims of circumstances: 'How would they be able to live soon without the public subsidy [of National Guard pay] and without work? Who would feed the wife and children?'[34]

Economic motives were neglected by idealistic pro-Commune historians for the same reason they were emphasized by contemporary counter-revolutionaries, who referred mockingly to the Fédérés as *les trente sous* (the National Guard daily pay). However, Commune officers too privately recognized the importance of economic motivation. The 'red' 177th battalion put it bluntly: 'the thirty sous or they'll do a bunk'.[35] Higher wages were offered to specialist artillerymen and engineers: 'to get them we have to pay them', explained the National Guard chief of staff.[36] Fédérés refused to

---

33. Gould (1991) and (1995); for some criticisms, see Tombs (1997).
34. Appert (1875), p. 8.   35. Report, SHA Ly 83.
36. Letter from Col. Henry, 9 April, SHA Ly 31.

dig trenches for only 50 centimes extra. A member of the Central Committee of the National Guard urged cutting off the pay and rations of *refractaires* (men who did not turn up for service) to make their wives put pressure on them, and this was done – a far from negligible means of pressure as the National Guard was regularly distributing hundreds of tons of food to the population. Moreover, in some *arrondissements* public assistance (given through ration cards for bread and soup) was refused to *refractaires*' families. On the other hand, it was well known that men who had jobs in sectors still functioning, such as transport, utilities, engineering or retailing, were more likely to avoid National Guard service, and this was sometimes accepted by their officers. Some were given official exemptions if their work was indispensable – though the National Guard high command was unwilling to extend this, as Courbet wished, to artists!

The other theme is that of community pressure. Gould estimates that in between a quarter and a third of all court martial cases, the accused or witnesses mentioned 'social influence or coercion' as a motive. All regular National Guard units were recruited locally and organized into *arrondissement* legions: we have already seen how Haussmannization had created large socially homogeneous areas (above p. 24) where political loyalty and neighbourhood pressure were predominantly in one direction. Companies formed during the German war had been drawn from two or three streets or blocks of houses. Since the summer of 1870 it had become the principal means of local social integration and 'male bonding'. During the Commune men who had enlisted in units outside their own districts (suspected of being a ploy to evade service) were ordered to leave them and join local battalions.[37] The organization of Fédéré service was focused on the *arrondissement* legion: routine duty was in their own streets, with occasional tours of duty at the nearest sector of the city ramparts, in barracks or in the suburban forts and trenches, followed by a return home. The Commune authorities encouraged their visibility in the streets and squares. Regular parades, ceremonial presentation of new red flags to battalions, 'beating the retreat' with drums and bugles, impressive funerals (in the workers' friendly-society tradition) for comrades killed fighting the Versaillais, and military-band concerts in open spaces and theatres to raise money

37. A vast quantity of muster rolls from the siege and the Commune survive, often giving age, occupation and address: see AP series D 2R⁴ cartons 1–158 and SHA series Ly cartons 37–93. For the order to enlist in local units, see *Murailles*, vol. 2, p. 470. Gould (1995) suggests that a 'network of cross-district enlistment' developed (p. 154), but that seems to me a misinterpretation of the evidence.

for the wounded and dependants (battalions even collectively adopted orphans) – all these activities must have strengthened links with the local community. Membership of the National Guard could give even rank-and-file members unprecedented power in everyday situations (above p. 108).

We should think of the Fédérés not as whole categories – 'workers', 'socialists' – nor even as random samples of those groups, but as thousands of little clusters of neighbours, friends and comrades. To give a few concrete examples. Of 48 identifiable officers and NCOs of the 102nd battalion (13th Legion), 16 shared a house with at least one of the others. Of the 102 men of the 2nd combat company of the 184th (13th Legion) – a more mixed unit because formed from among the younger men of the battalion – nearly half lived in four streets; the captain, the lieutenant and three other men lived in the same house. It is easy to imagine the kind of influences operating: friendship, honour, shame, intimidation. Sometimes the details are odd: five officers or NCOs of the 102nd lived in one house, where the chief tenant (who sub-let to the other residents) exercised a good deal of influence over his sub-tenants, even going to pick up their dole money from the welfare bureau; and when he was elected lieutenant in the 102nd, he got four of them to enrol.[38] Pressure was particularly strong in certain streets or houses: 'we lived in a house where all the tenants were in insurgent battalions. Every day I was a target of insults and threats; the women were always saying that I was young, and that it was shameful to stay at home.'[39] Women could put effective pressure on men, nagging other mothers and wives to get their menfolk to go: 'she used the rudest language to me because I didn't make my sons march'.[40] Men put pressure on other men, as *refractaires* were particularly resented. A Versaillais spy reported that when the Guard at La Villette mustered, 'the men who had already assembled in the street shouted up at the others, calling them cowards and do-nothings to get them to come down'.[41]

Many new officers were elected after the insurrection began, largely manual or white-collar workers. 'Red' battalions especially seem to have been predominantly commanded by workers. The 15 officers and NCOs of the 2nd combat company of the 184th battalion, mentioned above, were all (with one possible exception) workers, mainly in their twenties. This gave them a marked increase in local status. For example, the Mercier family were immigrant building

---

38. SHA 6e CG 229.   39. SHA 19e CG 120 (Beauté).
40. SHA 5e CG 92 (Juhel).   41. Gould (1995), p. 179.

workers recently arrived in the 13th *arrondissement*. The eldest son, aged 24, a former soldier, was elected commander of the 184th battalion. His father became a company delegate; his younger brother then deserted from the Versailles army to become paymaster; and the two young officers got married on the same day to neighbours – a sign of their new place in the community. 'Before the Commune Mercier was in a precarious situation; during the Commune this improved.'[42] The jealousy such 'improvement' could arouse testifies to its reality: a female neighbour remarked cattily to a brilliantly uniformed Fédéré colonel, a cobbler by trade, 'That suits you better than hammering old shoes!' This status was governed by a characteristically male culture, which valued physical courage, patriotism and fraternal solidarity, and to which the experience of the war had given a strongly military gloss. To fulfil comrades' expectations and justify a prestigious position provided a powerful motive for persisting in a dangerous adventure.

To summarize, the active Communard *peuple* were those who, predisposed by political sympathy and social status to accept the language of radical republicanism, chose for various reasons, including economic need, neighbourhood pressures, National Guard loyalties and the need to justify newly acquired status – strongest of course in those districts where sympathy for the Commune was predominant – to remain active in a revolutionary movement whose prospects of success grew steadily less, and whose number of wholehearted supporters dwindled.

Women in revolution

So far we have looked primarily at masculine activities and values. But the participation of women was for contemporaries one of the Commune's most distinctive and even defining features. It has recently become so again for historians, and this high degree of interest justifies a specific discussion here. The sympathies of mostly conservative and invariably male nineteenth-century commentators and mostly progressive and ofen female twentieth-century historians are poles apart, but their analyses are basically similar: that women's involvement in the Commune represented a fundamental subversion of bourgeois society, a shocking rejection of conventional morality, a deliberate affront to social propriety, an assertive crossing of gender

---

42. SHA 20e CG 402 (Mercier).

boundaries, a flouting of patriarchal authority. 'Many of them, attracted by theories of socialism developed in the clubs, believed that a new era was about to open,' wrote a Versaillais army officer; 'women called upon other women to join them in a struggle . . . to create a future envisioned as promising greater freedom for all,' agree late-twentieth-century academics.[43] The *pétroleuse*, the mythical female 'petrol-bomber', became perhaps the most powerful symbol of Communard revolt.

The passionate interest of the Commune's contemporaries complicates historical investigation. The whole saga of the Commune is coloured by myth, but no aspect more than this one. Contemporary perceptions were influenced by fear, disgust, hatred, prejudice and prurience. This distorts the evidence, including our major source, court martial files. Versaillais propagandists and prosecutors searched for, selected or invented evidence that Communard women were promiscuous, violent, threatening, loud-mouthed and sacrilegious; that they burnt buildings, desecrated churches, carried weapons, terrorized neighbourhoods, fought on barricades and killed soldiers. The prosecution statistics indicate the extent of the credulity and prejudices of the authorities. In the heat of the chase they arrested over 1,000 women (having summarily shot an unknown number of others) but had to release 80 per cent of them without charge; only 133 were convicted, in spite of relentless efforts to produce evidence against them.[44] Many women truly active during the Commune were never arrested because they did not fit Versaillais stereotypes, and so they disappear from our ken.

There is a danger that historians looking for evidence of significantly radical attitudes or actions may accept propaganda material or sensational hearsay as fact. Though few if any now believe that *pétroleuses* set fire to houses or gave poisoned drinks to soldiers, several are inclined to portray women as preaching the violent overthrow of 'bourgeois morality', forming armed battalions and defending barricades. But is the evidence for the latter acts any more reliable than that for the former?

Women's real, and not merely figurative, involvement in violence has been put forward by recent analyses as being of unprecedented importance: 'The right to inflict violence . . . was no longer a man's domain.'[45] This 'called into question a basic assumption of nineteenth-century western civilization'.[46] We must be careful not to ignore the

43. Col. Gaillard, in Rougerie (1964), p. 114; Jones and Vergès (1991), p. 719.
44. Appert (1875), pp. 312–13.   45. Johnson (1994), p. 294.
46. Gullickson (1996), p. 85.

difference – hard though it sometimes is to establish – between imaginative 'representations' of women (several historians have presented contemporary drawings as fact, for example), and a range of evidence telling us something about who really existing women were, and what they believed, said and did.

The broad outlines of women's activities have long been known.[47] During the late 1860s, after twenty years of silence, women began again to speak at public meetings. Some were active in political movements, including the International and its associated food cooperative La Marmite. During the German siege, patriotic effort and the struggle for existence brought more women into the activities of committees, clubs, hospitals and local welfare organizations. Many were involved in war work, especially manufacture of uniforms. As noted above there were even proposals – widely scorned – that women should form a military unit, the 'Amazons of the Seine'. Wartime activity was the 'training ground' for their role during the Commune.[48]

During the 18 March events, women played a leading part in obstructing troops and encouraging fraternization and disobedience – a familiar part of the ritual of political demonstrations, in which the presence of women and children at the front of the crowd was a way of deterring violent repression. By some accounts, women were implicated in the capture and killing of the two generals at Montmartre. During the Commune itself, hundreds remained active in local politics and welfare activities, including public speaking and setting up specifically women's clubs. Several activists, mainly socialists, founded a city-wide organization, the Union des Femmes pour la Défense de Paris et les Soins aux Blessés, which eventually organized several hundred or even a few thousand women in cooperatives manufacturing uniforms, and working in hospitals and in schools. Women also served with National Guard units as *cantinières* (providing food and drink) and nurses. Some women certainly wore uniforms, usually as *cantinières*, and carried weapons. There were again, as during the German siege, calls for women to fight; and a few may even have done so, as had happened during the 1830 and 1848 revolutions.

The discussion in recent work has turned less on the facts of women's activities – though much certainly remains unknown – than on the precise significance of their ideas and actions in the context of women's history. Two subjects have attracted recent

47. See Thomas (1967).   48. Schulkind (1985), p. 135.

attention: the Union des Femmes, as the principal women's organization, and the activity of women as fighters. The first, because it has been seen as a new departure in political self-confidence, cultural assertiveness and ideological ambition. The second, because it has been suggested as a rejection of taboos and a revolutionary assertion of equality and citizenship.

The Union des Femmes was set up following a public appeal by 'a group of *citoyennes*' published in the Commune's *Journal Officiel* on 11 April (appendix 3). It called on the women of Paris – 'descendants of the women of the great Revolution who . . . brought Louis XVI back captive' – to be ready to 'conquer or perish' in the cause of world revolution. This appeal was a defiant response to a public appeal for peace by another group of women. Typical of the full-blooded romantic rhetoric of the time, it echoes with references to past revolutions and to the familiar republican nationalist vision of France leading world liberation. It is couched in strongly gendered language: for example, 'we, mothers, wives, sisters of the French people'. An appeal to emotion, not a plan of action, it would probably not be intended or understood as a literal call for women to fight: if it talks of using paving stones to crush traitors (presumably a reference to the throwing of objects from windows on to Charles X's soldiers in 1830), it also envisages the moral effect if the enemy dared to fire on 'a crowd of unarmed women' at the gates of Paris. Other calls to arms and individual or collective proclamations of women's willingness to fight clearly carry an inspirational and provocative message. Similarly metaphorical declarations had been made during the war against Germany.

The Union enjoyed official backing, and developed as the principal interlocutor with the Commune on behalf of women. Some of its main organizers were members of the International, and male Internationalists on the Commune Council, such as Fränkel, the Labour Delegate, were allies and associates. The Union set up committees in every *arrondissement*, whose members, mostly workers, were paid a small salary and provided with facilities by the *mairies*. Its main practical job was to organize women's cooperatives to make uniforms. As we have seen (above pp. 95–6), these hardly had time to get off the ground, but the Union's leaders saw them as the nucleus for a wide, even international, socialist women's industrial network. The provision of work on decent terms (even though some workers complained that they spent a lot of time waiting around) must have been a powerful incentive in attracting unemployed and destitute women to the organization. It certainly brought in some hundreds, all of whom were by the Union's statutes auto-matically affiliated with the International. Cooperative production was also a solution to part of the problem of inequality of women's pay: as all earnings would go to the workers, women would logically receive (as the International had demanded in the 1860s) equal pay for work of equal value. The Union was also involved in recruit-ing teachers for the Commune's planned secular girls' schools. Martin Johnson has argued that the Union also gave much atten-tion to defence, as its title implied, though fewer details are so far known here.[49] They recruited *cantinières*, and asked to be permitted a more active role in caring for Fédéré wounded, both by replacing nuns in the city hospitals and by nursing in the fighting zone.

This brings us to our second theme, women as combatants. Some groups and individuals were keen to be armed, both to intimidate grass-roots anti-Communards and to round up National Guard deserters. An age-old wartime role for women was to encourage or shame men into fighting, and one way was to offer to take up arms in their place, as when a member of the Women's Legion of the 12th *arrondissement* declared to backsliding males 'You're nothing but idlers; I, a woman, have more courage than all of you.'[50] Militant women seem to have been much occupied in chasing up Fédéré deserters, which may be why a much higher proportion of women than men were later prosecuted for 'offences against the person', largely of a minor nature.[51] Some women called for women's battalions to occupy defensive positions and release men to go into battle. Some certainly carried weapons, as was widely publicized at the time: *la générale* Eudes (the young wife of one of the Blanquist leaders) was a celebrity on both sides of the conflict, and some other women were known to wear uniform and carry pistols and daggers. There were certainly some small demonstrations by women – reports usually mention 25 to 100 – carrying flags, and in May there are accounts of a march of 500 women to the Hôtel de Ville to demand rifles, some of which were reportedly distributed by a member of the Committee of Public Safety. Johnson has discovered a women's group in the 12th *arrondissement*, associated both with the local committee of the Union des Femmes and with a club at St Eloi's church, which tried to set up a women's 'legion',[52] though it is not known whether this was unique or typical. There are many

49. Johnson (1994).   50. Ibid. (1994), p. 290.
51. 12.96 per cent of women were prosecuted for *crimes contre les personnes* com-pared with 1.24 per cent of men. Appert (1875), p. 338.
52. Johnson (1994).

contemporary reports of women carrying rifles and taking part in the defence of barricades during the final week of street fighting.

A wide range of interpretations of these activities is possible. Schulkind claims that the Commune was 'the first French regime to make use of women in positions of responsibility'.[53] This principally involved the few hundred women who sat on the committees of the Union des Femmes. They were skilled workers from the textile and book trades, some schoolteachers and a small leavening in key positions of established political activists. Jones and Vergès point out that they were given complete control over production and finance, which went further than subsequent proposals made at the 1876 workers' congress for women's cooperatives run by their 'fathers, brothers or husbands'.[54] Yet their activities during the Commune were confined to certain areas. The programme of the Union accepted the separation of 'women's work'. The areas of administrative responsibility it was given by the Commune – teaching, clothing manufacture, nursing, child-care – were in no way unconventional. Part of the motivation was anticlericalism: the Union's job was not to replace men in running hospitals and schools, but to replace nuns. But was any Communard woman offered greater responsibilities than any number of Mother Superiors?

Several recent commentators have stressed the importance of women's involvement in combat, arguing that it was a claim to equal citizenship and a conscious and shattering act of transgression: 'The right to inflict violence [was] crucial for constructing citizenship'; 'Women . . . had repudiated all the values of dependency, submission and domesticity demanded by the nineteenth-century bourgeois moral code.'[55] There are two problems here. First, some women had already fought in 1830 and 1848, and had been applauded as heroines rather than condemned as transgressors of propriety. Second, during the Commune women neither asked for, nor were they offered, equal political rights, which seems to disprove the idea that involvement in combat was part of a claim for citizenship. Women could speak and petition, but not vote or take decisions. Was this proof that Communards were far from any idea of equality? Or might Communard women have been so radical that they had gone beyond a concern with mere suffrage?

Women's presence in . . . the Commune exceeded both the conceptualization of women as workers and as citizens. It represented

53. Schulkind (1985), p. 136.   54. Jones and Vergès (1991), p. 722.
55. Johnson (1994), p. 294; Barry (1996), p. 146.

the politicisation of sexuality, the sexualisation of work, and the critique of universal suffrage as a fiction not because women had been denied this right, but because their citizenship could not be contained within the neutral territory of the state.[56]

This seems to involve reading back from later anarchist attitudes. In 1871 there was no disenchantment with voting. Indeed, voting was envisaged as the foundation of the democratic restructuring of government, administration and justice (as we saw in the previous chapter) through a perpetual succession of elections. Women would presumably have been excluded from this planned revolution. Why was there no demand for the vote? There seems to have been no grass-roots pressure: did most women accept the prevailing view of full citizenship as a masculine activity? Among the avant-garde elite, did they agree with the view of their male counterparts (which would prevail for the next seventy-five years) that women were in general too Catholic and conservative to be entrusted with the vote? This would have been an understandable view given the relatively small number of active Communardes and the hostility they sometimes encountered from other women.

This unassertiveness over political equality must surely influence our overall interpretation of Communarde attitudes and activities. In particular, it raises a question mark over the claim that women's involvement in combat meant 'that some women sought to expand their rights through what was traditionally a defining characteristic of citizenship, the bearing of arms'.[57] Why demand citizenship by fighting but not by voting? Could it rather be that participation in fighting was, as Edith Thomas suggested some years ago, often the act of 'individual women, involved in the battles by accident'?[58] Or was it another aspect of the community solidarity I have already emphasized?

Some recent historians have tried to clinch the argument that women's participation in fighting in 1871 had a significance far beyond what had happened in earlier revolutions by claiming that 'only during the Commune did women form organized, armed units which engaged in combat'.[59] Barry declares that women 'breached gender taboo by establishing an officially recognized war battalion'; and he later reinforces this to 'whole battalions of women'.[60] Thus organized in their own independent units, women

---

56. Jones and Vergès (1991), pp. 718–19.   57. Johnson (1994), p. 294.
58. Thomas (1967), p. 159.   59. Johnson (1994), p. 283.
60. Barry (1996), pp. x, 99, 123.

combatants were no longer 'mere appendages on the barricades', as Shafer rather ungenerously describes *cantinières* and nurses,[61] but women warriors acting autonomously and collectively. 'Truly, the civilized world had been turned upside down.'[62]

The example generally put forward as the most indisputable, most important and most spectacular action by a women's battalion was the defence of the Place Blanche on 23 May. This is presented not merely as a significant myth: 'in legend and history,' Gullickson assures us, 'the Place Blanche was defended only by 120 women'.[63] The story comes from Lissagaray's romanticized narratives of *la semaine sanglante*, and he in turn based it on a Commune newspaper article, though his two versions differ markedly. Alain Dalotel, in a careful review of known evidence, demonstrates that accounts are inconsistent and evidence fragmentary.[64] There is reason to believe that women were present, as at many other scenes of combat, but this is quite different from the story of a women's battalion fighting alone. Some members – Dalotel says 50 – of the Union des Femmes decided to go and help in the defence of north-eastern Paris, and one of its leaders, Nathalie Le Mel, was at the Place Pigalle, near the Place Blanche. She later denied having participated in the fighting, but only tended the wounded, 'the only older woman', according to one witness, 'amid a group of young girls, all armed with rifles and wearing ambulance nurses' armbands as well as red sashes'.[65] Dalotel's conclusion is that the women's battalion at the Place Blanche did not exist.

Other evidence, I believe, confirms this judgement. The Versailles troops filed detailed reports on every barricade taken. The soldiers who took the barricade in the Place Blanche said nothing about women defending it,[66] which would be an extraordinary omission if indeed they had had the unprecedented experience of a long and bitter battle against a battalion of women who, according to Lissagaray, held up the Versaillais attack for several hours. But the soldiers reported that there had been no significant resistance and that the barricade was quickly occupied. The writers of these reports, eager for decorations and promotion, were not inclined to hide their light under a bushel and habitually reported every

61. Shafer (1993), p. 99.   62. Barry (1996), p. 146.

63. See, e.g., Barry (1996), p. 124; Johnson (1994), p. 291; Gullickson (1996), p. 109.

64. Dalotel (1997), pp. 341–55.   65. Thomas (1967), p. 132.

66. Reports in SHA Li 116, esp. *journal de marche* of 1st division, 5th army corps, and 'renseignements relatifs aux barricades'.

skirmish. In short, in the absence of any evidence to the contrary, this seems to have been one of the many myths spawned during those dramatic days. This was also the view of a rank-and-file Fédéré writing soon after the events: 'I saw neither *pétroleuse* or any other fighting women, with the exception of the regular *cantinières*, *ambulancières*, &c. I utterly disbelieve in their existence.'[67]

Women were certainly present in the fighting as nurses and *cantinières*. The place of women in warfare had been curtailed since the eighteenth century, but the French army and the National Guard still had their famous *cantinières*, who marched with the troops and supplied them with food and drink. Although many men found *cantinières*' uniforms titillating – and the Communards, fond of uniforms, introduced some exotic versions – they can hardly be seen as a revolutionary transgression of gender boundaries, as several historians have suggested: they were copied from the regular army. The *cantinières* were part of the often close comradeship of National Guard units, which we have already noted; they often appear prominently in Fédéré group photographs. By definition, they were individual women integrated into male institutions, not women acting collectively. Like their male comrades, they were present for a variety of reasons: political sympathy, economic need and community solidarity. They served alongside their neighbours, friends and relatives, while also earning a living. Some acquired an important position within their battalions, like Marguerite Lachaise, who was publicly praised by her comrades for her 'most praiseworthy and virile [*sic*] conduct in remaining all day on the battlefield, despite the hail of shells, tending and bandaging the wounded'.[68] Such acts probably gave rise to many of the accounts of women Fédérés.

The attempt by the Union des Femmes to organize female military nurses to serve in the combat zone might be seen as part of a modern international trend; and it met the same resistance from some National Guard surgeons as Florence Nightingale had encountered in the Crimea. The Commune, however, encouraged them, being eager to replace nuns who were suspected of lowering the morale of Fédéré wounded or helping them to malinger. Yet not all Communards welcomed the presence of women. One legion delegate carrying out a front-line inspection in May reported jeers and murmurs from the men (who were not allowed to bring their wives to the outposts) when an officer arrived with 'a street-corner

67. *Macmillan's Magazine*, vol. 24 (May–Oct. 1871), p. 402.
68. *Cri de Peuple*, 11 April, quoted in Vuillaume (1971), pp. 65–6.

woman'; he complained of the presence of 'beautiful ladies with chignons' at the first-aid station 'as if they'd just come from the hairdresser'; and reported that 'the whores and the ambulance women could . . . seriously compromise the Commune's defence'.[69]

As individuals, some *cantinières* and even nurses – the distinction was not always in practice clear – carried and may even have fired guns. Some were certainly killed in action or shot or bayoneted on capture. In some cases their possession of weapons may, as several historians suggest, have been a conscious demand for equality of citizenship; in others, doubtless a result of personal solidarity or spontaneous desperation. The female celebrities who liked splendid uniforms with pistols and daggers were an eccentric few. We may choose to see them as a bold avant-garde in the pursuit of equal rights to inflict violence. Or we might interpret their somewhat absurd (including to contemporaries) comic-opera militarism, festooned with weapons, sashes and plumes – one dressed in baggy colonial-army breeches, an embroidered crimson velvet hussar's tunic, gold-tasselled boots, and a blue sash supporting two pistols – merely as a Slavonic form of radical chic, particularly affected by upper-class Russians and Poles. Perhaps too it was a sign of the difficulty of knowing how to behave as a woman revolutionary when political rights were still so limited.

On occasions, *cantinières* and other women were prominent as mascots or 'living allegories' (in Maurice Agulhon's phrase), leading parades and carrying flags. This could happen in fraught and dangerous circumstances, as Victorine Brocher, a socialist and *cantinière*, related:

> We were trying to rally a few friends on the place [de la Bastille]. The idea came to me of hoisting our flag on top of the central barricade to summon them to us. . . . When we climbed on to the barricade I quickly flourished our flag; one of my friends wanted to follow me. [A] bullet cut him short.[70]

Such acts – whose potency is demonstrated by their frequent appearances in the iconography of 1871 and that of other French and foreign revolutions – would have had several resonances. They made conscious or unconscious reference to peacetime ceremonies and to familiar political symbolism. Dalotel suggests that women symbolized the beauty and invulnerability of the cause. They would surely be seen as embodiments of the home and community that

69. SHA 4e CG 888 (Bignard).   70. Brocher (1977), p. 197.

was being defended. They appealed to male honour, protectiveness, vanity and sometimes, no doubt, desire. One who was hypersensitive to this iconic significance – he had been an art critic – was the notoriously anti-Communard writer Maxime Du Camp:

> the woman – the female – exercised an extraordinary influence over the males. Dressed in the short skirt that displayed her legs, the little kepi . . . perched on the side of her head . . . she strolled boldly among the fighters like a promise . . . proud of her uniform and her rifle, she outdid the man in extravagant bravado.[71]

Some women fired shots. But I know of no suggestion of any training being given in firing or maintaining weapons – Louise Michel later said that she practised in boulevard shooting-galleries. Leading Communardes, including Nathalie Le Mel and Marguerite Lachaise, who openly admitted supporting the revolution, building barricades and supplying ammunition (acts which carried heavy penalties), steadfastly denied shooting guns. Why should we not believe them? The military courts, little reputed for clemency, on the whole did: only a dozen women in all were sentenced to transportation with confinement (*déportation dans une enceinte fortifiée*), the penalty for using weapons in an insurrection.[72]

In short, women were present amid the fighting, but the nature and scale of their involvement probably did not exceed that in earlier revolutions: after June 1848, 118 women were sentenced for insurrectionary acts; after May 1871, 133.[73] There is little or no evidence that women claimed the same functions as men, or engaged in autonomous and collective military action. On the contrary, accounts suggest a consciously gendered role and discourse.

Most basically, should we be struck by how many women were involved, or how few? There were over 170,000 women wage-earners in the city: historians have identified a few hundred female Commune activists. Even though the Commune's attitude was certainly more positive than that of earlier revolutionary governments, women were extremely under-represented in revolutionary organizations. Barry, surveying women's participation in nineteenth-century politics, concludes that the activist minority tended to be single or widowed without dependents, with radical menfolk, or with exceptional personalities.[74] Some writers get round the problem of numbers by making abstract assertions about cultural transformation during the Commune – 'an experience of generativity, as an appropriation of

---

71. Du Camp (1878), vol. 1, p. 300.   72. Appert (1875), p. 312.
73. Barry (1996), p. 50; Appert (1875), p. 312.   74. Barry (1996), p. 20.

"space as created by an interaction, as something that our bodies reactivate, and through this reactivation, in turn modifies and transforms us".[75] Political clubs are emphasized in this context. Not only did they involve a substantial female constituency, with several thousand regular attenders, but they often addressed specifically female issues and demands, for example divorce and religion. Moroever, they have seemed – not least to shocked male contemporaries – to represent a cultural revolution, with women occupying a new 'public space' and saying the previously unsayable. In 1848, say Jones and Vergès, women pleaded; in 1871 they demanded.[76] But were clubs any more than talking shops for letting off steam, as they had been in 1848? Moreover, there are signs that the clubs were becoming both marginalized and segregated. That audiences seem to have become smaller and increasingly female – though few women were involved as organizers or speakers[77] – may show that men were losing interest, or were otherwise occupied. Club activities were relatively little reported in the main Communard newspapers. Few if any of the women's demands that had been discussed in clubs since the 1860s (such as changes in the Civil Code on marriage) led to action or even discussion by the Commune.

It can hardly now be said, after the research of recent years, that the history of Communard women has been neglected. There is still near silence, however, on the role of non-Communard women, many of whom were no less assertive in hostile circumstances, trying to prevent their menfolk from fighting and calling for peace negotiations. Much of women's activity – as during the French Revolution – was in defence of religion. Especially in dechristianized areas such as Paris, religion was predominantly a female activity: there were 5,400 nuns (mostly involved in teaching and social work) to 1,460 priests and brothers, and about ten times as many women as men attended church. Anticlericalism had a correspondingly misogynistic element: Catholicism was criticized for making men effeminate, and also for interfering in the patriarchal relations between husbands and wives. Several historians have argued that part of the attraction of religion for women was that it did indeed provide them with opportunities for relatively autonomous activity. Defence of religion was therefore defence of a 'female space', especially as most male clergy, exposed to violence or the threat of National Guard conscription, hid, escaped or were arrested.

75. Jones and Vergès (1991), p. 716, quoting Katherine Ross.
76. Ibid., p. 731.   77. Johnson (1996), p. 173.

Nuns resisted being expelled from their work in schools, hospitals and and welfare institutions, sometimes successfully. An unknown nun was still running poor relief in the 16th *arrondissement* at the end of April, and we have noted their continued activity in the 13th. Nuns staffing the Hôtel Dieu hospital are said to have agreed to wear red sashes in order to remain at their posts. Many braved armed intrusion into their convents by National Guards searching for treasure, arms, secret tunnels and evidence of hideous crimes (this was the area of greatest left-wing credulity). Some National Guards were impressed: one left a convent repeating 'They're so poor! So poor!'[78] One of Paris's most famous women, Sister Catherine Labouré (later canonized) and clearly an outspoken character, distributed Miraculous Medals to Fédérés:

> Where do you think you're going?
> Looking for a medal.
> But you don't believe in God or the Devil! What do you want it for?
> Tomorrow we're going into action, it will protect me.
> Here you are then, and let's hope it converts you.[79]

Catholic lay women, individually and collectively, were also active. There was literally a defence of female space when political clubs, abandoning secular public meeting halls, took to meeting in churches. Club members too were largely female, which meant that bitterly antagonistic female groups – Catholic and anticlerical – each with a small male 'clergy', competed, sometimes roughly, for possession of a traditional women's domain. A group of young Catholic women thought of blowing up one club meeting, but were dissuaded by a priest. Some mothers tried to stop the secularization of schools, sometimes physically attacking the Union des Femmes' new teachers. Madame Passenaud, a local milk-seller, bought objects from the vandalized church of Notre Dame des Victoires to prevent their destruction. Women petitioned and demonstrated against the arrest of popular clergy. Most famously, stall-holders of Les Halles secured the release of the parish priest of neighbouring Saint-Eustache, who – safe under the protection of his formidable parishioners – celebrated High Mass on Easter Sunday. Similarly, women carrying a red flag marched to the Hôtel de Ville to demand the release of the parish priest of Saint-Séverin. And 2,000 women – the largest women's demonstration of the Commune – demanded the reopening of Saint-Sulpice.[80] What Communard and anti-Communard

78. Marion (1981), p. 98.   79. Ibid., pp. 105–6.
80. APP Ba 364–6, report 12 May.

women had in common was a determination to claim rights and responsibilities seen as specifically theirs.

Was the Commune a breakthrough for women, as much recent writing has argued? Even the Empire had allowed women to make speeches in public, and the Government of National Defence had encouraged a range of women's wartime activities. In this context, similar activities during the Commune seem less than revolutionary. Michel Perrot has argued that throughout the nineteenth century women were always in the forefront of spontaneous community action, but when activity focused on formal electoral politics, organized labour or military organization, they were 'relegated to first aid and refreshments'.[81] The Commune followed this pattern: its formal structures were male, while women were active at its community grass-roots, and in the National Guard mainly as nurses and *cantinières*. Hence, the assertion by Jones and Vergès that 1871 was an 'aporia', unlike the immediate past or the immediate future, seems erroneous.[82] Communard women never mounted an action comparable in importance with the march on Versailles in October 1789, though some mentioned that as a precedent. The nearest equivalent was undoubtedly their involvement in the spontaneous community protest of 18 March. But there were no steps to include them in the formal political structures of the Commune.

The others: neutrals, opportunists and enemies

We have already noted the relative abstention of the middle and upper classes – some 150,000–200,000 adult males and their families. It is easy to understand the opposition of conservative and/or Catholic ideological opponents of democracy, equality and secularism, and also those (such as senior officials, landlords, large shareholders) whose economic interests as *oisifs* really were threatened by Communard socialism. Their attitude was always clear: 'What is the meaning of the term Revolution? It is the cry of Satan, "I shall not obey", erected into a principle, a right.'[83] But many middle-class Parisians were not counter-revolutionaries (they were non-churchgoers and republican voters), and fitted into the politically approved category of 'hard-working bourgeoisie'. They had shared the patriotic fervour of the siege. Many despised the '*capitulards*' and 'Prussians of Versailles',

81. Perrot (1979), pp. 140–1.
82. Jones and Vergès (1991), p. 716.   83. Roberts (1973), p. 8.

as did their working-class fellow-citizens. Even moderate Parisian papers criticized the National Assembly and supported the elections of 26 March, and 40,000 or more voted for non-revolutionary yet strongly republican candidates – an act of at least partial hostility towards Versailles. As the very moderate paper *Le Soir* wrote a week after the insurrection broke out, 'men of order and legality' were close to rallying to the insurgents because of their anger with the National Assembly's 'inertia . . . lack of political tact [and] barely concealed aversion to Paris'. Many were economically threatened by the Assembly's measure on commercial debts. An alliance with the middle class is precisely what many Communards hoped to encourage, as we have seen, but it only worked with a quite small proportion of the middle classes, the *bourgeoisie populaire* of shop-keepers, clerks and artisan-manufacturers, even though many Parisians of all classes seem to have believed that the Commune might defeat Versailles. Why?

The clearest ideological barrier to middle-class participation in the Commune could be summed up as a far more fearful and negative attitude towards the 'revolutionary tradition' of 1789 to 1848. These events were seen as occasions of conflict and terror rather than of liberation and fraternity. Whatever the Commune might say, revolution was seen as an inevitable threat to property – a view going back at least to the socialism of 1848: it had become a cliché to refer to the revolt of 'the have-nots against the haves' (*ceux qui n'ont rien contre ceux qui ont quelque chose*). Scepticism about revolution would also mean doubting that the Commune could ultimately win against Versailles and possibly the Germans too – support fell sharply when civil war began – and hence concluding that civil war could only weaken France in the face of the enemy, rather than regenerating it by successful revolution.

Second, a sense of social superiority made the middle classes suspicious or fearful of a regime which proclaimed social equality and gave unprecedented power to workers, who were often portrayed in the familiar stereotype of the 'dangerous classes', violent, drunken, ignorant and criminal. Consequently, those who thought of themselves as *bourgeois* rather than *peuple* were painfully aware that the Commune threatened their status, even if they shared its republican and patriotic views and its suspicion of Versailles. Class differences were often expressed in geographical terms reflecting the differences embodied in Haussmann's Paris. Communards were often referred to as 'Belleville people' or 'Montmartre people'. City-centre Commune local authorities complained of the rowdy behaviour of 'Belleville' Fédérés on their territory and tried to keep them out. Louis Rossel, former officer and War Delegate, tried to express sympathy, but it was tinged with disgust: 'frail, ugly, small, deformed . . . they are fighting so that their children may be less feeble and depraved than they are'; and he concluded that the Commune proved 'the working class's incapacity for government'.[84] The extreme verbal and physical violence and hatred poured out against the Communards after their defeat is eloquent testimony to the fear and resentment that was inspired less by the reality of the Commune and the Communards than by the stereotypes they evoked.

Yet few opponents of the Commune openly resisted it. An underground movement of conservative National Guards planned an uprising once the Versailles troops attacked. A handful volunteered to fight for Versailles, including a company led by the well known left-wing activist Ulrich de Fonvielle. But most preferred to leave the city or wait for the Versaillais to rescue them. There was an exodus after 18 March continuing that already begun after the end of the German siege, and a trickle of escapes after fighting began. From the end of the Prussian siege to the end of the Commune, probably one-third of the total Paris population left.[85] But many were kept in Paris by jobs, businesses or families. Men under 20 or over 40 were not liable to combat service in the National Guard. If they lived in predominantly middle-class *arrondissements* the pressure even on those of military age was in practice small, though the danger of being rounded up in the street increased during April when a census was started to identify deserters – a long job which had limited practical results, but frightened Goncourt: 'Here I am under the necessity . . . of hiding away as if in the time of the Terror.'[86]

Several prominent radical and some socialist politicians made a principled – or at least calculated – decision not to participate in the Commune, even while sympathizing with many of its aims. Apart from the election of some mayors to the Commune as moderates, there was no attempt – perhaps no opportunity – for established politicians to take over or influence its leadership as in 1830 or 1848. No prominent republicans hurried to the Hôtel de Ville to proffer their services. Those who kept out or soon withdrew included those who had headed the poll in Paris in the 8 February National Assembly elections – the veteran socialist Louis Blanc, Victor Hugo, the Garibaldis – and other prominent left-wingers such as the

---

84. Rossel (1960), p. 256.   85. Egrot (1953–54), p. 104.
86. Goncourt (1969), p. 263. See also Wright (1977).

journalist Henri Rochefort, Georges Clemenceau (mayor of the 18th *arrondissement*), Proudhon's chief disciple Henri Tolain, the young war hero General Cremer, and the prominent socialist Jean-Baptiste Millière. This abstention left the Commune free to follow a more revolutionary path, but it also made it even more difficult for it to win significant recognition or support outside Paris.

Their courses of action were not identical: Blanc and Tolain remained as advocates of compromise within the National Assembly at Versailles; Hugo had already resigned; Rochefort stayed for a time in Paris; Clemenceau temporarily withdrew from politics; Millière resigned from the Assembly and refused to stand for the Commune, but remained in Paris as a mordantly critical supporter without an official role. They all, however, wanted the conflict to be stopped by pressure from outside – especially from republican opinion in the provinces – leading to negotiations between the two sides broadly on Paris's terms. They criticized both sides for intransigence – 'we were not at all for Versailles, not wholly for Paris, let's say for Sèvres'. Several organizations were set up to promote a negotiated peace. The Ligue d'Union Républicaine des Droits de Paris and the Union Nationale du Commerce et de l'Industrie were the most prominent. Freemasons took a similar position. These groups probably judged that the Commune, however justified they thought its basic demands, could not win, either politically against a National Assembly newly elected by universal suffrage, or militarily, and that the consequences of its defeat would be disastrous: 'the improbable success of the Commune will bring back the Prussians; the hardly doubtful success of the government will be the signal for an intense reaction'.[87] However, many Communard leaders claimed – at least after the event – that they had never believed in victory either, so this calculation of prospects of success may not have been the only decisive factor. What other reasons could there have been? Most obviously, as noted above, that left-wingers who held back from the Commune did not share the apocalyptic revolutionary mystique which believed that popular fervour could triumph over any odds and that even a failed revolution marked a step forward – or at least they believed that such revolutionary mystique belonged to history. In other words, they were part of the republican mainstream that, learning from the failures of 1848–51, placed their hopes in electoral, not insurrectionary, politics. This divergence within the republican movement had become explicit during the 1860s.

87. Gaillard (1966), p. 10.

Much of the Paris population adopted a wait-and-see attitude. The Commune was, after all, the government, with power and patronage, and much of the prestige that these conferred. Many of its demands seemed just or reasonable. It was by no means clear that it would not win: every previous insurrection that had managed to seize control of Paris had been victorious. As one rather confused Fédéré greengrocer – who had fought on the government side in June 1848 – explained to an equally puzzled court martial after the Commune's defeat:

> I was a National Guard under Louis-Philippe, under the Republic, under the Presidency, under the Empire, under the Government of National Defence. I didn't think I was doing anything wrong by still being a National Guard under the government of the Commune.[88]

Some middle-class men sought jobs in the Commune's civilian administration, which paid them a salary and kept them out of the firing line; the Versailles authorities did not regard this as very heinous. Bodies such as the Artists' Federation took advantage of the revolution to advance their aims (above p. 100), but by no means all members were revolutionaries: few had a history of political militancy, and many had done well during the Empire. So they refused to regard Courbet as having special authority within the Federation just because he was a member of the Commune.[89] This willingness to collaborate with the Commune as long as it was successful was probably widespread. Many 'bourgeois' National Guard battalions were determined to keep going in a similarly autonomous way while performing as little duty as they could; some even paid their men from their officers' pockets. This prevented or delayed their being disarmed and disbanded; in the meantime it protected their members from being enrolled in 'red' battalions. It also enabled them – something especially dear to shopkeepers' hearts – to guard their own districts and keep 'the Belleville people' out.

Such collaboration could go quite far. As was noted earlier, in the 2nd *arrondissement,* nearly twice as many men performed National Guard duty, at least for a time, as voted for Communard candidates. Several of their battalions did fight, even while probably a majority of their men were not whole-hearted Communards. Several received commendations for bravery under fire, none of whom had any record of political militancy. Here we doubtless see the result of official pressure by the authorities, financial need and

88. Rougerie (1964), p. 102.   89. Sanchez (1994), p. 85.

group solidarity as well as political sympathy. Without acquiescence by a large part of the middle class – who were, after all, armed – it is hard to see how the Commune could have governed Paris and survived as long as it did. However, as soon as the Commune began clearly to collapse, such support evaporated.

CHAPTER FIVE

The Last Struggle

The civil war determines the chronology of the Commune from early April onwards. Appointments, dismissals, factional disputes and even most reforms, as we have seen, were by-products of the struggle for survival. The ability to organize its defence determined the time the Commune could survive. Willingness to fight was the acid test of commitment and mobilization, and allows us to see more about who really took part in the Commune, and why. Finally, it is the armed struggle and its bloody conclusion that dominate the 'memory' of the Comune, and which make it the end point of a certain revolutionary tradition.

The defeat of the people in arms

A core belief of revolutionaries was that the armed people, fighting on their home ground, buoyed up by patriotism, fraternity and zeal for justice, could defeat the armed forces of counter-revolution fighting only through ignorance, compulsion or self-interest. In the stirring words of Charles Delescluze, written at a critical moment in the Communards' struggle,

> When the People have rifles in their hands and paving stones under their feet, they have no fear of all the strategists of the monarchist school.[1]

Without this belief, popular revolution against the armed forces of the State becomes unthinkable. The invincibility of the People had been proved – at least according to legend – during the Great

---

1. Proclamation, *JOC,* 22 May.

Revolution. Not only had they stormed the Bastille, but they had thrown back the pipeclayed regiments of the European monarchies in 1792 – a memory to which Communard orators frequently referred. They had defeated Charles X's guardsmen in 1830 and Louis-Philippe's gendarmes in 1848. There were worrying counter-examples, especially the June Days of 1848. But conditions in 1871 were more propitious: thanks to wartime mobilization, the People were now armed, organized and led as never before. They had held Paris against the Germans and – so patriots said – but for the treachery of their leaders, would have seen them off as their grand-fathers had in 1792. The events of 18 March convinced them, besides, that the army was unwilling to fight against the People.

The tragic events of the spring of 1871 put these beliefs to the test, and destroyed them. Since then, survivors, revolutionary theorists and historians have tried to work out what went wrong and who was to blame. Are they right to assume that the Communards could and should have won? That with more dynamic leadership, harsher discipline or greater zeal the revolution would have triumphed? Or should we pose a quite different set of questions: with no effective help from outside, facing the regular army and a mostly hostile France, and with the German army able to intervene if necessary, how did they resist so successfully for nearly two months? And why did they not realize that in the long run their position was hopeless?

THE COMMUNE GOES TO WAR

Fighting had begun on 2 April. This followed a week of confused attempts by the mayors and deputies of Paris to find a peaceful compromise, and then several days of tense waiting after the Commune was installed. Blanquist National Guard generals Eudes, Duval and Brunel (appointed by the Central Committee on 24 March) were contemplating an offensive, but little had been done apart from moving up a few battalions. The Versaillais response led to the first skirmishing in the western suburbs, following which five Fédéré prisoners were shot – the first ominous sign of carnage to come. The Commune reacted with indignation:

> The royalist conspirators have *attacked*! Despite the moderation of our attitude they have *attacked*! No longer able to count on the French army, they have attacked with the pontifical zouaves and imperial police . . . Charette's Chouans, Cathelineau's Vendéens, Trochu's Bretons.[2]

2. *JOC*, 3 April.

This stirring echo of the 1790s shows vividly how the Commune envisaged the struggle (above pp. 118–20); it also served to explain the worrying fact that the army, so unaggressive on 18 March, had actually fought.

The Commune's response was immediate, and was meant to end the conflict with one blow: a *levée en masse* and a *sortie torrentielle* against Versailles, as so often urged as the way to defeat the Prussians. During the afternoon and night, drums beat, bugles blew, battalions and batteries mustered, food and ammunition were collected, and early on 3 April, three columns probably totalling about 30,000 or 40,000 men marched on Versailles from three directions, led by generals Eudes, Duval and Bergeret. But all three blundered to a halt well clear of their objective: the furthest advance seems to have been by 14 men of the *Francs-tireurs de la Marseillaise* who hoisted a red flag on Bougival steeple, four miles north of Versailles. This was due less to resistance by Versailles troops, few of whom were engaged and who suffered negligible casualties, than to confusion, tiredness after 12 hours and more on their feet, inexperience, lack of planning and leadership, poor communications, failure of supply and general unpreparedness on the Fédéré side.[3] They seem to have expected to be able simply to walk to Versailles, and were in no way ready or able to fight a battle. The irresistible *sortie torrentielle* had turned into 'confusion, talking, drinking and panic'. When the Versaillais cautiously advanced, most of the remaining Fédérés scattered. The Commune ordered the city gates closed to hold back their flight, but groups forced their way in whenever an ambulance passed through. Again some prisoners were taken, and again several were killed, including General Duval and the revolutionary hero Gustave Flourens. An embittered Fédéré commander reported: 'it is impossible to hold out longer . . . with men who are indisciplined, drunk and without their officers, who abandoned them this morning. Without discipline, no soldiers; with election of officers, no leaders.'[4]

For many commentators, most influentially Marx, the Communards had thrown away their chance of victory. Instead of waiting to be attacked, they should have marched on Versailles as soon as the revolution began, and captured or dispersed the government, the National Assembly and their troops. This may simply be wisdom after the event – though not long after the event in Marx's case, as he privately predicted as early as 6 April that the Commune

---

3. A later account by Eudes shows that no preparations had been made. Institut Français d'Histoire Sociale 14 AS 99 bis (manuscript note).
4. Bergeret to War, 0h10, 4 April, SHA Ly 3.

had missed the bus. Or it may not be wisdom at all. How could rank-and-file Fédérés have been rallied for an unprovoked attack on Versailles after 18 March, when the revolution seemed to have triumphed, and there was widespread desire for a peaceful solution? Some Fédérés told their officers that 'only the riffraff' were staying with their units and that 'decent men should go back home'.[5] Moreover, as the sad fiasco of 3 April showed, even when anger had been aroused by the first Versaillais attack, the numbers ready to fight were not so great as to be overwhelming, yet too great to be effectively commanded: a crowd of men with rifles was not an army. Even small numbers of Versaillais gendarmes and soldiers, in positions previously fortified by the Germans, were able to stop them. If, by some miracle, the Fédérés had reached Versailles, they would have discovered that their enemies had retreated out of reach to Rambouillet; and quite probably German troops would have threatened their rear. Victory at a stroke was not on offer.

Instead, defeat was staring them in the face. Paris, far from bursting with enthusiastic armed revolutionaries, was practically defenceless. On 4 April, only 45 men were guarding the Neuilly gate, and there were only 1,300 men in reserve at the Hôtel de Ville. On 6 and 7 April the Fédérés lost the outpost of Courbevoie and the strategic Neuilly bridge because they had only 1,100 men available. Desperate appeals for reinforcements produced only 700 more, while three battalions refused to advance. Even in the 'red' working-class districts, men were reluctant to turn out when the drums beat. At Montmartre, it took six to eight hours to muster men, and the legion commander reported that 'they do their duty deplorably . . . citizen guards use any excuse to abandon their posts and return to Paris'.[6] Fédéré officers knew that when their men had had enough they would simply go home: it was common to demand one day's leave after two days on duty. These amateur soldiers grumbled at camping in the wet and were upset by dirt and lice. Those who stayed took no notice of orders, demanded endless reinforcements and used up huge quantities of scarce ammunition. Something had to be done to make the National Guard capable of defending the city.

THE MILITARIZATION OF THE NATIONAL GUARD

That something was an attempt by the new War Delegate, General Gustave Cluseret, who replaced Eudes on 3 April, to turn the

5. Report 23–4 March (Fort Bicêtre), SHA Ly 121.
6. *Ordre du jour*, 6 April, SHA Ly 85.

National Guard into an army. Cluseret, aged 47, the son of a colonel, had been a regular officer – he had even fought against the June rebels in 1848. He had subsequently become a revolutionary adventurer, not untypical of the band of footloose French, Polish and Italian soldiers who offered their services to progressive causes, and who were to provide the Commune's high command and some of its staff officers. Cluseret had been made an acting brigadier-general while briefly serving the Union in the American Civil War, though he had spent most of his time in New York fighting a journalistic campaign against Lincoln. He had been involved with Fenian conspiracies in the 1860s, joined the International and had contacts with the anarchist Bakunin. During the German war he had tried to organize revolutionary military forces in Lyons. He is usually cast as villain in histories of the Commune, arrogant, indolent, incompetent and blamed for defeat. Yet he seems to have been the only man to have thought about how the Commune could survive, rather than trusting in the miraculous power of Revolution, or fantasizing about an invincible *levée en masse*. His conclusions, however, were not inspiring: to stay on the defensive, hold out as long as possible behind Paris's formidable forts and ramparts, and hope that the Versaillais would give up first, or else that the Germans (with whom he began to negotiate) or the Provinces would mediate. His attempts to militarize the Fédérés, though much more accepted by the citizens in uniform than is usually suggested, were resented by some influential Communards.

First, efforts were made to create discipline. Politically unreliable battalions were progressively disbanded and their men drafted to other units. Fédéré battalions were ordered to organize combat companies (*compagnies de marche*) from men aged 18 to 40, who would live in barracks rather than at home. Legion disciplinary tribunals were set up, and also a central court martial for serious offences. Incompetent or insubordinate officers were removed. The results disappointed their promoters. The combat units were slow to form, further delayed by the filthy condition in which the barracks they were to occupy had been left by the wartime garrison. The Commune refused to sanction harsh penalties and the court martial ceased to function. The legion tribunals did not meet. Dismissed officers were often reelected by their men. Though much could be done by officers through example and by proving their own competence, in tougher cases of indiscipline they had few sanctions – mainly a few days in the cells and loss of pay. But efforts were made to establish conventional military routines: reveille at

6:00, fatigues at 7:00, parade at 9:00, roll-call at 11:00, and so on. By mid-May, there was a reserve of 7,000 men in barracks.

Second, Cluseret was determined to promote officers with military experience, rather than the political activists or easy-going neighbourly men who were often elected – in some companies, a high proportion were innkeepers. Eventually, probably three-quarters of the legion colonels or lieutenant-colonels were former regular officers, NCOs or soldiers, as were many of the Fédéré staff officers. Many had combat experience in Africa, the Crimea or Italy, and several held the Legion of Honour or the Military Medal. The generals appointed by Cluseret in place of the Blanquists continued to command the defence to the end. Two were Poles, in exile as participants in the Polish revolt of 1863: Jaroslav Dombrowski (Dąbrowski), 35, formerly a captain in the Russian army, and Walery Wróblewski, 29, who had been earning a living as a piano teacher. The third, Napoléon La Cécilia, 36, a teacher, was of Corsican and Italian background, a former Garibaldian officer who had been a colonel of *franc-tireurs* during the war. The young Colonel Louis Rossel, 26, the half-Scottish son of an officer, was a patriotic deserter from the regular army, who, after serving as chief of staff, became Cluseret's successor as War Delegate from 1 to 9 May. Written examinations were imposed on aspiring staff officers, with essay titles such as 'Causes of France's defeat in 1870' and 'Advantages and dangers of a standing army'. The results could be interesting (above p. 122), though the ability to ride a horse outweighed literary skills. According to a Versaillais report, three-quarters of all Fédéré officers were former soldiers. Probably few had a record of political militancy, and most of them seem to have dropped out of politics again after the Commune.[7]

Third, a military administration had to be created. The National Guard had to be armed, equipped and supplied with food and ammunition. Existing stocks had to be found and used, and new supplies manufactured. The part-time National Guard had to be mobilized and counted, its units ordered into action, reinforced when necessary, and relieved when tired. They could only fight if properly armed, clothed, supplied and rested. Progress in a few fraught weeks seems impressive, in spite of what nearly all historians from Lissagaray onwards have said. By the middle of May, some front-line units were being relieved every 48 hours, and even daily, though the staff's aim was five-day tours of duty. Supply was effectively organized under

7. See Martinez (1981), pp. 152–4.

Varlin, Avrial and the Blanquist May brothers. Twenty tons of fresh meat and 40,000 litres of wine were distributed daily during May to units on active service – enough for over 100,000 men. They were reported to be pleased with the quality of the meat, cheese, brandy, sugar and coffee, but did not like rice and thought salt meat was provided too often – so the Intendance decided to make it into sausages. Quantities were sometimes plethoric: Fort Vanves received 10,000 fresh meat rations for its garrison of 800; at Fort Issy (which according to Lissagaray had run out of food and ammunition) the Versaillais captured 119 cannon, 2 powder-magazines, 13 tons of biscuit, 800 kilos of rice, 600 kilos of bacon, 1,300 litres of brandy and 'equipment in abundance'. Moroever 40,000 rations per day were being distributed to 200 guardposts within Paris.[8] Cannon, rifles, machine-guns and shells were being manufactured; and gunboats and armoured trains were in action, and seriously disrupting the Versaillais advance. Staff officers – led by the unsung 'Colonel Henry' (the engineer Henry Prod'homme, 26, described by the military prosecutors as 'very intelligent, even-tempered and cheerful') and Rossel – were needed to see that the Fédérés actually turned up and obeyed orders. This permitted commanders to use what was perhaps the most effective means of discipline, given that the Commune would not permit the customary harsh military penalties: economic pressure (above p. 129). Most National Guards and their families depended on their pay and rations for subsistence, so the general staff began to withold them from units not doing their duty, and counted the actual number present when battalions reported, which determined how much pay and rations they received. One Commune official suggested that to find men they should adopt the 'revolutionary' method of offering 5 francs per day to National Guards with the promise of 1,000 francs bonus when the revolution had triumphed.[9]

Of course, the National Guard never became a regular army. It always kept its political and democratic character, electing its officers and NCOs, and also company delegates to look after the men's interests. Orders were always discussed and sometimes disobeyed if they seemed unreasonable. Units often failed to appear, refused to obey orders or simply went home when they had had enough. In the 'red' 18th Legion, the disciplinary tribunal itself failed to turn

8. Egrot (1953–54), p. 170.
9. Information on National Guard administration is drawn mainly from SHA Ly 29, 30, 32, 33, 76, 93, 119, 121.

up. Most men would turn out for duty inside Paris; fewer for service in the front line; and fewer still would stay there long, though absentees often returned after a break. Front-line units insisted on regular leave and threatened to strike. Over-zealousness could prove as much a problem as backsliding, when keen commanders constantly demanded reinforcements and ammunition, angrily refused to obey orders they disapproved of and even left their posts on missions of their own devising. Eager amateur gunners blew the breeches off their cannon.

Drunkenness, negligence and corruption remained endemic. Drunkenness was accepted as a fact of life – 'you know what the National Guard is like' – and it was decided for reasons of morale not to make public reprimands.[10] There are some spectacular examples. During the night of 14 May, four battalions left a threatened section of the ramparts unguarded while they pillaged the wine-cellar of a nearby Jesuit college, got roaring drunk, and dressed up in the school's theatrical costumes. The staff realized that many battalions overstated their strength, sometimes to draw extra pay, equipment and rations; the surplus was sold. Sentries could be bribed to let deserters escape from the city.

Yet it is misleading to stress only the failings. There was a cadre of determined, able and conscientious men who gave the National Guard its backbone. Many, as noted, were skilled and experienced soldiers who had served their time in Napoleon III's army or other armies; this doubtless explains what a Versailles officer called the 'extraordinary shooting' of Fédéré artillery, which caused the attackers great difficulty. The number of men actually serving or available for service greatly increased during April and the first half of May. We have seen that about 30,000 marched in the 3 April sortie. If we consider these the Fédéré hard core (recalling that only 54,000 had voted No in the October 1870 plebiscite – a test of revolutionary support), it is striking that a month later the National Guard staff estimated that it had 170,000 men under arms, of whom 80,000 were in the combat companies, 10,500 were garrisoning the southern forts, and several thousand reserves were in barracks. The full strength was never available simultaneously, nor could the Fédérés be used for coordinated large-scale operations. And clearly many of them were not strongly committed to revolutionary ideology. This doubtless explains much of the indiscipline described above.

10. Garrison commander to Min. of War (n.d.), Executive Committee to War (n.d.), SHA Ly 5.

But without enrolling the lukewarm, and organizing food, armament and regular rotation, it would have been impossible to hold several miles of trenches day and night for weeks on end against unremitting Versaillais pressure.

We saw in the previous chapter how community solidarity and pressure helped to induce men to take part in the Commune, and how important the National Guard was within the community (above p. 131). To this must be added the further dimension of specifically military camaraderie and pride. 'We were all militarists then,' recalled one Blanquist later. Many men had been together since the previous August or September, and had faced the Prussian siege together. Many who had not known each other before must have become firm friends. A 'young English gentleman of good family' conscripted into a Fédéré unit wrote, 'I can never forget the kindness I met with from them.'[11] Funerals of comrades were important and moving ceremonies; sometimes the whole battalion demanded to attend, which caused problems for the high command. Battalions had identities: their numbers were often well known; some had nicknames (like 'the armoured 101st' or 'the shiny-boots battalion'); some adopted small variations of uniform, such as plumes or coloured piping. Many had group photographs taken, with their buglers, drummer-boys and *cantinières*, posing in front of barricades or the demolished Vendôme Column brandishing flags, rifles and bayonets. One legion commander, Combatz, argued against forming new combat regiments because it would break the local links of existing units, bring in unknown officers and destroy the *esprit de corps* of battalions that were proud of their flags and numbers, and had 'their legends, their revolutionary aura'.[12] Rossel, as president of the court martial (which the Commune would not allow to pass death sentences), tried punishing a pusillanimous battalion by having all their right sleeves cut off: 'all those fellows were sobbing, and the guards surrounding them seemed more upset than if they'd had to shoot them'.[13] Military pride must have been especially strong for those who had been elected officers, NCOs or delegates, many of them former soldiers. They were keen to defend their performance under fire, and demanded to have their exploits publicly recognized. A Versailles spy saw Fédéré officers leaving the Hôtel de Ville 'rubbing their hands with pleasure' because their battalion had been mentioned in dispatches,[14] and the Commune press

11. *Macmillan's Magazine*, vol. 24 (May–Oct. 1871), p. 386.
12. Note (n.d.), SHA Ly 36.   13. Rossel (1960), p. 245.
14. APP Ba 364–5, report 25 April.

contained frequent disputes about the relative prowess in action of various units.

A revealing sign of the prestige of National Guard rank was what Cluseret called 'the mania for gold braid'. It affected all levels. The Commune solemnly debated whether its members who were not officers should be allowed to wear swords. Many loved parading on horseback wearing their red sashes (gold-fringed for the Commune, silver for the Central Committee) – very like the Legion of Honour regalia worn by ministers and generals on the other side. Fédéré officers demanded expensive pistols (tens of thousands were issued), 'chic carbines' and patent-leather riding boots. Some even fought duels, in best aristocratic fashion. Others ran up large bills with expensive military tailors – 8,000 francs for the staff of the Blanquist General Eudes (several years' salary for a skilled worker), to the disgust of austere revolutionaries such as Jourde and Varlin, who angrily refused to authorize payment. Individuals or little groups of comrades liked to be photographed in military poses, sometimes in front of a martial backdrop, resplendent with jackboots, revolver and sabre. Sérisier, the famous commander of the 101st and later of the 13th Legion,

> proud of his braid and his authority, had himself photographed in colonel's uniform, revolver in belt, kepi at a jaunty angle, right arm resting on his drawn sabre. . . . He enjoys showing off like this, scaring the timid.[15]

The photograph still exists; there are many similar. More than one Fédéré was convicted after the defeat of the revolution on the evidence of photographs, uniform buttons, badges of rank or patent-leather swordbelts kept as souvenirs. Status created obligations: self-respect required that behaviour should match the image, and that the confidence and respect of comrades should not be betrayed. 'As long as he remained a corporal he showed little ardour in serving the Commune,' ran the verdict on one Fédéré; 'as soon as he was elected an officer he wanted to be worthy of his colleagues and became actively engaged in the insurrection.'[16]

How might we judge the effectiveness of this amateur Parisian army? Most writers deplore its indiscipline and incompetence, and, as we have seen, it was far from perfect. Its chain of command was confused, and orders and counter-orders arrived from all directions.

15. Vuillaume (1971), pp. 99–100.   16. SHA 3 CG 2001 (Boniface).

There was no way of coordinating or deploying its full strength, so that it had to fight piecemeal and could only react to events rather than initiate them. Many of its members got drunk and shirked their duty. But can any hastily improvised insurgent army (and indeed many regular armies) avoid such failings? We should beware of pro-Commune writers seeking scapegoats for failure, and counter-revolutionaries eager to brand the whole Commune as a drunken orgy. Instead of comparing the Fédérés implicitly with some imaginary ideal of a serried mass of unflinching revolutionary purists, we should think of them in comparison with historical realities. Alongside the extravagantly chaotic and drunken state of the Red Army during the Russian civil war, or the sometimes farcical insurbordination of the Republican militia during the Spanish civil war, they seem paragons of self-disciplined efficiency. And this without the sanction of the firing squad. Their largely forgotten organizers deserve some belated credit, though admittedly their efforts rested on the existing organization of the National Guard and the huge stocks of arms and supplies built up during the war. The tragedy of their situation was that, however tireless their efforts, their chances of survival were slim.

DEFENDING *PARIS LIBRE*

Improved organization and supply meant that the Fédérés were securely holding the formidable system of forts, trenches and ramparts protecting Paris to the south and west. They had vast quantities of arms and ammunition, including heavy artillery, gunboats and armoured trains, with which they kept up a spectacular display of fireworks, reassuring to their friends and of at least some danger to their enemies, who could only operate by night. In numbers, until well into May they were roughly equivalent to the available Versailles forces, which were composed mainly of demoralized and inexperienced conscripts. The Versaillais were forced to undertake a slow and tedious siege, digging miles of trenches and bombarding the forts and ramparts.

However, once the siege started, the days of Paris's defence were numbered. Though the Fédérés could stage a defence and use their firepower in daylight, they were not capable of mounting counter-attacks strong enough to disrupt the besiegers' elephantine advance in the hours of darkness. Cluseret's idea was to create a defence in depth to wear out the attackers, and he ordered armour-plated barricades from Paris factories. But the Commune leadership wanted more action and also feared that Cluseret was becoming too powerful. After a near disaster when the key position of Fort Issy was temporarily abandoned by its garrison on 30 April, although Cluseret had reoccupied it in person, he was dismissed and arrested on 1 May, and has been a convenient scapegoat ever since. His successor was Rossel, self-assured but inexperienced and a martinet. He frequently indulged in threats, and published a damaging order to 'sabre' or 'cannonade' Fédéré runaways. His answer to the military crisis was to order a great offensive to put the Versaillais to flight and relieve Fort Issy. Nineteen battalions were mustered for this enterprise, but Rossel decided it was not enough; and when Issy finally fell on 9 May he published a flamboyant letter of resignation blaming National Guard disobedience and the Commune's weakness (above p. 6) and disappeared. These public conflicts, and the loss of the fort, were the first unmistakable signs for Parisians that the war might be turning against them.

During the next ten days, it definitely did. The Versaillais brought their trenches and batteries ever closer to the city ramparts, which came under heavy bombardment and were periodically abandoned by the defenders. The disparity in numbers also grew. Versaillais forces rose eventually to 130,000. The Fédérés lost probably about 10,000 killed, wounded or captured. Their combat units fell from 80,000 to 50,000, with the legions from the working-class districts showing the sharpest falls, for they doubtless suffered the highest attrition. Morale too seems to have slumped: battalions considered unreliable were marched to their action stations by 'red' units with loaded rifles; but 'red' legions too were discouraged. Angry wives protested about casualties and tried to keep their men out of the fight. Only in May, as the position worsened, were serious attempts begun to round up *refractaires*. House to house visits, the beginning of a census, and discussion of an identity-card system alarmed middle-class men who were trying to make themselves inconspicuous. A Fédéré lieutenant wrote to his wife on 12 May:

> nothing changes in my unhappy position I am as hard up as could be and I am having to accept the rank they are offering me to be able to eat I haven't a penny. . . . I have pawned my watch if anything happens to me you'll find the receipt in the chest of drawers. . . . It's a sad thing to see a civil war among Frenchmen. . . . I really ought to have stayed in the village. . . . God help us![17]

17. SHA Ly 130.

Rossel's successor as War Delegate, the veteran Jacobin Delescluze, urged his commanders to hold their trenches and launch counter-attacks; he would not countenance withdrawal inside the city walls. But Dombrowski reported that 'the battalions sent for combat . . . return immediately to Paris in disorder'.[18] Although the Communard press continued to print news of victories, staff officers reported that the most shell-swept stretches of the ramparts were often undefended, while the Versaillais trenches were now only a stone's throw away. Last-minute efforts were made to build a second and third line of defence inside Paris. Delescluze, a civilian with no military experience, realized despairingly that exhortation was no longer enough:

> Bad news. . . . La Cécilia, abandoned by a large part of his troops, asks to evacuate. . . . It is certain that if the position is as I am informed, it is no longer tenable. . . . If only the men came, if those who came stayed, all could be saved. . . . I am asked for men, for gunners, there is nothing. It's tragic.[19]

It is unclear how many people realized the true position, and when. Certainly, no Commune leader publicly suggested asking the Versaillais for terms, which Thiers had several times hinted at. Did they fail to realize their plight? Sometimes. The Communard press constantly reported victories. Many seem to have believed it. Paul Lafargue, a visiting socialist, wrote at the beginning of May (just as the war was turning definitely against the Commune) that 'Paris is becoming invincible . . . already possess[ing] a well organized citizen army supplied with victuals and munitions; and each passing day adds to the importance and solidity of that army.'[20] Versaillais spies reported that some people talked openly of defeat, but others still expected to win. This was certainly so for Courbet, who airily assured his family that 'In our spare time we fight the swine at Versailles. We take turns. . . . They could fight as they are doing for ten years without being able to enter our territory.'[21] Even the less optimistic 'realized that it couldn't last, but counted on some last-minute compromise'.[22] Some even hoped that Versailles and the Commune would form a last-minute alliance against the Germans. The Artists' Federation was happily organizing competitions, having official stationery printed, and thinking of organizing a Universal Exposition in Paris; as late as 17 May it began recruiting art teachers.

18. Dispatch to Delescluze, SHA Ly 2.
19. Delescluze to Committee of Public Safety, 20 May, SHA Ly 29.
20. Derfler (1991), p. 101.   21. Courbet (1992), p. 417.
22. Henri Maret in *La Revue Blanche*, 12 (1897), p. 261.

Was there more here than simple wishful thinking? Little is known about how Communards envisaged the outcome of the conflict. After the event (which of course weakens their testimony) several leaders claimed never to have believed in victory, and to have seen the struggle only as a heroic gesture to inspire future generations. Tomanovskaya wrote to Marx as early as 24 April, 'I am pessimistic and . . . expect to die on a barricade one of these days . . . it is going to be a matter of luck.' But she, like most Communard leaders, managed to escape. Versaillais repression may have been less comprehensive than usually supposed, especially where respectable-looking ladies and gentlemen were concerned. Or they may have been astonishingly lucky – unless some had prepared bolt-holes in anticipation of defeat. The verdict of the socialist Commune member Andrieu was severe: 'Those who saw the danger remained silent so as not to attract attention to their escape plans. . . . Most of the other members *did not believe in the danger.*' They probably underestimated the consequences of holding out: the Commune member Dereure said later that 'we did not think that the repression could be so ignobly cruel'.[23] Rank-and-file Fédérés suffered the consequences.

Perhaps the Communards did not know how to stop: they had so deeply committed themselves over the years to revolution as the inevitable and historic form of progress that they could not pass up such a favourable opportunity when Paris and all its resources fell into their hands. Perhaps the leaders thought they had gone too far, and led their followers too far, to contemplate surrender. A few of the most courageous leaders, such as Delescluze, Gambon, Ranvier and Vermorel, did make discreet and tentative approaches to groups urging 'conciliation' with Versailles, but these came to nothing.[24] Perhaps their belief in the historic necessity of revolutionary victory caused them to hope desperately for some final reversal of fortune. For if victory was not possible in the favourable circumstances of 1871, then the whole idea of revolution by armed insurrection might as well be abandoned. Even after their defeat, this admission remained taboo.[25]

ON THE BARRICADES

Paris was irretrievably lost in a few hours during the evening and night of 21–2 May, when the first Versaillais forces swarmed over

23. Tomanovskaya in Schulkind (1985), p. 154; Andrieu (1971), p. 116; Dereure in *La Revue Blanche*, 12 (1897), p. 276.
24. Nord (1987), pp. 12, 20.   25. See Martinez (1981), p. 206.

the abandoned south-western ramparts. Somehow, the Fédéré commanders and the War Delegate Delescluze did not realize or dared not admit the seriousness of what was happening. Delescluze forbade giving the alarm and denied reports of the Versaillais invasion. So the army was able to overrun the newly constructed defence lines, surprise thousands of sleeping Fédéré reserves, and occupy the western districts of the city almost without resistance. Many lukewarm Fédéré units decided that the game was up, and surrendered or went home without a fight. One captured officer gave the army the password and persuaded his men to surrender.

Next morning, 22 May, Versaillais cannon fire made further denial impossible. Delescluze published a stirring proclamation calling for a *levée en masse*:

> Enough of militarism! No more staff officers braided and gilded on every seam! Make way for the people, for the bare-armed fighters! The hour for revolutionary war has struck!

But no great mass uprising took place: enthusiasm for the Commune had for weeks been fading, and many of its supporters must have felt that they had done enough and the cause was hopeless. Delescluze's rejection of 'militarism' has been blamed for undermining what was left of Fédéré organization. Many staff officers took their cue and disappeared. Some simply fought in the streets, where Dombrowski was fatally wounded. In any case, the National Guard had always been a loosely coordinated confederation of battalions, without at the best of times a command structure that would enable it to function like an integrated army. Now most units had to fend for themselves.

Companies and battalions maintained some cohesion, even if their numbers plummeted with the disappearance of those who now felt acutely that discretion was the better part of valour. The faithful mustered and began to look to the defence of their own districts. Attempts at coordination were made. Some felt relief that the decisive moment had come. They were now fighting the way they thought they knew, with 'paving stones under their feet', and could perhaps repulse the half-hearted regular troops and save the revolution. So all over Paris little groups of men and women – from a few dozen to a few hundred, perhaps roughly 10,000–20,000 altogether – began to build barricades, for the last great revolutionary battle in French history.

Barricades had become the preeminent symbol of popular resistance since they were first used on a large scale in Paris as recently as 1830 (above p. 19). They had many purposes and meanings, and a symbolic power not wholly explicable in utilitarian terms. Most basically, they were intended to hamper the passage of enemy troops, horses and guns, perhaps while defenders fired or threw objects down at them from roofs and windows. But they could also form ramparts, marking off 'liberated' territory from no-man's-land: hence the many photographs (often taken just after 18 March) of triumphant groups of Fédérés posing heroically on them. Barricades turned streets and neighbourhoods into protected spaces, and their inhabitants into a garrison. Barricades were rallying points attracting defenders to them, and sometimes focuses for a defensive network of fortified houses, snipers' positions, ammunition and food stores and field dressing stations, often in neighbouring shops or bars. Their construction was often a community act, in which neighbours or passers-by would contribute a paving stone. But they also attracted danger, which other neighbours preferred not to see in their vicinity, so the builders were sometimes acting under duress.

About 900 barricades were built all over the city,[26] including those prepared in advance, such as the useless defence lines in western Paris and the huge, much-photographed, redoubts facing the Place de la Concorde, constructed laboriously and impressively by the Commune's Barricades Commission. The biggest concentration was in the eastern districts, where support for the Commune was strongest and which had time to prepare before the Versailles troops arrived: there were 78 barricades in the 11th *arrondissement*, 76 at Belleville and Ménilmontant, 111 at La Villette. Some were miniature fortresses of paving stones, turf and sandbags, with moats, cannon, machine-guns and even mines, built to command the strategic points designed by Haussmann: avenues, squares and crossroads. In small sidestreets were the classic barricades of revolutionary tradition, little walls of paving stones, thrown up spontaneously by bands of neighbours. Most barricades were like this. Of 44 barricades at La Chapelle, for example, only 2 were listed as 'big'; of 45 in the 14th *arrondissement*, only 4 were big; and of the others, only 30 had been built high enough to shelter the defenders.

Meanwhile, the Versailles invaders – some 120,000 men – poured in and pursued an inexorable seven-day march across the city from south-west to north-east. A few strongpoints held out in western and central Paris, such as the strongly fortified Place de la Concorde.

---

26. See statistics compiled by city highways department, AP VO (NC) 234, and on detailed reports of barricades captured by army units in SHA Li 116, Lu 7.

But places expected to prove strongholds of the revolution, such as Montmartre, were scarcely defended. Often there was a grotesque disparity in numbers. In the central 2nd *arrondissement*, the few dozen dutiful Fédérés who manned barricades (a fraction of the 1,600 men who had voted for Communard candidates in the 16 April election) confronted 25,000 Versaillais, so numerous that they blocked the streets. Not suprisingly, most barricades did not hold out long: of the 93 barricades captured by one army division during the week, only 10 were strongly defended, and 41 were not defended at all. The heroic legend of every street being barricaded and held to the last is just that: a heroic legend. After firing a few shots, most defenders retreated; many went home, throwing away incriminating evidence: 'in a few minutes [the street] was transformed into a huge depot of arms, ammunition and uniforms'.[27] In the 2nd *arrondissement* alone, 13,000 rifles and 450,000 cartridges were later collected, many from cesspits and sewers. At least one battalion disarmed itself, and the armourer handed its rifles over to the advancing troops.

Those determined to fight on sooner or later came under a hail of shells and bullets from several directions. Barricades could reassure and protect, but they also immobilized their defenders, who could no longer manoeuvre, but only wait passively for hours or even days to be attacked. The army sidestepped frontal assaults, preferring to cannonade from a distance. Under artillery fire, the barricade was a death-trap, as fragments of paving stone or rubble flew like shrapnel. Meanwhile the attackers trickled through alleys and courtyards and smashed through the internal walls of buildings until they could outflank the now useless barricades and fire down on their exposed defenders from upper windows and roofs. This tactic had already been practised in 1848. So the barricade was associated not only with the power and triumph of the people in arms, but also with their vulnerability and defeat: a painting by Meissonnier had already fixed the image of the smashed barricade strewn with corpses.

If surviving Fédérés took too long to retreat or surrender, they were likely to be surrounded and shot down on the spot as rebels taken carrying arms:

the fusillade redoubled, and the troops coming from behind... pushed all the rebels back towards the ramparts; they only had time to fire one cannon shot. But in their flight they met two other army

27. Rouffiac (1873), p. 153.

columns [which] cut off their retreat and massacred them; at the corner of the street 26 Fédérés lay scattered on the ground.[28]

The Fédérés sometimes barred their enemy's way by setting fire to buildings: for example, in the Rue de Rivoli in the centre and the Rue Vavin on the Left Bank, which were largely destroyed. Other fires were probably caused by cannon shells, which certainly caused vast damage: the Versaillais were in no mood to spare Paris. But most of the biggest fires were started as deliberate symbolic acts. There had been much talk ever since the Prussian siege of 'burying ourselves beneath the ruins of Paris rather than surrender'. The rhetoric was put into practice, though by individuals (many of them Blanquists), not as the result of a concerted decision. In the choice of symbolic targets, in stone as well as flesh and blood, Communards were showing what and who they thought were their true enemies (above p. 123).

The strongest defence came in the eastern quarters, where the Fédérés were most numerous, and where there had been most time to prepare. The remaining members of the Commune, and Colonel Henry with the remnants of the National Guard staff, tried to set up an organized defence in the north-eastern districts, summoning all units to concentrate in the 11th *arrondissement*. General Wróblewski continued to command the southern forts and trenches, until on 25 May his men insisted on returning to Paris. Many preferred to defend their home ground south of the Seine as long as they could, rather than join a common defence. There were attempts to hold out on the Left Bank, especially round the Pantheon, the Place d'Italie and the Butte aux Cailles (which Lissagaray's account made into an epic), but by the evening of 25 May, those still able and willing to fight were concentrated on the Right Bank.

Here geography and Haussmannization helped them. From the Place de la Bastille via the Place du Château d'Eau to the Place de la Rotonde at La Villette broad squares and avenues and long straight vistas gave fields of fire, and the Canal Saint-Martin provided a moat or (where it was covered) a glacis. We still know little about the rank-and-file defenders and their leaders. They included the Jacobin veterans Delescluze and Gambon. Three who were wounded in the fighting were the young journalist Vermorel and two former regular soldiers, Lisbonne and Brunel, both legion colonels. Several accounts stress the prominence of Commune members Eugène Varlin, Gabriel Ranvier (representative of Belleville and member of

28. Statement of witness, SHA Ly 132.

the Committee of Public Safety, a small businessman, freemason and Blanquist) and Alexis Trinquet (a cobbler, also from Belleville). The remants of National Guard headquarters under Colonel Henry also played a part. Together they brought the Versaillais advance to a halt, and inflicted the heaviest casualties of the week. This was certainly the most organized defence mounted by the Fédérés. An eye-witness account by one of them, written soon after the event, relates orders being given, supplies of ammunition and food being organized and tours of inspection of 'fifty or sixty' barricades by staff officers.[29] The centre of the defence was the Place de la Bastille:

> there were men running to and fro, some hurrying to the parapet of the Canal to discharge their rifles, others returning to their posts for fresh supplies of ammunition; guns being dragged about, guns being dismounted, guns being loaded, guns being fired from all sides; in fact, guns in every possible position. Every now and then an officer with his orderly would cross the Place at full gallop; then at a more leisurely pace would come an omnibus with the red cross flag, then an ammunition waggon, then an ambulance waggon – and all this to a rattling accompaniment of musketry mixed with the sound of trumpets and the booming of cannon.[30]

Only when large Versaillais forces pushed round to their rear were the barricades at the Bastille and the Place de la Rotonde taken on 26 May, and the last few thousand defenders were surrounded in the streets of Belleville, Ménilmontant and Popincourt, not far from the scenes of major fighting in June 1848. A map of the main barricades of the 20th *arrondissement* (Figure 5.1) shows that they created a coherent defence with big barricades covering every main crossroads – proof of coordination on a fairly large scale, involving several thousand people, and doubtless organized by remaining members of the Commune and Fédéré commanders.

The situation was now evidently desperate. The hope that a mass uprising of 'bare-armed fighters' would make the city invincible had proved an illusion. The expectation that the Versailles troops, once inside Paris, would again prove unreliable was no less false. Delescluze and three other Commune members had tried on 25 May to leave the city to contact the Germans and ask for mediation – the first attempt at any kind of political strategy since Cluseret's explorations in April. But they were turned back at the city gates by angry Fédérés who suspected them of trying to save their own skins, and this humiliation was one reason why Delescluze went alone, in top

29. *Macmillan's Magazine*, vol. 24 (May–Oct. 1871), p. 401.   30. Ibid.

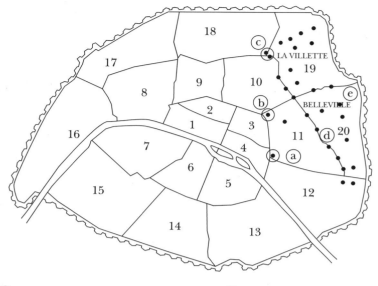

Figure 5.1   *The Communard defence of eastern Paris*

Legend:
- ⊙ Main defensive positions
- • Large barricades
- ⓐ Place de la Bastille
- ⓑ Place du Château d'Eau (now de la République)
- ⓒ Place de la Rotonde (now de Stalingrad)
- ⓓ Père Lachaise cemetery
- ⓔ Rue Haxo
- ∩∩ City ramparts

hat and red sash, to seek death on an abandoned barricade – the only member of the Commune to die in the fighting. The Germans were anyway in no mood to help. They even turned back people trying to escape through their lines – for many, a death sentence. Thousands of Fédérés laid down their arms as the ring of force closed inexorably round them. The last dozen members of the Commune met in Belleville, decided on a final desperate appeal to the Germans, but then resolved instead that for the sake of history and the 'greatness' of the Commune, they must go down fighting 'without negotiation or compromise'.[31]

The last barricade combats, and the last running fights, took place on 28 May, in a few streets off the Faubourg du Temple and the Exterior Boulevard at the foot of Belleville and Ménilmontant – the site of riots in 1869–70, and one of the battlegrounds of June

31. *PVC*, vol. 2, p. 517.

1848. One of the last sizeable skirmishes was at a barricade at the bottom of the Rue de Belleville, defended (in the words of a Versaillais officer) by 'all that is most resolute in the quarter'. Vallès later described it:

> We reply with rifle and cannon to the terrible fire directed at us. . . . In all the windows, our men have put mattresses, which smoke under the impact of bullets. From time to time a head pops up behind the balustrade, and fires. . . . A moment of calm. A parley, to tell us to surrender. . . . 'M[erde]!', bawls our commander, upright on his cobblestone dais. But suddenly, the windows are abandoned, the dam breaks. . . . 'We've had it! Run for it!'[32]

The Versaillais charged and, in the bureaucratic prose of an army report, shot 'all those still offering resistance'. The rest, chased through the streets, showed a white flag and 150 surrendered.[33] It is not certain when or where the very last shot was fired. Tradition places it near the intersection of two Belleville backstreets, the Rues Ramponeau and de Tourtille, a few yards from Vallès's barricade, where, according to Lissagaray, a lone Fédéré held out a quarter of an hour, and managed to escape at about 1 p.m. However, army reports refer to fighting near Ménilmontant church later that day, and place the final skirmish in the Rue de Tourtille at 6 p.m.

It is not possible to say exactly how many Fédérés fought, or how many were killed. There are some indications of the order of magnitude of participation. About 900 barricades were built (compared with 600 in August 1944), but only about 100 were seriously defended. The Versaillais lost about 3,500 men killed or wounded – some 500 per day. So several thousand Fédérés must have fought at any one time during the week. Some thousands must have been killed or wounded in the fighting – surely rather more than the Versaillais, given the superior organization and tactics of the latter – and a large number were summarily executed. Officially, 15,083 were recorded as arrested during that week, 4,500 of them in the last two days of fighting; but not all these had been active combatants. These indications suggest that the Communard Benoît Malon's estimate of 20,000 active Fédéré combatants in all is as good a guess as any. But it must be remembered that the level of involvement varied greatly: some did as little as putting a few stones on a barricade, while others fought day after day as they retreated from Auteuil to Belleville. All this suggests – unsurprisingly – that the intensity of

---

32. Vallès (1972), pp. 319–20.   33. Report of 136th regt, SHA Li 116.

actual fighting during 'Bloody Week' was of a comparable order with that of the shorter June Days insurrection of 1848, very much more intense than that of the 'Three Glorious Days' of July 1830 and considerably more extensive than in the 'National Insurrection' of August 1944.[34]

The ways in which the Fédérés responded collectively to the Versaillais invasion show how they related to the city as a whole and to their local communities. They did not rush to stem the Versaillais incursion into western Paris. Nor did they assemble at the Hôtel de Ville. That is to say, their instinct was not to defend the city as a whole, or its political buildings or central districts. Nor on the other hand did they retreat *en masse* to the (temporarily) safer eastern quarters to prepare a last-ditch collective defence. Their instinctive rallying point was their locality. Contrary to prevailing myth, however, this did not mean that everyone defended his own street: most small barricades, as we have noted, were not defended. The cohesion of battalions and legions often led to a wider geographical focus: the *quartier*, the *arrondissement*, or even a broader space marked out by the urban topography of thoroughfares, squares, waterways, slopes and open spaces, some natural, some designed by Haussmann and his planners. *Arrondissements* were defended mainly by their local Fédéré units, who often tried to establish some coordinated defence, centred on the *mairie* or some other obvious landmark, or the main intersections or roads which sometimes formed the *arrondissement* boundary.

When they gave up the fight, relatively few from the western and central districts – perhaps two or three thousand – retreated to the eastern districts, whether to elude the Versaillais or to fight on, or both. Most rank-and-file Fédérés, stripping off their uniforms and throwing away their weapons, tried to disappear into the shelter of their own communities, helped by families, friends, not infrequently employers: they could see no escape in the anonymity of the city. Whether or not they were betrayed to the Versaillais – and there were many *dénonciations* during the first few days – probably reflected the amount of resentment the Commune had generated within their community, whether individuals had made enemies, and also perhaps

---

34. Casualties among the insurgents in 1830 were 500 killed and 850 wounded (compared with 150 soldiers killed); in June 1848, over 1,400 killed (compared with about 200–300 soldiers killed and about 1,000 wounded); in 1944, 1,500 killed and 3,500 wounded (though the poorly equipped and demoralized Germans suffered worse). Pinkney (1988), p. 149; Tilly and Lees (1975), p. 186; Levisse-Touzé (1994), pp. 78–9.

the level of ferocity shown by the Versaillais, for the price of one's own life or liberty might be the betrayal of a neighbour.[35] Except for those who were – or could pass as – 'respectable', and could be helped by others of similar status who could provide shelter, money and passports, or at least vouch for their good behaviour, the city was a poor hiding place.

The Commune and the problem of political violence in France

The storming of the Bastille in July 1789 began a period during which the political life of France was by far the most violent in Europe. Precise figures are incalculable. The civil conflicts of the 1790s cost hundreds of thousands of lives; a modest estimate for those killed and seriously wounded during the nineteenth century would be 60,000. The last days of the Commune were the bloodiest episode of post-Revolution history. It was also the last occurrence of mass violence of comparable concentration in time and space.[36]

The general reasons for this history seem clear. First, in 1789 the State lost what Max Weber considered its defining characteristic: the monopoly of legitimate violence. The use of violence by political factions became the most effective way of asserting power. Revolutionaries by definition regarded insurrection both as a right and as an effective political tactic. No regime deriving its power from revolution could absolutely deny that insurrection was sometimes justified. Consequently, separate, and usually more lenient, treatment was given under most regimes to political offences: for example, the death sentence for political crimes was abolished in 1848. The revolutionary appeal to violence was effectively countered not by the law, but by the State's demonstrating its own superior capacity for violence outside legal restraints. These have been called 'founding massacres', by which a new regime proved its ability and determination to rule: April 1832, June 1848, December 1851, May 1871. Once the monopoly of violence was thus established, it was common to give pardons or amnesties to defeated enemies.

35. This is my impression from individual Fédéré files, and it also seems to be reflected in statistics of arrests, which show most Fédérés being captured soon after the army arrived in their respective home districts. Appert (1875), pp. 266–91.

36. The Franco-French violence of 1943–44, in which about 9,000 were assassinated or summarily executed, was spread over the whole country and was obviously intensified by the conditions of war.

A threat to the power of the State from outside – by war – increased the danger of internal violence, and often its ferocity, when factions accused each other of colluding with the enemy. Many of the bloodiest political episodes have coincided with war or immediately followed it: the 'September massacres' in 1792, the Vendée revolt and its repression in 1793–94, the 'White Terror' of 1815, the muted civil war of 1943–44, and, of course, 1871. Once universal suffrage had proved an effective creator of legitimacy after 1848, a way both of denying in principle the right to revolt and of deterring or defeating it in practice, the link between war and major violence grew closer: only when failure in war weakened the legitimacy and power of the State was its monopoly of legitimate violence seriously threatened – as of course in 1870–71 – and its own use of violence to reassert that monopoly heightened, and also made to seem more justified by the need to defend the existence of the State in the face of both foreign and internal enemies.[37]

Because the threat, and fear, of political violence were ever present, the nineteenth century saw a consistent attempt to reduce, control or at least hide the level of everyday violence in society. Political violence was not principally understood in the sort of political terms outlined above, but diagnosed anthropologically as a manifestation of social or cultural sickness. There was understandable horror at the idea of an outburst of orgiastic violence like that of 1789 or 1792, what Alain Corbin has termed 'Dionysiac' violence – a violence that is enjoyed by jubilant crowds stringing up or butchering their victims. Anything that was believed to excite such appetites was gradually stopped or hidden: cruel public punishments (branding and the pillory) were abolished after the 1830 revolution, and public executions were made less public (an unsuccessful compromise); public slaughtering of animals was forbidden; public cruelty to animals was outlawed after the 1848 revolution; visits to the Morgue to see corpses were made more difficult.[38]

Yet in every revolutionary period tales of horrors *à la* 1792 were manufactured and eagerly believed. They fitted conservative mythology of a brutal underworld surging out to pillage, torture and kill. This partly explains, and certainly was used to justify, harsh repression

37. This can be seen even in recent years. The worst recent example of State violence inside France, the killing of over 150 Algerian demonstrators by the police in Paris on 17 October 1961, was closely linked with the Algerian war and its hatreds. The far more extensive May 1968 events, in contrast, led to only five deaths throughout France.

38. See Corbin (1992), pp. 90–101 and Chauvaud (1991), pp. 234–6.

in June 1848, December 1851 and May 1871. The 'forces of order' tried to blur the distinction between political and criminal offences. There were relentless (if rarely very successful) attempts by the authorities to discover criminal backgrounds among rebels and accuse as many as possible of 'common-law' crimes, such as murder, arson or looting. There was an avowed determination to purge society of what were seen as its dangerous elements. The fact that the law treated political violence with relative restraint did not prevent – perhaps it even encouraged – summary mass execution of rank-and-file revolutionaries in 1848 and 1871, and mass deportation without proper trial, as in 1848 and 1851. As one army officer put it in 1871, 'the government should not have the right of mercy . . . a drumhead court martial must function at once, otherwise they will tell us that it is too late to execute the guilty, and we shall have to start all over again with the same men.'

The final struggles of the Commune saw the climax of this history of violence: a massacre of thousands by the Versailles forces, and also (on a vastly smaller scale) killings by Communards that were described as, and sometimes were, examples of the sort of 'popular violence' that had caused *frissons* of horror since the 1790s, and which was arguably more a feature of rural than urban culture. This ended the period of periodic mass violence that had lasted eighty-two years. As we have seen, no comparable violence was to occur for another seventy years, until after another defeat by Germany.

THE ESCALATION OF VIOLENCE, JANUARY–MAY 1871

A series of incidents created anger and a desire for revenge, making a peaceful outcome to the long political crisis less easy. They also began to designate enemies. Civil bloodshed had been carefully if narrowly avoided during most of the war against Germany. But on 22 January 1871, the Blanquist-led attack on the Hôtel de Ville (above pp. 59–60) was repulsed with several deaths by Breton Gardes Mobiles, seen by the Left as benighted reactionary peasants. On 26 February, a policeman was lynched near the Bastille. On 18 March, Generals Lecomte and Thomas were shot at Montmartre. This was an act for which conservatives and the government insisted on punishment. These were uncontrolled actions by anonymous men and women, prominent among them demobilized soldiers and deserters. On 22 March, Fédéré sentries fired on a crowd of anti-Commune demonstrators in the Rue de la Paix, killing several. During the first skirmish, on 2 April, an army doctor was killed by Fédérés, and in reprisal five captured Fédérés were shot – the first of thousands to be slaughtered. The news of these killings helped to mobilize the Fédérés for their attack on Versailles on 3 April, after which more prisoners were killed, including the Fédéré General Duval and Gustave Flourens.

Understandably, there were calls in Paris for reprisals, and on 5 April a decree on hostages was passed, in the hope of preventing summary execution of Communard prisoners by threatening to execute a triple number of 'accomplices of the Versailles government'. But the Versaillais continued to kill small numbers of prisoners, especially deserters and foreigners. The Fédérés probably also shot a small number of suspected spies and perhaps an army prisoner. However, the hostage decree remained a dead letter until after a report that a Fédéré nurse had been raped and murdered by soldiers. A succession of hostages were then arrested, most famously the Archbishop of Paris. This did much to undermine provincial republican support for the Commune, though it may also have inhibited Versaillais killing.

If we look away from official debates and proclamations to the grass roots, there were vocal demands for a popular revolutionary government willing to use arbitrary power and violence. 'Why is the Commune so soft?' was a typical reproach. The socialist paper *La Révolution Politique et Sociale*, affiliated with the International, not only supported the Committee of Public Safety, it also printed a selection of 1793 decrees to inspire it. Clubs voted motions calling for authoritarian actions, repression of opposition, arrest of hostages, executions. Important elements within the Commune – especially some Blanquists and Jacobins – were tempted to go along with this tradition. However, in spite of vocal demands from club audiences, only 14 hostages were officially tried by tribunal and none was executed under the authority of the Commune, although some were killed in the dying days of the revolution, mainly on the initiative of Blanquists or as a result of spontaneous violence (below p. 178). So the tradition of the Terror of the 1790s was still alive, but more in words than in acts.

Despite their admiration for the 1790s, most leaders of the Commune, like other revolutionary leaders of the nineteenth century, were determined not to go down the terrorist path – a scruple for which Marx, Lenin and Trotsky later criticized them. Hence, there was an immediate motion to abolish capital punishment, and although this was not adopted, the Commune always refused to sanction executions, not only of hostages but also of National Guards sentenced by court martial for dereliction of duty. A grass-roots initiative was taken by a committee in the 11th *arrondissement* (where public executions took place), who on 6 April burnt the guillotine in front of the statue of Voltaire outside their *mairie*.[39] One testimony from a hostile witness: a priest was protected from violence by a Fédéré officer who said to him, 'I know the priests are our enemies [but] we're not thieves or murderers.'[40] There was an emotional Commune debate over holding prisoners *incommunicado*: on one hand, Blanquists argued the necessity of security in time of war, but others rejected the use of methods which they had condemned during the Empire. Consequently, Parisians under the Commune – with the main exceptions of Catholic priests, captured policemen and unwillingly conscripted National Guards – were rarely subjected to oppressive authority and not at all to revolutionary violence.

On the other hand, some Commune officials and the press accused the clergy of spying for Versailles as well as rape and murder. Meanwhile, the Versailles army separated out among its prisoners leaders, volunteers, deserters, foreigners and criminals. With both thus defining their target groups, the scene was set for carnage.

'BLOODY WEEK' (21–8 MAY) AND ITS AFTERMATH

Carnage duly began soon after the army invaded the city on 21 May and began a deliberate purge.[41] Orders were given, probably informally, to shoot on the spot insurgents captured carrying weapons, and this was often interpreted as meaning anyone suspected of having fought on the barricades, even including the wounded. The panicky rumour that *pétroleuses* were setting fire to houses added another category of people to be shot on sight. A young American girl witnessed one anonymous death:

> two of the soldiers were half-dragging a man who was on his knees . . . screaming to be spared. . . . The soldiers kicked him to make him get up, and hit him on the head, so that you could hear the blows across the street. Someone . . . called out to the officer not to shoot him before so many women and children, so they pushed and kicked him until they came to the end of the street, and there they shot him. . . . I saw a little boy of about five years of age go up and kick the man while he was begging for pity.[42]

39. Bird (1997).   40. Lesmayoux (1871), p. 11.
41. For details, see Tombs (1981), chap. 10.
42. *Macmillan's Magazine*, vol. 45 (1892), p. 66.

In addition to summary slaughter, some twenty drumhead courts martial – of at best dubious legality, and probably total illegality – were quickly set up to try less black-and-white cases, and firing squads in prisons, parks and barracks systematically dispatched hundreds sentenced to death. Anyone suspected of having fought, of being an army deserter, a leader of the Commune, a foreigner, a criminal, a volunteer (for example, being outside the age of compulsory National Guard service or serving in one of the special volunteer units) or an arsonist was particularly at risk of execution. The total of those killed after capture runs into thousands, and the Fédérés were soon aware of what was being done.

A few responded by shooting some of their own prisoners. The provocation was extreme: many hundreds of Fédérés had been slaughtered before any of the hostages were killed. Even then, reprisals were never authorized by the remnant of the Commune. The four main incidents (there was sporadic shooting of suspected spies and traitors) were either the initiative of a small number of individuals, particularly Blanquists (notably the young Commune members and public prosecutors Théophile Ferré and Raoul Rigault), or were a result of the spontaneous rage of rank-and-file Fédérés and bystanders in a traumatic and confused situation. Some Communards may have been determined that if they were to die, they would take some of their foes with them. This again demonstrated with grim eloquence whom they instinctively felt as the enemy: priests and policemen. The Blanquists, concludes Hutton, fought their 'last battles . . . against the symbols of the enemy rather than the enemy itself'.[43]

The most notorious act was the execution of the Archbishop of Paris, Georges Darboy, and three other hostages on 24 May at La Roquette prison (shortly to become one of the worst Versaillais execution grounds). This was undertaken on the initiative of Ferré and the Blanquist-manned court martial: 'their deeds corresponded directly with their ideological vision of the world'.[44] On 25 May came the massacre in the 'red' 13th *arrondissement* of Dominican priests and their staff from a suburban boarding school at Arcueil. They had been arrested on suspicion of spying and brought back to Paris. It is far from certain that anyone planned to kill them: they were brought out to help build barricades as the Versaillais troops were arriving, and in confused and panicky circumstances were shot down in the Avenue d'Italie as they tried to run. A few escaped

43. Hutton (1981), p. 90.   44. Ibid., p. 76.

by being sheltered by neighbours. By a bitter irony, one who got away was wounded by approaching troops, who then killed him on the assumption that his wound proved that he had fought for the Commune. On 27 May another bishop, Surat, and three other hostages were recognized as they tried to escape through the working-class La Roquette district, and shot nearby – an unplanned and unauthorized act. A young woman and several boys from the nearby juvenile prison were among the killers.

On 26 May occurred the most gruesome of the Fédéré killings. Fifty hostages were taken to Belleville as the Versaillais advanced, again at the initiative of Blanquist officers: 10 priests (including some Jesuits, long the target of anticlerical mythology), 36 gendarmes and 4 Blanquist militants identified as police informers. They were marched in procession through the streets of the last refuge of the increasingly desperate insurgents. In the courtyard of the local National Guard headquarters, a new housing development in the Rue Haxo, they were set upon by a crowd of men and women who shot them down 'like rabbits'. The manner of this violence – impulsive, circumstantial, uncontrollably brutal – may recall some of the acts of the Revolution, as it did to contemporaries. One of the killers later excused it as 'an act of revolutionary justice, like at the Abbaye' (one of the sites of the 1792 September Massacres).[45] But what is striking about Communard violence as a whole is its comparative rarity and brevity, the lack of sanction by the leaders except for a small number of Blanquists, and the near absence of the gleeful carnivalesque rituals of popular violence in an earlier age. Horrified Commune leaders (unlike the Versailles authorities) made valiant efforts to prevent the killings, regarding them rightly as a disaster for their cause. As Vallès put it, they hoped to go down in history unstained by 'the filth of the abattoir'.[46]

These killings encouraged, and provided a pretext for, Versaillais massacres, presented as just reprisal. It was, in fact, Versaillais violence that marks out 'Bloody Week' as the worse civil violence in Europe between the French and Russian revolutions. Army commanders intended (in their own words) 'to purge the country of all the scum that is spreading grief and ruin everywhere', to destroy a 'revolutionary army' that they thought was centred on the 'dangerous people . . . people of the lowest class that makes up the dregs of the present population', 'ex-convicts, drunks, pimps, *déclassés*, in short, all the vermin of the *faubourgs*'. The fragmentary evidence so

45. Vuillaume (1971), p. 136.   46. Vallès (1972), pp. 285–6.

far uncovered[47] suggests that around 10,000 people were killed in combat or by summary execution, though most writers have suggested much higher figures, usually based on Lissagaray's estimate of 17,000–20,000. There was a widespread belief that the Seine had been reddened by the torrent of blood pouring down the gutters: literally impossible, but eloquent testimony to the impact of 'Bloody Week' on contemporaries.

Journalists – especially foreign journalists, notably the *Times* correspondent – and some Versailles ministers began to be alarmed at the scale of the slaughter. But many applauded what they believed – correctly – to be a decisive crushing of revolution, the liquidation of 'all the scum that is spreading grief and ruin everywhere'. The slaughter was witnessed and applauded by conservatives. Goncourt wrote, 'It is good that there was neither conciliation nor bargain . . . such a purge, by killing off the combative part of the population, defers the next revolution by a whole generation.' An Anglican clergyman visiting Versailles was told, 'No half-measures this time. Europe will thank us when it's over.'[48]

Nearly 40,000 people were rounded up, marched off to Versailles and held in camps in harsh conditions before being shipped off to provincial prisons or coastal hulks. Several hundred died. Manhunts and new arrests continued. Most prisoners were released after lengthy investigation. But over 12,500 were tried by specially created courts martial, the proceedings dragging on for several years. It was, remarks Rougerie, the biggest repressive enterprise in French history.[49] Some 10,000 were found guilty, the vast majority of political offences (e.g. 'usurpation of public functions', 'participation in armed bands aiming at the overthrow of the State', 'wearing uniform and carrying visible weapons', 'using weapons in an insurrection'), which carried a graduated punitive tariff: imprisonment, penal servitude, simple transportation, transportation with confinement. Ninety-five men and women were sentenced to death, mostly commuted to hard labour for life, for 'common-law' capital crimes, principally homicide or arson. Twenty-three (all men) were executed: 17 for murder or manslaughter, 4 for arson of inhabited buildings and 2 soldiers for desertion to the enemy. This is, of course, a very small number compared with the thousands slaughtered during or immediately after

47. E.g. reports by the city highways department on numbers of corpses found and buried within Paris. AP VO (NC) 234. For details and a discussion of other estimates, see Tombs (1994).
48. Goncourt (1969), p. 312; *Fraser's Magazine*, 4 (July–Dec. 1871), p. 232.
49. Rougerie (1964), p. 20.

the fighting: as noted earlier, the law did not allow capital punishment for political offences. The main result of the massive judicial repression was the transportation to a penal colony in New Caledonia of over 4,000 insurgents.[50] This, like the massacre applauded by Goncourt, was meant to remove dangerous elements from society for good – a drastic remedy first applied after the insurrection of June 1848 and again after that of December 1851.

Even given the rather haphazard nature of the Versailles repression, 'the combative part of the population' – which we might roughly equate with the 15,000 extreme-Left voters in 1869 or perhaps the 52,000 who had voted for Blanqui in the February general election – had suffered a crushing blow. Their leaders too had been eliminated. Of the members of the Commune, one, Delescluze, died on a barricade (above pp. 169–70) and another, Vermorel, died of his wounds; 5 were caught and killed by Versaillais troops, most notably Varlin; and 1, Ferré, was executed after court martial for his role in the killing of hostages; 16 were transported, 3 imprisoned (plus Blanqui, who had been arrested before the Commune began) and 2 released; 48 escaped, mainly to Britain, Switzerland or Belgium.[51]

Paris and much of France remained under martial law. The International was outlawed. Bismarck used the fear of revolution to persuade the emperors of Austria, Russia and Germany to sign the Dreikaiserbund. Britain and Switzerland were the safest havens, and there Communard exiles continued an often acrimonious political existence, quarrelling with each other and with Marx, who dismissed them as 'beggars' (two of them married his daughters). For most, exile was a wretched, poverty-stricken time. Many, disillusioned by the Commune, dropped out of politics. Vallès was not alone in hating English food, weather and the mildness of its working class. But several refugees made surprisingly successful careers in an England suddenly sympathetic to the survivors of 'Bloody Week'. Colonel Brunel, General La Cécilia and others taught French at Eton, Sandhurst, Woolwich and Dartmouth. The dynamic Colonel Henry set up a business, as did at least 50 others in London, one of them employing 15 other Communard exiles.[52] One of the major political demands of republicans inside France over the next nine years was for an amnesty for Communards: releases on grounds of

---

50. For details, Perennès (1991), p. 524 and *passim*.
51. Rougerie (1964), pp. 63–4. See Martinez (1981), for slightly different figures.
52. Maitron *et al.* (1967–71), *passim*, and Martinez (1981), pp. 152–3, 245.

'clemency' were not sufficient. Amnesty was finally granted in 1880: the last few hundred transportees and exiles returned.

The violence of 'Bloody Week' left potent memories. The Commune's legislative and administrative innovations were mostly forgotten. The Hôtel de Ville and the Palais de Justice were rebuilt. The ruins of the Tuileries were turned into a garden. The long and bitter fighting in the suburbs was soon barely recalled. But though physical traces of the barricades were swiftly removed, the fighting on the barricades created an image of dauntless popular resistance. And the slaughter of Fédéré prisoners became a compelling symbol of bourgeois ferocity. As Marx wrote perceptively, if portentously, only days after the event, Paris's 'martyrs are enshrined in the great heart of the working class. Its exterminators history has already nailed to that eternal pillory from which all the prayers of their priests will not avail to redeem them.' The priests, however, were otherwise engaged: they had their own martyrs to commemorate – the archbishop, the other clergy (one a candidate for beatification[53]), the two generals at Montmartre and even the humble slaughtered policemen. Two more expiatory churches were added to the two that Paris already had to atone for its revolutionary sins.[54] Soon the 'Fédérés' Wall' (below p. 195) became the shrine to the victims on the other side.

Violence therefore became something to be commemorated, but not repeated. The dominant 'memory' of 1871 was of disaster. As a Fédéré prisoner put it succinctly in a scribbled note: 'mortte notre povre république'.[55] It would be wrong to see this as a sea-change in French political culture: throughout the nineteenth century civil conflict was always regarded with alarm, and those who actively tried to start revolutions were always few and rarely successful. As we have seen, in March 1871 many even of the extreme Left embarked on a revolutionary course with foreboding. 'Bloody Week' dramatically confirmed the dangers of 'the bare-armed fighters' trying to wrest

53. Henri Planchat, a Brother of St Vincent de Paul working in the Charonne quarter, killed in the Rue Haxo massacre.

54. The Expiatory Chapel, almost demolished by the Commune, still commemorates the deaths of Louis XVI and Marie-Antoinette; the 'chapelle Bréa' in the Avenue d'Italie, commemorating a general killed in June 1848, also narrowly escaped destruction by the Communards but succumbed to the urbanism of the Third Republic. The post-Commune additions were a church (still standing) in the Rue Haxo adjoining the site of the massacre, and, of course, the Sacré Coeur basilica. Decided on during the Prussian war, it now took on a new significance, for it was built where the insurrection broke out on 18 March, and where the two generals were shot.

55. SHA 6 CG 229.

power by force from a government elected by universal male suffrage and backed by a large army equipped with modern weapons. Although the extreme Left continued to herald revolution and the reestablishment of the Commune, and the Blanquists especially threatened to take up arms and build barricades during the political conflicts of the 1880s, they carefully avoided actually doing so. In practice, they sought other tactics – the ballot box and the strike – which inexorably led them away from armed revolt. In this sense, we may accept the conclusion vividly formulated by François Furet: 'the last great uprising . . . the one which created the most fear and shed the most blood . . . formed the ultimate exorcism of a violence which had been an inseparable part of French public life since the end of the eighteenth century . . . in this Paris in flames, the French Revolution bade farewell to history'.[56]

56. Furet (1992), p. 506.

CHAPTER SIX

Consequences, Representations and Meanings

Great events leave a wake of memory, legend and controversy. The Commune is an acute case because it immediately provoked durably important ideological interpretations while also generating deep emotions, so much so that it has often been suggested that the Commune's 'myth' is more important than its reality. Artistic, ideological and historical representations overlapped. Relatively dispassionate investigation was therefore difficult, and almost sacrilegious. As late as the 1960s and '70s, pioneers of archival research such as Jacques Rougerie were vehemently attacked for bringing inappropriate 'objectivity' to the subject. Even recent works on the Commune are – presumably unknown to their authors – hybrids of fiction, polemic and history. Eugene Schulkind noted two decades ago that although the Commune is 'one of the most vigorously debated nineteenth-century subjects . . . it is also one whose documentation has still to be studied thoroughly'.[1] This is still largely, if decreasingly, true.

The categories adopted in this chapter – political consequences, representations and contemporary historiographical questions – are attempts to simplify and make comprehensible complex and interlocking themes. The first section presents the most visible and I think least problematic political consequences of the Commune. The second section discusses representations, including art, literature, ceremony, ideology and history – different forms but with much similarity of content. Ideological and historical works are treated together (though some could equally be considered alongside works of fiction) and at greater length on the grounds that they had greater repercussions. In the third section, for reasons of

---

1. Schulkind (1978), p. 331.

convenience I have separated present-day historiographical debates from those of earlier generations. In the conclusion, I exercise the author's privilege of the last word.

Political consequences of the Commune

DID THE COMMUNE SAVE THE REPUBLIC?

Communards were republican – 'fundamentally, radically and, dare one say, solely'.[2] They fought to defend the Republic and its Parisian stronghold against monarchists and 'rurals'. Survivors and sympathizers later claimed that, however high the price, and however many the disappointments in other areas, there at least they had succeeded: 'the coming of the Republic [was due] to the will of the Parisians [whose] fathers and grandfathers sacrificed themselves for it, and for which they endured the horrors of the second siege and terrible repression'.[3] Was this really so? The argument is twofold. First, that the government and the Assembly were poised to restore the monarchy, and second that the resistance of Paris prevented them. It is not quite clear how. Bourgin hints vaguely that the royalist Assembly 'lost something of its confidence'. It is often suggested, moreover, that Thiers had been forced to promise provincial republicans that he would safeguard the Republic in order to dissuade them from supporting the Commune.

These are not convincing explanations of the policy of the government and the Assembly, whose acts can be accounted for in quite other ways. First, the Assembly had already agreed in the 'Bordeaux Pact' of 19 February not to decide the form of France's constitution until the immediate problems caused by the war had been cleared up – in practice, until the German occupation troops had withdrawn, which turned out to be in 1873, and it took until 1875 to vote a constitution. Second, Thiers had probably already decided that the only viable form of government for France was a republic, and had chosen as his key ministers republicans of long standing. Third, the real obstacle to a monarchist restoration was division between Orleanists and Legitimists, aggravated by the intransigent absolutism of the Bourbon pretender the Comte de Chambord, which made his restoration unacceptable even to most royalists.

The outbreak of insurrection in Paris was not, therefore, the only obstacle to a restoration. On the contrary, the danger posed

2. Rougerie (1988), p. 122.   3. Bourgin (1971), p. 121.

by the Commune was probably the only thing that could have united the royalists sufficiently to have brought a restoration about. Had the Thiers government looked like weakening in its resistance or losing the civil war, it was openly canvassed that the Assembly would appoint an Orleans prince as head of government as a prelude to full restoration. Furthermore, the German army was stationed east of Paris, and had the Commune looked like winning there was a good chance that the Prussians would have intervened and possibly tried to restore Napoleon III – Bismarck certainly threatened this to the Versailles government. It was royalist fears of a possible resurgence of the Commune that caused them to overthrow Thiers in 1873 and make a final effort to bring about a restoration – which again was wrecked by Chambord himself.

Ironically, it was the *defeat* of the Commune that was necessary to preserve the Republic, for it proved the viability of the 'conservative republic' headed by Thiers, Favre, Picard and Ferry. Soon after 'Bloody Week', the 'founding massacre' of the Third Republic, the republicans won 99 out of 114 by-elections. This increase of support among provincial voters gave them a majority by the end of the decade. As one veteran republican wrote to Gambetta, 'what does the failure of the republicans in Paris matter . . . compared with the immense importance of the triumph of the Republic among *les ruraux*?'[4]

DID THE COMMUNE END PARIS'S PRIMACY?

Parisians suffered cruelly during 'the Terrible Year' of 1870–71. All in all, the repatriation of immigrants, economic dislocation, death, transportation, imprisonment and flight were reported to have caused a fall in the population of some 300,000;[5] however, the number voting in the 2 July by-elections was only 38,000 lower than in February, presumably because most who had quitted the city came back. Did the devastation have long-term consequences? As far as possible, signs of the tragedy were expunged. Frédéric Chauvaud has noted how the authorities after every civil conflict made haste to clear away visible traces – corpses were removed, barricades demolished, damage repaired. Only a few days after the Commune ended, many scandalized observers reported that Paris seemed astonishingly normal. With the exception of the Tuileries – too

4. Huard (1996), p. 218.
5. *La Situation industrielle et commerciale de Paris* (1871), pp. 19–20.

monarchical a symbol – all the damaged monuments were restored. Boime has argued (largely on circumstantial grounds) that subsequent artistic representations of Paris set out to obliterate the memory of the Commune – an idea proposed some years ago by Horne. In 1878 a major Universal Exposition was held, confirming the city as the world's principal centre for international gatherings. It was frequently asserted that 'Paris was herself again'.[6]

The Commune was not a political watershed for Paris. In the city council elections and the National Assembly by-elections in June, radical Parisian republicans – those who had sympathized with but not participated in the Commune – still did reasonably well, and were to play an important political role over the next generation. It was three decades after the Commune that Paris moved to the Right, a consequence of political circumstances and social and economic change – the continuing movement of industry to the suburbs (begun under Haussmann) and the expansion of the middle class and the service sector.

The Commune and its defeat did, however, have important effects on Paris's political role within France. First, Parisian self-government under a mayor, conceded by the Government of National Defence, was abolished: the city remained under the tutelage of the Prefects of Police and of the Seine until Jacques Chirac became mayor in 1977. The National Guard – one of the institutions by which Parisian power had been asserted since 1789 – was abolished immediately after the fall of the Commune, and public order was henceforth guaranteed by a large garrison commanded by a military governor. The National Assembly sat at Versailles until 1879, and it insisted that the President should also reside there. Joint sessions of the two chambers to elect a President or revise the constitution continued to take place at Versailles, safe from pressure from the Paris population. The 1875 constitution created a senate which deliberately under-represented the cities. In all these ways, the power and status of Paris, which until then had acted as a 'proxy' for the population of France in making the major political choices for the country, was both materially and symbolically reduced. Never again did Paris determine the form of government, even symbolically: General de Gaulle deliberately refused to accept the traditional acclamation of the Parisian people on the balcony of the Hôtel de Ville at the Liberation in August 1944. Unlike Louis-Philippe in 1830, Lamartine in 1848 or the Commune, he would

6. Giard (1966–68), p. 50; Chauvaud (1997); Boime (1995); Horne (1965), p. 427.

not accept that his authority had been conferred or legitimized by the people of Paris.

THE LEFT AND THE 'PROLETARIAT': ALIENATED AND IRRECONCILABLE?

Did the defeat of the Commune create an embittered and alienated working class, conscious of having suffered what a leading Communard called 'the third defeat of the French proletariat'? And did it and its leaders turn towards class politics and international proletarian solidarity in place of its traditional, and betrayed, patriotic republicanism?

The crushing of the Commune put the revolutionary and socialist Left temporarily out of action. During the 1870s, workers were represented by moderate trade unionists and radical republicans. Only in 1879, after the republican victory over the Right, could a socialist workers' congress be held, at Marseilles. But after the 1880 amnesty, some former Communards returned as intransigent revolutionaries, occupying leading positions in the various socialist parties, and insisting on no compromise with the treacherous 'bourgeois republic'. The Blanquists above all retained a following in Paris, and were often regarded as a sort of Communard old comrades' association, led after Blanqui's death in 1881 by authentic Fédéré combatants, General Eudes and Commandant Granger. A Marxist party, founded in 1879 and led by Jules Guesde (a journalist imprisoned for supporting the Commune in print), emphasized class struggle. The former *déporté* Jean Allemane founded a revolutionary workers' party in 1890, the Parti Ouvrier Socialiste Révolutionnaire, dedicated to industrial action and decentralization along Commune lines. From the 1880s, a loose (of course) anarchist movement, the very epitome of political alienation, featured former Communards such as the increasingly famous Louise Michel.

However, the overall picture is more complex and ambivalent than this might suggest. First, most Parisians rallied to the mainstream republican cause in the 1870s: the Versaillais enemy was always identified first and foremost as monarchist. Even Thiers, who had committed himself to the Republic, was given a huge public funeral in Paris in 1877. Many prisoners and exiles, satisfied with the new Republic, were willing to petition for clemency. Intransigent revolutionaries remained a minority, supported by about 40,000 voters in the mid-1880s. This was a small minority of Paris workers, and it does not suggest that they had been collectively alienated from the

Republic, however embittered they may have been against the Right. Most workers – including prominent Communards – supported anticlerical radicals, reformist socialists or moderate republicans. Blanqui himself considered the radical parliamentarian Clemenceau (who had avoided involvement in the Commune) to be his heir as revolutionary chief.

Over the years, many prominent Communards took their places on the Left of the republican spectrum: they neither shunned it, nor were they shunned by it. Several became deputies or senators. They included the 'Jacobins' Gambon, Pyat and Meilliet, members of the Committee of Public Safety deeply involved in the military effort; Humbert, former editor of *Le Père Duchêne*, a radical deputy and chairman of the Paris city council; and the socialists Amouroux, Allemane, Camélinat, Cluseret, Vaillant (leader of the neo-Blanquists) and Malon (one of the most influential advocates of reformist 're- publican socialism'). Others obtained minor political appointments, such as Avrial as a railway inspector, Andrieu as a vice-consul, Arnould (founder of the Central Committee of the National Guard) as a Paris city architect, Longuet as inspector of modern language teaching for Paris, and the Blanquist police official Da Costa as author of textbooks for the city's schools. Paris, naturally, was fer- tile political territory, and a string of well-known Communards were city councillors, several serving as chairmen in the 1880s and 1890s, including the former Blanquist police official Lucipia, sentenced to death for complicity in the killing of hostages. One of Courbet's paintings was bought for the restored Hôtel de Ville, whereas (a sign of how times had changed) an anti-Communard painting of 'the apotheosis of the mob' was excluded from the Salon of 1885 – ten years earlier it had been Pichio's anti-Versaillais *Le Triomphe de l'ordre* that had been banned.[7] The great statue of the Triumph of the Republic, erected in 1899 near the spot where Delescluze had been killed, was sculpted by a former Fédéré officer and leading member of the Artists' Federation, Jules Dalou.

The political choices of those who refused to be reconciled with constitutional politics also show the ambivalence of the Commune's legacy. Insurrection had clearly ceased to be a viable strategy. When faced with a possible opportunity for revolution, the extreme Left took diverging paths. During the Boulanger crisis of 1885–89, which seemed to offer a chance of overthrowing the regime, the Parisian revolutionaries split amid bitter recrimination. Some Blanquists

7. Sanchez (1994), pp. 416, 427.

and 'Possibilist' socialists finally supported the 'bourgeois' republic. Most Blanquists, including their leader, Granger, rallied to General Boulanger, figurehead of radical populist nationalism. (Few knew that he had been one of the first to murder Communard prisoners.) In the dramatic Paris election of January 1889, a socialist candidate from the anti-Boulangist revolutionary faction won only 17,000 votes against Boulanger's 245,000 – and he then joined the Boulangists. The Marxists, clearest exponents of proletarian internationalism, were never strong among the ex-Communards in Paris, and did not dare to put up a candidate against Boulanger; indeed, three of their first parliamentary deputies were elected on a Boulangist ticket. Radical nationalism thus survived the Commune's defeat. Several prominent former Commune supporters remained prominent in nationalist circles thereafter.

At the time of the Dreyfus affair (1894–1906), the extreme Left were again forced to examine their attitude towards the the 'bourgeois' Republic: were they indifferent to its fate on class grounds, or should they defend it against the Right? Former Communard leaders such as Vaillant and Allemane could not stomach the appointment in 1899 of General de Galliffet, most notorious of the butchers of 'Bloody Week', as minister of war in the Government of Republican Defence. Yet they did not oppose the government in parliament. As at the time of Boulanger, some ex-Communards took the nationalist side, including Cluseret and Rochefort, while several, including 'the Red Virgin' Louise Michel, maintained some links with them.[8] In 1914, practically the whole Left, including the Marxists led by Guesde, some prominent anarchists and the former Communard leaders Vaillant and Allemane, joined the 'sacred union' to defend the nation and the Republic against Germany – convincing proof that the working class and its spokesmen had not gone into internal exile.

A more difficult question is whether the strong appeal of Communism to part of the French Left and working class after 1920 is a delayed manifestation of post-Commune alienation. This may seem doubtful after a lapse of fifty years, especially as most of the older generation of socialist leaders, including recognized standard-bearers of the Communard tradition such as Allemane, did not join the Communist Party. Moreover, the sociological and geographical support for Communism was not identical with that for the Commune. On the other hand, the Communist Party made the Communard

8. Varias (1997), p. 71.

heritage an important part of its discourse and ritual; indeed, it practically took it over – 'The Commune is ours,' declared party leader Jacques Duclos. Thus the party presented itself as the culmination of the French revolutionary tradition. Communists were able to claim justification for their own changing strategies either by stressing the 'class war' interpetation of the Commune, or by invoking its patriotism.

Representations

WORDS AND IMAGES

A manichaean conflict of stereotypes was deliberately created as Communards and Versaillais strove to deny each other political legitimacy and moral respectability. These shaped the way that events were understood at the time and since. In the Versaillais press, in instant histories and in memoirs, the Communards were represented as criminals, madmen, drunkards, vagrants, prostitutes and foreign agents; at best they were shown as unbalanced fanatics or simpletons led astray by utopian fantasies or cynical leaders. The Communard press replied by describing the Versailles assembly as antiquated rural reactionaries, the government as evil bloodthirsty monsters, the army as brutal mercenaries or archaic 'Chouans', and the whole lot as treacherous '*capitulards*' and 'Prussians'.

This was a great age of political caricature, renewed during the effervescence of the 1860s. The great Daumier and Doré were still working. A new generation had appeared, including André Gill and Pilotell (both active Communards), and, on the other side, Bertall and Cham. Communard artists caricatured the members of the government – Thiers especially becomes a grotesque dwarf, both absurd and sinister – and portrayed male and female revolutionaries as noble and sublime, shedding their blood unstintingly for the cause. Pro-Versailles artists showed Fédérés as ugly, dirty and drunk, or else as dandified middle-class bohemians.

At a time when photography could not capture movement, drawings were still the means of dramatic visual communication, and artist-reporters as well as political cartoonists put similar stereotypes into their pictures in French and foreign newspapers, broadsheets and books, which were propagated throughout the 1870s. This was particularly important at a time when theories of physiognomy, according to which bodily form represented moral condition, were widely accepted. It was easy to make the subject's appearance confirm or contrast with his or her political claims. Ugliness signified degradation and vice; beauty, nobility. Artists were used to conveying messages about corruption, penitence, madness, hatred, idiocy or honesty into their drawings, which became allegories masquerading as descriptions. Every picture told a story.

One of the most powerful visual themes for both sides – and one of the most studied in recent years – was that of women, inspiring, shocking and often titillating. Conservatives, in articles, memoirs, letters, eye-witness reports and drawings in the French and foreign press, portrayed Communard women as drink-sodden prostitutes, sinister hags, mannish viragos, frustrated spinsters, trigger-happy cross-dressing adventuresses, even beautiful but dimwitted idealists. Ugliness conveyed messages about character, drinking habits and social class. Beauty sometimes suggested girlish naïvety, sometimes professional promiscuity. All these images were put forward as proofs of female incapacity for politics and war. The burning of parts of Paris during the last struggles provided the most powerful contemporary images, encapsulating many of the themes of anti-Communard propaganda: criminality, destructiveness, terror, and the the fear of rampaging women. These were now caricatured as *les pétroleuses*, vicious harpies cackling with loathsome pleasure in destruction, and who – entirely imaginary though they were – became probably the most memorable symbol of the Commune.

The Versaillais massacre was the corresponding image of horror from the Communard point of view, shared by many non-Communard sympathizers. It was expressed in drawings, paintings, song and poetry.[9] The violence was represented mainly as impersonal, the act of a military machine, with few of the perpetrators – General de Galliffet the exception – ever being identified by name or shown facially. The ultimate responsibility was placed on the government, especially Thiers and Favre, who were accused of deliberately planning a vast bloodletting – something that many conservatives had indeed welcomed. The image of the barricade, once, as in Delacroix's *Liberty Leading the People*, a symbol of triumph and hope, had again become, as in 1848, 'an image of horror', without hope or future: 'a wall against which all hope is extinguished', as in the paintings by Manet, an eye-witness.[10]

---

9. This fitted into an existing massacre genre, most famously represented by Daumier's lithograph *Massacre in the Rue Transnonain* (1834) and Meissonnier's painting *La Barricade* (1848), and in literature by Hugo's *Les Misérables* (1862) and *Les Châtiments* (1870).

10. Genet-Delacroix (1997), p. 120.

Yet the sickening reality of the slaughter was to some extent euphemized by the romantic conventions of the time: both Communard writers and some conservatives (for whom it was a symptom of fanaticism) described men, women and children going to their deaths 'joyfully', with proud defiance: 'Feel my pulse, see if I'm afraid.'[11] Hence, it could be either a pro- or an anti-Commune writer relating that 'young women, pretty of face . . . a revolver in their hands, fired at random and then said, with proud mien, elevated voice, eyes full of hatred: "Shoot me at once!"' It is in fact a present-day historian, quoting, seemingly as factual description, a left-wing contemporary who is in turn quoting a right-wing contemporary.[12] We are seriously told that 'women and children [followed] their menfolk to the execution place, demanding to die with them'.[13] Compare the harrowing description by a young American girl, a rare eye-witness account, given earlier (p. 177).

Important means of Communard expression during and after the events were poetry and song. Commune members Jean-Baptiste Clément and Eugène Pottier were the two most famous writers. Several of their songs from the 1880s are threats of retribution at the next revolution: the message is that 'the Commune is not dead', and 'Beware of revenge, when all the poor take a hand.' This fitted the angry Blanquist and anarchist politics of the time. The two most famous songs were different in tone, however. Pottier's 'L'Internationale', seemingly written at the time of or just before the Commune though not published until 1887, is an optimistic versification of Communard beliefs, its opening lines and chorus a stirring call to action in the final revolutionary struggle. Its setting to music as a jaunty marching song in 1888 helped it to become the most popular socialist anthem in the 1900s. Clément's 'Le Temps des cerises', never widely known outside France, is a wistful love-song, written in 1867, whose link to the Commune is that Clément rededicated it to an unknown Fédéré nurse. It came to be sung ritually at the annual commemoration of the Commune at the Mur des Fédérés. Its evocation of a bygone 'cherry time' that leaves 'an open wound in my heart' became a lament for the brief springtime of revolution brutally snatched away. These two songs, the most famous expressions of the popular memory of the Commune, neatly summarize its contradictory legacy: fidelity to a revolutionary tradition, and realization that the tradition was over.

11. Lissagaray (1972), p. 371.
12. Barry (1996), p. 143, quoting Lissagaray quoting Francisque Sarcey.
13. Ibid.

No novels featuring the Commune appeared in France for nearly two decades. First to break the silence was Vallès's autobiographical *L'Insurgé* (1886). Several appeared from the 1890s onwards, including Zola's *La Débâcle* (1893), the end of his Rougon–Macquart cycle, and those by Geffroy (1904), Paul and Victor Margueritte (1904), Decaves (1913) and Deffoux (1913). They took a more detached political view than writers a generation earlier, finding good and bad on both sides, and emphasizing the tragedy of civil war: the Marguerittes' book was dedicated 'To the victors and the vanquished of the Paris Commune, whose sacrilegious battle under the eyes of the foreigner finally tore France apart.'[14] This resembled the 'republican' view in historiography (below p. 204) and can perhaps be taken as expressing a broad consensus. Yet their descriptions of the Commune, in spite of sympathetic intentions, continued some of the themes of the conservative writers and caricaturists of the 1870s: destructiveness, political utopianism, and even drunkenness, criminality, chaos and insanity. In Zola's novel, the burning of Paris under the eyes of the gloating Germans is the climactic set-piece; and amid the flames, with ponderous symbolism, a decent but enraged Versaillais soldier kills a Fédéré who turns out to be his closest friend. Here, as in other contemporary novels, the Commune ceases to be a political conflict and becomes an allegory. This permitted an optimistic conclusion round the themes of redemption and renewal, sometimes in the sentimental form of love conquering death. In Zola's case, it takes the deeply reactionary form of sick urban modernity being overcome by sane rural tradition:

> It was the healthy part of France, the reasonable, the thoughtful, the peasant part, that had remained closest to the land, which snuffed out the mad, angry part, spoilt by the Empire, unbalanced by dreams and pleasures. . . . But the bloodbath – of French blood – the abominable holocaust, the living sacrifice amid the purifying flames, had been necessary. . . . The crucified nation was expiating its sins and would be reborn.[15]

The First World War, which brought new preoccupations, pushed *l'année terrible* into the background. Silence was broken outside France by the Soviet film *Novii Vavilon (The New Babylon)* (1929), with music by Dmitri Shostakovich, and by Bertolt Brecht's play *Die Tage der Commune* (1937), examples of the purposeful Communist takeover of the Communard tradition, and its further reduction from historical complexity into ideological simplicity.

14. Wood (1978), p. 74.   15. Zola (1971), p. 496.

The approach of the centenary aroused new interest. A combination of 1960s sensibility and sociology brought out the idea of the Commune as popular festival, a carnival of liberation often explicitly compared with May 1968. Several new novels appeared, sympathetic to the Commune as a revolt of the people against the villainous bourgeoisie, and including sentimental portrayals of love, heroism, villainy and death – traditional themes in Commune literature. This was also the perspective taken by the only film in English, Ken McMullen's *1871* (1990).

In summary, this diverse range of representations established certain stereotypes and certain dramatic episodes in popular awareness, in France and to some extent outside; and these have tended to depoliticize and allegorize the conflict. It becomes a manichaean confrontation of good and evil, often within a simplistic framework of class war, with inexorable doom prefiguring redemption.

COMMEMORATION

In the later years of the 1870s, Commune sympathizers held dinners, lectures and even dances every 18 March to celebrate the hopeful beginning of the insurrection. The first rally at the 'Mur des Fédérés' ('Fédérés' Wall') at the Père Lachaise cemetery took place on 23 May 1880, apparently because the government had forbidden a demonstration at the traditional gathering-place of the Left, the Bastille. An annual May pilgrimage to the Wall developed thereafter into the great Communard ceremony. It drew on the established practice of using funerals and cemeteries to avoid restrictions on political assembly: speeches could be made and even the forbidden red flag carried.

The ritual also showed that it was the Commune's end, amid fire and slaughter, that had left the strongest impression. The Mur (part of the south-eastern boundary wall of the vast cemetery) represented both popular heroism and bourgeois ferocity. Heroism, because it was (mistakenly) taken to have been one of the last, if not the very last, Fédéré strongpoint during 'Bloody Week'. Bourgeois ferocity, because it was in reality one of the places where condemned Fédérés had been executed. This was represented in an apocalyptic painting, the previously mentioned *Le Triomphe de l'ordre*, by Ernest Pichio (1875) of a mass of young and old, women and children being mown down by *mitrailleuses* (machine-guns – an important detail, because it showed the ruthless mechanical nature of the killing) and falling into an abyss – one of the most powerful and widely known images of 'Bloody Week', often imagined to be a realistic portrayal. Moreover, the Wall was near one of the mass graves where (as in all the big Paris cemeteries) the bodies of hundreds of victims of the repression had been anonymously disposed of. The Versailles army had tried to forestall individual commemoration – for example, by ordering Delescluze's body to be buried without identification in a mass grave – but they could not prevent collective commemoration.

There were soon numerous poems, songs and pictures featuring the Wall. The mid-1880s saw clashes between Communards and the police. Wreaths were hung on the Wall, usually with simple dedications, such as 'To the martyrs'. Those with too partisan a message – 'To our brothers murdered by the Versaillais' or 'To the victims of militarism' – were removed by the police, though 'To the victims of bourgeois ferocity' was vague enough to pass muster. Even those who regarded themselves as intransigent revolutionaries came increasingly to centre their activities on the commemoration of a past 'too pure to sully with the petty passions of contemporary politics'.[16]

The late 1880s saw the beginning of a different kind of politicization, as rival left-wing groups competed for the Communard heritage. There was a clash between pro-Boulangist and anti-Boulangist Blanquists in 1890; between anarchists and the rest; and between Dreyfusards and nationalists a decade later. The Wall was no longer, as hitherto, a place of reconciliation for the Left. The annual pilgrimage was regulated by strong forces of police, and rival groups came on different days. Reformist socialists such as the Possibilists and later Jaurès and his followers also came to the Wall, to pay tribute to the victims of a civil war whose recurrence they were determined to avoid.

From 1905 the Socialist Party (SFIO) and from the 1920s the Communists turned the occasion into a show of strength, which corresponded to a dwindling of Communard 'memory' proper as Communards aged and died. This is shown also in some novels of the 1900s, in which the Commune is seen as an old men's memory. Elderly Fédérés even found themselves jostled aside at the Wall by party militants. From the 1930s onwards, commemoration, like the rest of the Commune heritage, was an increasingly Communist preserve, though other left-wing parties, notably the SFIO, tried to

16. Hutton (1981), p. 140. See also Rebérioux (1984) and Tartakowsky (1991) and (1998), from whom this section is largely drawn.

maintain their place. The victory of the Popular Front in 1936, when the two parties were in alliance, saw the biggest ever rally at the Wall. One of the last surviving Communards, Zéphirin Camélinat (d. 1932), the symbolic Communist candidate for the Presidency of the Republic in 1924, was the living symbol of the Party's attachment to 1871. He, and later his daughter, became its masters of ceremonies at the Wall. But in the late 1930s and during the war, fascist groups too tried to claim the heritage by honouring the Communards as 'victims of the Republic' and nationalist rebels.

The meaning of the Commune tradition, and of the Wall, was again modified by the Second World War. The Communards' anti-German patriotism was emphasized as a forerunner of the Resistance, with Versailles cast as a proto-Vichy – a theme also present in the historiography of the period. The rally in 1945 was led by Camélinat's daughter and the leaders of all the main left-wing political and Resistance organizations. Monuments to Resistance heroes and to death-camp victims were built near the Wall, and Communist leaders and notables were buried close by. The Commune was thus absorbed into a greater saga of international left-wing patriotic struggle and suffering as the Communists fought a 'battle for memory' against the Gaullists. Even the tricolour – in 1871 the Versaillais flag – was now carried. The centenary year of 1971 saw large demonstrations at the Wall, including by student Leftists; the body of the longest-surviving Communard, Adrien Lejeune, who had died in Moscow in 1942, was buried there. There were also ceremonies in Eastern Europe and in Communist-run towns in France, exhibitions and academic conferences. The Gaullist government notably abstained from participation. Since then, commemoration has gently declined. The Wall was listed as a protected historical monument in 1983. Interestingly, it still occasionally attracts demonstrators who are outside the mainstream Left.

The Commune is no longer politically contentious.[17] It has become an integral part of the French historical narrative, evoking the courage, fraternity and patriotism of ordinary people, and also

17. Another form of commemoration is through Paris street names. Few Communards – Varlin, Delescluze, Vallès, Michel, the uncontroversial ones – have been thus honoured, and only with small streets in eastern Paris and the former 'red belt' suburbs. A few others – Courbet, Vaillant, Rochefort – are probably being remembered for other activities, Courbet of course (with a street in the wealthy 16th *arrondissement*) as an artist. The significance of this is probably that while the Commune is famous, its individual participants are not.

part of the legitimizing legacy of the official Left. In 1981, after the socialist election victory, Pierre Mauroy became the first serving prime minister to lay a wreath at the Wall. In a recent speech, the socialist president of the National Assembly, Laurent Fabius, listed 1870–71, along with 1936, 1848, 1830 and 1789, as part of 'the countdown to emancipation', the matrix of 'the values that unite us'.[18] At a rally at the Bastille on 10 January 1996 to mourn the death of François Mitterrand (piquantly, a man whose role in history François Furet compared with that of Thiers), 'Le Temps des cerises' was sung by an American opera singer. There can be few more perfect examples of the taming of a myth.

IDEOLOGY AND HISTORIOGRAPHY

From the moment they were taking place, the events and meaning of 1871 were seized on as weapons in French and European ideological battles. The historical interpretations formulated had a very long life, and more than anything else have shaped what we think we know about the Commune.

The Commune and Marxism
The European-wide notoriety given to Karl Marx and the International by their supposed role in the Commune, and the Commune's influence on and exploitation by Marxist and Communist ideologists, were arguably its most important and lasting international consequences. The starting point was Marx's contemporary pamphlet, *The Civil War in France*, written in the name of the International in London during April and May 1871. Much of it is taken up with denouncing the Versaillais and the Empire in Marx's characteristic prizefighter style. But his essential point is that the Commune's historic achievement was to have destroyed the 'bureaucratic-military machine', the instrument of bourgeois capitalist oppression. So its significance was 'its own working existence' as 'essentially a working-class government', honestly and efficiently administering the city at 'workmen's wages', with all office holders subject to election and dismissal by the people. This self-government by armed workers was hailed by Marx, as we have seen, as 'the political form at last discovered' (the key phrase) which future revolutions would follow. Thus the Commune was 'the glorious harbinger of a new society', the dawn of a new revolutionary era. Its economic reforms were of

18. Opening speech at exhibition 'L'Europe des images', 4 Feb. 1998.

secondary importance: in the circumstances, they 'could but betoken the tendency of a government of the people'.[19]

His private comments in a letter ten years later, in which he speaks dismissively of the Commune, whose majority was 'in no wise socialist, nor could it be', are not incompatible with his earlier view that it was essentially an experiment in workers' government. But his abandonment of heroic rhetoric about the Communards 'storming heaven', and his comment that they did not have the 'modicum of common sense' to reach 'a compromise with Versailles useful to the whole mass of the people', shows a different assessment of its historical significance, perhaps coloured by his quarrels with Communard exiles in London.[20]

Although Marx did not use the phrase 'dictatorship of the proletariat' in relation to the Commune, Engels and Lenin repeatedly did. For Marxists, the Commune was the prototype to be examined and diagnosed in order to produce a successful future model. So their analyses, following up brief comments made by Marx, focused on the Commune's supposed political and strategic errors as explanations of its defeat. Basically, these were seen as 'too great *decency*' and 'want of centralization and authority'.[21] Stressing disorganization and lack of powerful leadership was an important point, given Marx's conflict with Bakunin's anarchism during the 1860s and '70s. The insurgents should have attacked Versailles at once, Marx and his disciples repeated; and they should have seized the Bank of France as a hostage. These strategies were certainly not the panaceas that many writers, notably Lenin, alleged. Moreover, Marx only thought about the Bank ten years after the event – possibly getting the idea from Lissagaray – and then only as a way of forcing the Versaillais to negotiate. But later Marxist writers recast these comments into a ready-made formula for victory, which the Communards had foolishly neglected to follow. The importance of these arguments was as assurance to future revolutionaries that success was possible. They became a repetitive feature of French Marxist writing up to the 1970s, angrily dismissed by Serman as 'criticizing the Communards for not having followed . . . the enlightened advice of their historians'.[22]

---

19. Marx (1966), pp. 78, 72, 68. This Peking edition is the first to include the two preliminary drafts and Engels's 1891 introduction. See also letters written by Marx during the Commune, in Marx and Engels (1971), pp. 284, 285.

20. Letter to Ferdinand Domela-Nieuwenhuis, 21 February 1881, in Marx and Engels (1971), pp. 293–4. See also Thomas (1997), p. 506.

21. Marx to Wilhelm Liebknecht, 6 April 1871, in Marx and Engels (1971), p. 283; Engels, letter of 4 June 1872, ibid., p. 292.

22. Serman (1986), p. 10. See Paz (1972) for discussion of Marx's criticisms.

In the last quarter of the nineteenth century, most European socialists, including Marxists, in practice abandoned revolutionary tactics, and evolved towards constitutional politics. The orthodox theoretician Karl Kautsky, using the Commune's failure as an example, warned against premature revolution: socialism could come when the time was ripe, which meant in the indeterminate future, and ideally by peaceful means. The most important exceptions to this development were Lenin and the Bolsheviks, who interpreted the Commune differently to suit their political strategy for Russia and as a stick to beat their social-democratic enemies with, both before and after 1917. Lenin presented the Commune as a working model of a broad people's revolution, and used this as justification for his assertion that an alliance between workers and peasants was the route to revolution in Russia. Its failure had not been inevitable, but was the result of strategic mistakes. Communards had pursued 'contradictory tasks' – both patriotism and socialism. Patriotism was a sham: any war should be turned into a class war. As a historical analysis this was unreal: without the patriotic stimulus there would have been no Commune at all. Lenin added further characteristic criticisms, spicier versions of Marx: the Communards had 'stopped half way . . . led astray by dreams of . . . justice'; their 'excessive magnanimity' had prevented them from 'destroying' the class enemy through 'ruthless extermination', and so they themselves had been massacred. 'Lessons: bourgeoisie will *stop at nothing*. Today, liberals, radicals, republicans, tomorrow betrayal, shootings.' The Commune's defeat had not been an inevitable consequence of taking power prematurely (as Kautsky concluded) but was the result of excessive moderation. Yet the sacrifice of a few thousand lives had been worth it: to have surrendered would have damaged proletarian morale, while the bloody repression dispelled patriotic illusions and destroyed the naïve belief in class cooperation.[23]

The Commune, wrote Lenin, had demonstrated how 'the state begins to wither away' as bureaucracy is destroyed and power seized by the people. But the Leninist concept of revolutionary rule was very different from the usually amiable, semi-anarchic 'magnanimity' of the Commune: it would be marked by 'strict, iron discipline'. Trotsky stressed the chaos and lack of direction of the Commune, using this as an argument for Bolshevik dictatorship: 'We can examine the history of the Commune page by page, and we shall find

---

23. Newspaper article, 1908, and notes for lecture, 1905, in Lenin (1970), pp. 13, 20–23.

one single lesson: strong party direction is necessary.'[24] Lenin, Trotsky, Stalin and their apologists used the Commune's defeat as a justification for terror against class enemies, traitors, spies and indeed each other. In Trotsky's words, 'the Commune was weak. . . . We have become strong. The Commune was crushed. . . . We are taking vengeance.'[25]

The classic Marxist analyses were not all self-evidently wrong. Some of them (for example, the criticism of confusion and disorganization) were made by Communards at the time. But they contained many myths, illusions of hindsight and polemical distortions, as Engels privately admitted: for example, repeating contemporary propaganda as fact, assuming the actual application of measures that existed only on paper, misinterpreting or exaggerating acts and intentions, and blithely recruiting after the event any Communard they approved of into the Marxist or at least Internationalist camp.[26] Above all, they ignored difficulties. This is not to say that Marxists did not study the Commune seriously: Lenin took Marx's pamphlet with him in his flight to Finland in 1917, carefully compared the early stages of the Bolshevik regime with the Commune, and was triumphant when he passed its record of 72 days in power. But as works of history their writings are at best flawed, for they do not attempt to understand either the ideas or the practical situation of 1871, but impose a preconceived conceptual framework and draw desired conclusions.

Marxists balanced their criticism of the Commune by glorifying its heroism and importance as an epic of class struggle. Here, they took their cue from Marx's eulogy of the Communards as 'martyrs'. The Bolsheviks praised the Communards' daring in 'storming heaven' (in Marx's phrase), seen as justifying their own revolutionary strategy in contrast with the prudence of more orthodox Marxists. 'Communes' were for a time proclaimed in Berlin, Budapest and Canton.

It was furthermore important for the Bolsheviks to prove themselves true Marxists and standard-bearers of the European revolutionary cause, not barbarous Asiatic terrorists – 'Blanquists with

---

24. Trotsky (1921).   25. Sawer (1978), p. 256.

26. Engels, for example, in his important introduction to the 1881 edition of *The Civil War in France*, asserted that the Commune closed down pawnshops 'on the ground that they were a private exploitation of the workers'; that all Commune members and officials were 'subject to recall at any moment'; and that 'by far the most important decree of the Commune', that on workshops, was a transition to Communism. Marx and Engels (1971), p. 31. All these assertions were wholly unfounded.

Tartar sauce', as one French socialist put it. Hence, they went to great lengths to establish symbolic links with the Commune: Lenin's embalmed body was wrapped in a Fédéré flag; Soviet warships were named in the Commune's honour; and a fragment of a Fédéré banner was sent up in the first manned space flight. In return, the French Communist Party and its historians stressed the continuity between the French revolutionary tradition culminating in the Commune and the Bolshevik revolution of 1917. This usefully reconciled national pride with devotion to the USSR.

The Marxist-Leninist view, stressing the centrality of class conflict and the need for authoritarian party direction, was not accepted by most Communards or, for many years, by the French Left in general.[27] The democratic socialist leader Jean Jaurès, for example, always eager to soothe conflict and build bridges to democratic republicanism, rejected the Commune as a 'blueprint' for the future, while praising the 'daring and hope' of the Communards in their struggle for 'reconciliation through justice'.[28] Marx's *Civil War* was only published in France in 1901, and the elaborations of his views written in Germany and Russia did not become current in France until the 1930s. But from then on the Marxist view became the dominant orthodoxy in Commune history until the 1970s, influencing works as various as Winock and Azéma's *Les Communards* (1964), Edwards's *The Paris Commune 1871* (1971) and Schulkind's *The Paris Commune: The View from the Left* (1972). The centenary of 1971 was its swansong. Celebration, rather than analysis, was the main concern, epitomized in enormous semi-official publications such as that by Soria and that by Bruhat, Dautry and Tersen, more interesting for their illustrations than their ideas. But heretical voices could already be heard.

Communard accounts

If Marx was the first significant writer on the Commune, Communard exiles were quick to follow. The first books – by Benoît Malon and Pierre Vésinier, both members of the Commune – appeared within months. They were evidently polemical and often self-justifying rather than 'historical' in intent, reflecting the partial experiences of the writers, their wish to defend the Commune and themselves, to discover reasons for their defeat, and to stress the atrocities committed by the Versaillais. Understandably, they are

27. Hutton (1981), p. 103.
28. Jean Jaurès, La Guerre franco-allemande, 1870–71 (Paris, 1971), p. 292.

often marked by haste, confusion and emotion. Over the years there emerged many memoirs, some written in the heat of the moment, others recollected in relative tranquillity. Among the most interesting are those of Andrieu, Cluseret, Allemane, Lefrançais and Vallès (in the form of an autobiographical novel); Vuillaume's vignettes; and from rank-and-file Fédérés, those of Brocher, Baron and Sutter-Laumann.

Very different was Prosper-Olivier Lissagaray's *Histoire de la Commune*, published in Brussels in 1876, in an English translation by Eleanor Marx in 1886, and in France in 1896. Written by a Communard journalist, passionate, caustic, often unreliable, coloured by his own views, friendships and enmities, yet detailed, documented and readable, it is still after more than a century arguably the best general history of the Commune. Lissagaray stresses the drama and heroism of the struggle in a narrative in which legend and fantasy are effectively buttressed by an impressive marshalling of dates, times, places and statistics. His version of the Commune – quite compatible with the Marxist view – is of a heroic popular revolution defeated by a combination of error, disorganization, betrayal and Versaillais ruthlessness, but whose legend remains an inspiration for the future.

Counter-revolutionary versions

Just as quick off the mark in pursuing the battle on paper were counter-revolutionaries, who, moreover, had the incentive of royalties in what was clearly an eager market. Many dwelt on dramatized or invented descriptions of political clubs, fighting, arson, revolutionary women, orgies and the killing of hostages; the photographer Appert brought out a book of photographic reconstructions of such scenes. Their version of the Commune is of a violent, chaotic, drunken spree, without any political meaning or justification. This reflects the idea of the 'dangerous classes' going back to the 1840s if not earlier, and recalls propaganda in 1848 and 1851. A similar view was expressed in the Versaillais press, and was acted on by the army in carrying out its bloody purge – an act which counter-revolutionary writers subsequently excused, denied or explained away.

The view of the Commune, and of revolution in general, as a symptom of pathological individual and social tendencies was carried to a higher (or at least more elaborate) level in three volumes by Maxime Du Camp, *Les Convulsions de Paris* (1878). For him the Communards were a disgusting sub-proletariat of criminals, madmen and drunks, led by an antisocial leadership of ambitious and unbalanced fanatics. This view influenced the later analyses of revolution and crowd psychology by Hippolyte Taine and Gustave Le Bon, immensely influential in forming conservative perceptions of revolution. Also, aiming explicity to combat Communard versions of events, Du Camp minimizes the extent of the Versaillais massacres. Similar views could be found among conservative writers in the inter-war period. Now even mildly anti-Communard views are hard to find, with Rials's *Nouvelle histoire de Paris: de Trochu à Thiers, 1870–1873* (1985) the notable example. This is because most conservatives came to accept a broadly republican view of history, and even, by a significant reversal of loyalties, to sympathize with the Commune as a patriotic revolt against a weak and defeatist government.

Republican historians

The first 'republican' historians of the Commune sympathized with the Commune's republicanism, but disapproved of its revolutionary acts. They accepted the Versailles assembly as the legal authority, but deplored its royalism, which they tended to blame for the crisis. As during the events themselves, they saw negotiation as the only way of averting disaster. Louis Fiaux's *Histoire de la guerre civile de 1871* (1879) is therefore one of the few to have taken seriously and described in detail attempts to negotiate a settlement after 18 March. He and others also wanted to restore the political dimension to the Commune, and hence combat conservative dismissal of it as meaningless criminality.

The slaughter of 'Bloody Week' became a subject of polemic. Several writers in the 1870s replied to conservative accusations that the Commune meant bloodshed by showing that reaction was bloodier still. Exposing Versaillais atrocities became part of a campaign to obtain amnesty for Communard prisoners and exiles – a central theme of radical politics in the late 1870s. Camille Pelletan's *La Semaine de Mai* (1880) is the most detailed and powerful of such works. He showed the Communards as the victims, whose acts of violence under provocation were entirely outweighed by the callous brutality of the Versaillais. He therefore stressed (and almost certainly greatly exaggerated) the number of Communards killed, which he put at some 30,000 – higher even than Lissagaray's estimate. Other writers went even higher. It became a commonplace of republican historiography to insist that the Versaillais repression had been the worst in French history, worse than the Jacobin Terror, thus establishing the moral superiority of the Left in the 'Franco-French War'.

Later republican histories attempted the different task of integrating the Commune into the broad sweep of French history, which they wanted to present to a mass readership of schoolchildren and adults as progressive, unifying and culminating in the Third Republic. Lavisse and Rambaud's *Histoire generale du IVe siècle à nos jours* (1904) and Seignobos's *Histoire de France contemporaine* (1921), the standard textbook accounts, distanced themselves from the Versaillais, viewing the conflict as a shared national tragedy, condemning Versaillais as well as Communard violence, and even accepting Lissagaray's estimate of the death-toll. This non-*engagé* position links them to later generations of historians who attempted to conduct relatively non-polemical scholarly studies. Here Georges Bourgin was a pioneer. He edited the essential source, transcripts of the Commune's debates. (Given the level of interest in the Commune, it is remarkable how few of its documents have been published.) He also resisted Marxist historicism by stressing the contingent and improvised character of the insurrection in a little book still valuable for its balance and accuracy.[29]

A different theme was that of Communard patriotism, a powerful phenomenon still visible in the nationalist tendencies of many ex-Communards in the 1880s and 1890s. In historiography it was revived by the Second World War. The point being made was that the working class had always been patriotic, and the bourgeoisie always treacherous – something that many writers from extreme Right to extreme Left could agree on, now that the Communist Party was basing its claim to legitimacy as much on its wartime resistance activities as its class ideology. This view was reiterated by writers such as Maurice Choury and Henri Guillemin. Their particular heroes were lonely intellectuals with guns, nationalistic and romantically doomed soldiers of fortune such as Flourens and Rossel (subject of yet another recent biography[30]). Their villains were the Government of National Defence and the army generals as well as the Versailles government.

The most recent generation of French historians, most notably Jacques Rougerie, Jeanne Gaillard and William Serman, can properly be regarded as republican historians in their sympathetic emphasis on the republican motivation of the Communards – 'their programme seems not outmoded to republicans of all shades'[31] – as opposed to the stress on class conflict in Marxist versions. This

---

29. Bourgin (1971), first published in 1953.
30. Liger (1998).   31. Serman (1986), p. 571.

emphasis also distinguishes them from a heterogeneous collection of often non-French 'liberal' historians (as French scholars have termed them), who have tended to take a more detached, empirical or even ironical tone, such as Mason, Williams, Greenberg and Horne.

Contemporary historiographical questions

The decline of Marxism as an intellectual force and of the Communist Party as a power within the universities aided the new generation of 'republican' historians to place the study of the Commune on a scholarly footing, to destroy the old consensus, and perhaps create a new one. A different approach was the 'libertarian' view put forward by Lefebvre (1965) and Decouflé (1969), clearly influenced by the cultural trends of the 1960s, which presented the Commune as a *fête* in which the participants aimed not merely to change governments but to 'change their life'.[32] This approach has remained influential, especially among literary historians.

In recent years non-French historians have made a distinctive contribution in extending debate into new areas. Influenced by general trends in historical research, they have analysed the Commune as an event in women's history, and also investigated its cultural dimensions and its grass-roots dynamics. The richness of the archives makes it a fertile field for such studies.

DAWN OR DUSK?

Change was heralded in 1964 when Jacques Rougerie, on the basis of pioneering research in the records of the military courts, concluded that the Marxist 'myth' of the Commune, which presented it as significant only as a prototype for the Bolshevik revolution, had 'deformed and diminished' its reality. Far from engaging in a new kind of proletarian struggle, its participants were mainly craft workers whose political and social ideas were influenced by the past. Besides, social questions were a secondary consideration. In Rougerie's bold and provocative conclusion, 'the Commune is no more than the . . . culmination and end of the French revolutionary saga of the nineteenth century. Dusk, not dawn.'[33]

32. Lefebvre (1978), pp. 33–6; see also Lefebvre (1965) and Decouflé (1969).
33. Rougerie (1964), pp. 240–1.

This met with violent criticism from Communist circles, but in time it became the accepted view, echoed in Rougerie's later work and in the large-scale and outspokenly anti-Marxist general history by William Serman. They both stressed the essentially republican motivation of the Communards, although the republic they sought was 'democratic and social' – very different from that which emerged as the Third Republic. François Furet incorporated similar ideas into a trenchant post-Marxist overview of the French Revolution and its consequences. Thiers, by crushing the Commune, had 'tamed' the Revolution. Consequently, the more liberal elements of the heritage of 1789 were 'coming into port' in the form of the Third Republic. The defeat of the Commune ended the cycle of political turbulence begun by the French Revolution. This is a more absolute conclusion than Rougerie's, which, referring specifically to the end of a nineteenth-century saga, leaves open the possibility that the conflict continued in other forms in the twentieth: 'Dusk certainly! Dawn perhaps!'[34]

A REVOLUTION FOR WOMEN?

The role of women in the Commune has recently attracted intense interest. Several historians have advanced a similar hypothesis: that the Commune marked a turning point for women, especially working-class or socialist women. The main findings have been discussed in chapter 4, where I offered some qualifications.

As with so much of the Commune, the 'myth', originally created by anti-Communard writers eager to discover shocking instances of female activism or violence, impinges on the 'reality'. Cultural historians' concern with such representations may lead to a neglect of other kinds of evidence. These seem to me problems with Gay Gullickson's important analysis of representations of women in her *Unruly Women of Paris: Images of the Commune* (1996). Another problem is that earlier work, such as Edith Thomas's pioneering book *The Women Incendiaries* (1967), showed an understandable desire to rescue women Communards from oblivion, and so focused on the heroism of a few outstanding individuals. David Barry in his *Women and Political Insurgency: France in the Mid-Nineteenth Century* (1996) sets 1871 within the broader historical context of women's activity in insurrection since 1789, but his argument that 1871 was an unprecedented event for women is belied by the fascinating evidence he presents on earlier revolutions.

34. Rougerie (1971), p. 8.

There are problems in arguing that the Commune was somehow a crucial moment for women although it had so few identifiable consequences for them thereafter. Whether or how much the Commune was really a turning point in French women's history or whether – as before it and after it – they were usually kept within conventional bounds is a question yet to be decided. There has been insufficient archival research to permit an informed general assessment of the experience of women during 1870–71.

REVOLUTION IN THE CITY

Several sociologists and cultural historians have, as we have seen, pursued the idea of the Commune as a liberating *fête* emerging from the conflicts of Haussmann's Paris. The diverging routes taken from this starting point by Castells, Harvey and Gould have been discussed in chapter 1, where it was argued that they omit or underestimate the importance of the abnormal circumstances of 1870–71. Nevertheless, Gould's innovative attempts to conceptualize and measure the importance of the local community in mobilizing popular action, discussed in detail in chapter 4, deserve to focus more rigorous attention on the local and concrete, as opposed to the abstract and general.

There has long been a considerable French literature on the Communard 'grass roots', often thorough but of a rather antiquarian nature.[35] Some of my own work has attempted to explore ambiguities of Parisian identity and the local social and institutional context of Fédéré activity – points also discussed by Rougerie and Huard. Sanchez's study of the Artists' Federation gives insights into the working of an organization that both predated and in some ways survived the Commune. Johnson's major study of clubs and committees provides a new depth of detailed knowledge. But we still know remarkably little of what was actually happening before, during and after the Commune in the *mairies* and National Guard legions in the main centres of Communard support such as Montmartre, Popincourt and Belleville, always referred to but rarely investigated.[36] And yet these are the places where the biggest urban revolution of modern times happened – and where the French Revolution 'bade farewell to history'.

---

35. E.g. Choury (1967) and (1971); Rémy (1970).
36. Several important unpublished dissertations are practically inaccessible to scholars, e.g. Freiermuth (1972–73), Giard (1966–68), Marion (1981) and Rougerie (1955).

Conclusions

A revolution is by definition a turning point. Communards believed that turning history round was precisely what they were doing. 'It is the end of the old governmental, priest-ridden world,' declared the Commune. Pottier hammered home the message in 'L'Interna-tionale': 'It's the eruption of the end. Let us wipe out the past. . . . The world is changing its foundations'. If there are, in Namier's famous phrase, sometimes turning points when history fails to turn, the Commune, even in its failure, was not one of them. But its historical importance is far from that which its supporters wanted. To paraphrase Marx, people make history, but not in the way they choose.

The preceding chapters have discussed the Commune's ori-gins, its ideas and methods of government, its popular support, its mobilization for war, and its consequences and interpretations. The answers are not always simple or agreed – for example, as concerns the precise nature of the Commune's relationship with urban change or with the mass mobilization of modern war. Nor, if we assume that a revolution must be revolutionary in every direction, do the answers always seem consistent: the Commune was eager to change the power relations of politics, but not those of gender; it set out to end exploitation, but respected property. The reasons for such seeming inconsistency are not far to seek: the Communards were pursuing their ideas of progress, not ours; and they were acting within a particular set of circumstances that determined their priorities and their possibilities.

Historians often stress origins and consequences, and this book is no exception. But no event is reducible to what goes before it and what comes after it. The Commune, so often presented as a reincarnation of the past or as a harbinger of the future, remains extraordinarily and unexpectedly itself. Let us recall one striking instance. In August 1870, the Blanquists could raise 60 men for an insurrection; in May 1871, there were 80,000 insurgent Fédérés armed, equipped and organized. In explaining what brought about this utterly unpredictable shift, exploration of long-term conditions – the 'revolutionary tradition', economic developments, urban social structures, political organizations, republican and socialist ideologies – is certainly necessary. But the events themselves, during the entire episode of *l'année terrible*, possessed their own dynamics.

To take an individual case: François Godin, aged 51, a green-grocer and Fédéré sergeant, being interrogated after the event by army officers puzzled by the fact that he had 'an excellent record' and in June 1848 had fought *against* the insurgents.

> During the siege I belonged to the 133rd battalion. When the Commune was named, they told me that I absolutely had to carry on serving. I made sure that I sent my son away so that he could not be enrolled in the combat companies. Pressed from every side by friends and neighbours I'd served with during the siege, I didn't dare refuse; they were always coming to fetch me. I rejoined the artillery battery I'd been in at the end of the siege.[37]

Godin's story, which combines both striking continuity and no less striking change – or, more precisely, a continuity (as a National Guard) which utterly changed its significance (sufficiently to earn him transportation to New Caledonia) – is Paris in microcosm. The Commune was spontaneous, unplanned, uncharted, like Godin's part in it. It produced no pioneering ideological statement or programme. It was taken over by no organized party and had no preeminent leader. The most famous French revolutionary, Auguste Blanqui, who had spent forty years planning revolt and whom many Communards regarded as their chief, sat out this greatest of Parisian insurrections in a prison cell. In short, the Commune was the way in which the Parisian *peuple* improvised a response to the political, national and urban crisis of January–March 1871.

The crisis had been caused by an event external to Paris, the defeat of France by Germany. In that sense, it could be described as accidental. In particular, the siege of Paris produced circumstances that were, to put it mildly, extremely unusual – the radicalization and arming of the population. Without these circumstances a mass insurrection would have been impossible for most people even to imagine, let alone carry out. This does not mean that the insurrection is inexplicable or meaningless: indeed, it can neatly be fitted into a 'structuralist' model of revolution[38] – the weakening of the State leading to divided sovereignty and a contest for power – which resembles 1789 or 1917. But even to formulate such an abstract explanation shows how incomplete it is, for it leads on to further questions (addressed in chapters 3, 4 and 5): what aims were pursued, how and by whom?

At the abstract political level, the Commune resembled a war of secession of Paris against France, or at least against the unitary French state. It was fought in the name of the patriotic republicanism that was so powerful an element of Parisian political culture,

37. Rougerie (1964), pp. 100–2.   38. See, e.g., Skocpol (1979).

and which had been greatly stimulated by the frustrations and sufferings of the German siege. One of the toughest and bravest Communards, Alexis Trinquet, explained this with admirable clarity in a letter to the President of the Republic written from his New Caledonia labour camp, when, after the victory of the Republic in 1879, he finally consented to ask for clemency:

> Republican from childhood, I was brought up in the deepest love of the Republic and the Revolution. . . . After our disastrous defeat, amid the revolutionary turmoil, in those days of feverish ardour, I, like many others, saw the infant Republic being threatened in its cradle by the reactionary Bordeaux assembly. I shared the enthusiasm of the many who took up arms to overthrow the coalition of royalists and clergy.[39]

This attitude is evidently linked (as explained in chapter 1) with Paris's special position within France, and its history of political exceptionalism. But the open warfare that began in April 1871 was unprecedented and unplanned, and very different from the limited insurrections of the past. Again, we must look for explanation to the dynamics of the moment, to the changed perceptions and alignment of forces which led a quarter of a million men to vote on 26 March for a Commune, for *Paris ville libre*, with every expectation that a democratic city government would prevail, either peacefully or by force.

Philippe Riviale has lamented that revolutionary radicalism was weakened in this process: when revolution became secession it lost its way.[40] His idea can more plausibly be reversed: that revolution rode on the back of a war of secession. We might imagine as a thought experiment a purely political conflict between Versailles and a Paris led by Gambetta or Garibaldi. But that is not what happened: the initial demands for the safeguard of the Republic and the 'rights of Paris' at once took on broader revolutionary implications. This development too depended on recent political shifts: the discrediting of mainstream republican politicians due to their wartime failures, the takeover of the patriotic and republican cause by the extreme Left, and the postwar economic crisis that left most Parisians temporarily destitute and in need of what Serman sums up neatly as 'a sort of municipal war socialism'.[41] So when Paris was evacuated by the government on 18 March, the only people able to govern it were the revolutionary Left. Conservatives and moderate

---

39. Maitron *et al.* (1967–71), vol. 9, pp. 236–7.
40. Riviale (1977).   41. Serman (1986), p. 358.

republicans were unable to oppose them or influence them, and (apart from forlornly calling for negotiations) they largely abstained from political action or left the city. Hence, *Paris ville libre* came under the control of a revolutionary yet democratically elected government. This is an extremely rare phenomenon. It is explicable by the particular combination of elements which we have already seen: the deep ideological divisions within French political culture (in this case, between republicanism and royalism, both revived by the war), and the concentration of republicanism in Paris. Moreover, republicanism was most intensely concentrated in certain geographical areas of Paris and in certain Parisian institutions – local clubs and committees, and above all the National Guard.

Parisians' understanding of this new situation was influenced by their previous beliefs about politics, history and society – their 'political culture' in broad terms – and which inevitably included distortions and misunderstandings. Johnson has recently argued that we should analyse the Commune from this cultural viewpoint. He argues that it discloses a much more consistent and purposeful 'culturally and politically defined revolutionary community' which had planned to take power. Hence, he argues, to see the Commune in terms of accident and spontaneity (which he regards as coming from a narrowly political analysis) is misconceived.[42] It is certainly true that Communard leaders drew upon an ultra-democratic and socialist ideology inherited from the experience of opposition to the Second Empire, from the hopes and disappointments of 1848, and (more vaguely) from the inspiring myths of the 1790s. They respected legitimate property rights, and saw socialism as a progressive replacement of capitalism by 'association' of workers in cooperatives. As Vaillant summed it up, 'The essence of nineteenth-century revolution is that, wherever there is production, the producer shall receive the total benefit.'[43] This political culture was the familiar common denominator of mid-century radicalism.

We must remember, however, that political culture and the 'cultural community' to which it belonged were not static or fixed: they too had been transformed by recent experiences, and by sudden expansion of their opportunities for action. Their audience had been hugely increased: most of those participating in the Commune, even in quite prominent positions, had little or no political history, and afterwards dropped out of politics once again. The war had attenuated prewar economic and industrial conflicts and created

42. Johnson (1996).   43. Rougerie (1971), p. 187.

the conditions for a broad alliance of the 'people'. Their physical power had multiplied, as that of the State had weakened. The tissue of solidarities and obligations which had grown among Parisians over the previous months made it possible to mount and sustain a common effort. The tiny and fragmented 'revolutionary community' of the late 1860s was in no way prepared for this: these were people whose background was in cooperative movements, trade unions, secularist societies, unsuccessful election campaigns, speech-making and minor journalism. They had certainly talked about a revolutionary seizure of power, but until power was dropped into their laps on 18 March, they had no conceivable way of bringing it about. Then suddenly they had to administer a city and run a war. This is no doubt one reason for their frequent references to the 1790s, their only precedent for a war-making revolutionary government.

Inevitably, ideological, personal and practical disagreements emerged in the Commune, the press and the clubs. There were disagreements within the Commune over the priority given to social reforms, and over the extent to which the State should interfere in economic life and with property rights. There was a deep difference between, on one hand, the conscious and deliberate moderation of most of the leaders, determined to demonstrate that a modern democratic republic could work without degenerating into disorder, economic crisis and terror as in the 1790s; and, on the other, the verbal and sometimes physical extremism at grass-roots level, especially among committed club orators and their audiences, for whom the 1790s were a constant inspiration in what Johnson describes as a 'particular mixture of contentious democracy, boisterous fraternalism, and rhetorical violence'.[44] The most important manifestation of these differences was the split between 'Majority' and 'Minority' in the Commune over the Committee of Public Safety, which was simultaneously a debate between authoritarians and democrats and between traditionalists and modernists. Yet previous party affiliation is an imperfect guide to how Commune members chose: the situation was too new and complex.

Survival was at stake. The Commune's priorities were necessarily political, determined by its understanding of how political power worked: safeguarding the Republic, abolishing reactionary institutions (army, police, Church, bureaucracy), raising armed forces and democratizing government. Yet the need to beat Versailles forced a reordering of priorities as democratic and social experimentation

44. Johnson (1996), p. 13.

became both more difficult and less urgent. The desperate lack of time and the constant pressure of events meant that many announced plans were scarcely even begun. We might find it difficult to imagine the ultra-democratic administration and the economic panacea of 'association' actually working, and conclude that such plans do not in reality betoken (*pace* Marx) the 'tendency of a government of the people'. No matter: a crucial part of the Commune's later mystique lay in the virginal purity of its untried utopianism.

The Commune was, on the other hand, criticized by some of its own members and grass-roots supporters for being in practice too much like an ordinary government – 'keeping all the bureaucracy, changing only the men, leaving all the *octroi* officers busy in their booths'.[45] But that was a large part of its strength. Many non-revolutionaries obeyed it precisely because it was a government, while most rank-and-file supporters seem to have been satisfied that for the first time they had a real government which was on their side. Many poor people, Arnould recalled, could hardly believe it. The most effective leaders, such as Varlin, Vaillant, Jourde, Cluseret, Vermorel, Tridon and Avrial, were insistent on caution, practicality, responsibility and moderation, both as the only way of surviving, and as a necessary example of what a modern revolution should be: 'the triumph of science, work, liberty and order'.[46]

It was, however, the Commune's defeat, and what were diagnosed as the causes of defeat, that undeniably constitute its greatest historical significance. It remained an isolated Parisian event, with the minor exception of brief risings in some French towns: in striking contrast with 1848, 1830 and of course 1789, it inspired no revolutionary outbreaks abroad. In that sense, it showed that the French Revolution had already bidden farewell to history. The commune was part of no general European political or social crisis, which again shows its intimate connection with the purely German–French crisis. This is its real link with past and future revolutionary periods such as that of 1917–20: revolution emerged from war which undermined states and both mobilized and divided peoples.

Within France, 1870–71 was the 'dusk' of a revolutionary period that began in 1789 and which, arguably, would have ended in 1848–51 with the smashing of the 'June Days' revolt and the victory of authoritarian Bonapartist populism – had Bonapartism not been

---

45. Elisée Reclus, in *Revue Blanche*, vol. 12 (1897), p. 297.
46. *JOC*, 30 March, quoted in Lafargue (1997), p. 85. A good biography of one of these leading figures is Vermorel (1911).

destroyed in September 1870. This was, in the simplest terms, because the physical power of the State had been greatly increased by economic modernization and its political authority strengthened by universal male suffrage. Hence the Commune's survival was extremely unlikely. After its fall, the props that had supported it were removed: Parisian municipal self-government and the National Guard. Interestingly, it was in the aftermath of another defeat by Germany, which produced another armed Parisian resistance, that conservatives in 1944 began to fear a new Paris Commune.

The significance of the Commune's defeat was all the greater because it had not merely been a failed insurrection (of which there had been many), but it had actually held power at the very epicentre of the revolutionary tradition. It was therefore the defeat of a certain idea of revolution: insurrection in the street impelled by patriotic enthusiasm and directed by a leadership chosen by popular acclaim and expecting to govern by proclamations, decrees and speeches. Lafargue points out that this was in particular a defeat for the Jacobin tradition, because the neo-Jacobins had been given power and proved impotent. Johnson suggests an epitaph: 'the reign of the orators vanished'.[47]

Both inside and outside France the Commune contributed to division among those who saw themselves as forming the vanguard of progress. The defeat of France in 1870 and of the Commune in 1871 was one of several causes of the break-up of the International. In the years that followed, the experience of the Commune was a bone of contention between socialists who implicitly or explicitly abandoned revolution in favour of electoral politics and trade unionism, and those who insisted that violent revolution was the only route to socialism. Hence the importance of finding scapegoats and errors to explain away the Commune's defeat, which could never be accepted as inevitable. Next time, revolutionary power was to be more carefully prepared for and above all more ruthlessly exercised.

Thus, during their lives and after their deaths, the Communards were conscripted into many causes. Let us end by giving some of them – looking back a quarter of a century later – the last word.[48] The Commune was 'provoked by a feeling of patriotism first of all, and by the wish to prevent the monarchical form from taking over

47. Lafargue (1997), p. 95; Johnson (1996), p. 287.
48. Inquiry into the Commune, *Revue Blanche*, vol. 12 (1897), pp. 270, 277, 280, 367.

the country'. It aimed to 'set up a dictatorship, defeat Versailles, call a national convention and continue the war against Germany'. It was to be 'a precision instrument of economic transformation'. It was 'to show that working people could govern economically'. It was 'a sort of *jacquerie*, above all patriotic'. How diverse their expectations and intentions were; how unpredictable the consequences; and how divergent their retrospective understandings.

APPENDIX 1

Declaration to the French People

In the painful and terrible conflict which is imposing once again on Paris the horrors of siege and bombardment, which is shedding French blood, which is killing our brothers, our wives, our children crushed beneath shells and shrapnel, it is necessary that public opinion should not be divided, and that the national conscience should not be troubled.

Paris and the whole country must know the nature, the reason, the aim of the Revolution which is being carried out. And the responsibility for the mourning, the sufferings and the tragedies of which we are victims must fall on those who, after having betrayed France and sold Paris to the foreigner, are pursuing with blind and cruel obstinacy the ruin of the capital in order to bury in the disaster of the Republic and liberty the dual witness of their treason and their crime.

The Commune has the duty to affirm and clarify the aspirations and the wishes of the population of Paris; to define the character of the movement of 18 March, misunderstood, unknown, and calumniated by the politicians who sit at Versailles.

Once again, Paris is working and suffering for the whole of France, whose intellectual, moral and economic regeneration, glory and prosperity it is preparing by its combats and its sacrifices.

What does Paris want?

The recognition and consolidation of the Republic, the only form of government compatible with the rights of the people and the regular and free development of society;

The absolute autonomy of the Commune extended to all localities in France, assuring to each the integrality of its rights and to each Frenchman the excercise of his faculties and his aptitudes as man, citizen and worker;

The autonomy of the Commune, only limited by the equal right to autonomy of all the other communes adhering to the contract, whose association is to assure French unity;

The rights inherent in the Commune are:

The vote of the communal budget, receipts and expenses; fixing and distributing taxation; directing local services, organizing its judiciary, internal police and education; the administration of the assets belonging to the Commune;

The choice by election or competitive examination, with accountability and permanent right of supervision and dismissal, of magistrates and communal officials of every grade;

The absolute guarantee of individual liberty, of liberty of conscience, and liberty of work;

The permanent intervention of the citizens in communal affairs through the free manifestation of their ideas, free defence of their interests: these rights will be guaranteed by the Commune, alone responsible for supervising and assuring the free and just exercise of the right of assembly and publicity;

The organization of urban defence and the National Guard, which elects its leaders and alone watches over the maintenance of order in the city.

Paris demands nothing more, under the heading of local guarantees, on condition of course that it finds in the great central administration, delegated from the federated communes, the realization and practice of these same principles.

But, by the use of its autonomy and profiting from its freedom of action, Paris reserves the right to carry out as it sees fit in its own domain the administrative and economic reforms that its population demands; to create institutions suitable to develop and propagate education, production, exchange and credit; to universalize power and property, according to the necessities of the moment, the wish of those concerned, and the data provided by experience.

Our enemies deceive themselves, or deceive the country, when they accuse Paris of wishing to impose its will or its supremacy on the rest of the nation, and to claim a dictatorship which would be a real attack on the independence and sovereignty of the other communes.

They deceive themselves, or deceive the country, when they accuse Paris of aiming at the destruction of French unity, created by the Revolution, amid the acclamations of our forefathers, who flocked to the Fête de la Fédération from every corner of old France.

Unity, as it has been imposed on us until today by the Empire, the monarchy and parliamentarism, is no more than despotic centralization, unintelligent, arbitrary or onerous.

Political unity, as Paris wants it, is the voluntary association of all local initiatives, the spontaneous and free cooperation of all individual energies with a view to a common aim, the well-being, liberty and security of all.

The communal revolution, begun by popular initiative on 18 March, is inaugurating a new era of experimental politics, positive, scientific.

It is the end of the old governmental, priest-ridden world, of militarism, of bureaucracy, exploitation, market-rigging, monopolies, privileges, to which the proletariat owes its serfdom, and the fatherland its sufferings and its disasters.

So let this dear and great fatherland, deceived by lies and calumnies, be reassured!

The struggle engaged between Paris and Versailles is one of those that cannot be ended by illusory compromises: the issue cannot be in doubt. Victory, pursued with indomitable energy by the National Guard, will go to the Idea, to Right.

We appeal to France!

Given notice that Paris in arms possesses as much calm as it does bravery; that it maintains order with as much energy as enthusiasm; that it sacrifices itself with as much reason as heroism; that it has only taken up arms by devotion to liberty and the glory of all, let France cause this bloody conflict to end!

It is for France to disarm Versailles by the solemn manifestation of its irresistible will.

Called upon to benefit from our victories, let her declare herself in solidarity with our efforts; let her be our ally in this combat, which can only end with the triumph of the communal idea or the ruin of Paris!

As for us, citizens of Paris, we have the mission to carry through modern revolution, the most wide-ranging and fruitful of all those that have illustrated history.

We have the duty to struggle and to conquer!

Paris, 19 April 1871.
The Commune of Paris.

'L'Internationale'

Debout, les damnés de la terre!
Debout, les forçats de la faim!
La raison sonne en son cratère,
C'est l'éruption de la fin.
Du passé faisons table rase,
Foule esclave, debout! debout!
Le monde va changer de base,
Nous ne sommes rien, soyons tout!

C'est la lutte finale,
Groupons-nous, et demain
L'Internationale
Sera le genre humain.

Il n'est pas de sauveurs suprêmes,
Ni Dieu, ni César, ni tribun,
Producteurs, sauvons-nous nous-mêmes!
Décrétons le salut commun!
Pour que le voleur rende gorge,
Pour tirer l'esprit du cachot,
Soufflons nous-mêmes notre forge,
Battons le fer quand il est chaud!

C'est la lutte . . .

L'Etat comprime et la loi triche,
L'impôt saigne le malheureux.
Nul devoir ne s'impose au riche,
Le droit du pauvre est un mot creux.

Arise, the cursed of the earth!
Arise, slave labourers of hunger!
Reason is thundering in its crater,
It's the eruption of the end.
Let us wipe out the past.
Crowd of slaves, arise! arise!
The world is changing its foundations,
We are nothing, let us be everything!

It's the final struggle,
Keep together, and tomorrow
The International
Will be the human race.

There are no supreme saviours,
Neither God, nor Caesar, nor tribune,
Producers, let's save ourselves!
Let's decree salvation for all!
To make the thief hand back his loot,
To free the mind from prison,
Let's heat our furnace ourselves,
And strike while the iron's hot!

It's the final struggle . . .

The State oppresses, the law cheats,
Taxes bleed the unfortunate;
No duty is imposed on the rich,
The right of the poor is a hollow phrase.

C'est assez languir en tutelle,
L'Egalité veut d'autres lois:
'Pas de droits sans devoirs,' dit-elle,
'Egaux, pas de devoirs sans droits!'

C'est la lutte . . .

Les rois nous soûlaient de fumées,
Paix entre nous, guerre aux tyrans!
Appliquons la grève aux armées,
Crosse en l'air et rompons les rangs!
Bandit, prince, exploiteur ou prêtre
Qui vit de l'homme est un criminel;
Notre ennemi est notre maître:
Voilà le mot d'ordre éternel.*

C'est la lutte . . .

Ouvriers, paysans, nous sommes
Le grand parti des travailleurs;
La terre n'appartient qu'aux hommes,
L'oisif ira loger ailleurs.
Combien de nos chairs se repaissent!
Mais si les corbeaux, les vautours
Un de ces matins disparaissent
Le soleil brillera toujours.

Enough of subjection to authority,
Equality demands other laws:
'No rights without duties,' it says,
'For equals, no duties without rights!'

It's the final struggle . . .

Kings made us drunk with gunsmoke,
Peace between us, war to tyrants!
Let the armies go on strike,
Reverse arms, and let's break ranks!
Bandit, prince, exploiter or priest,
Whoever lives on man is a criminal;
Our enemy is our master:
That is the eternal watchword.*

It's the final struggle . . .

Workers, peasants, we are
The great party of those who labour;
The earth belongs only to men,
The idle can go elsewhere.
How many gorge on our flesh!
But if the crows and vultures
One morning disappear,
The sun will always shine.

Eugène Pottier
The text is generally assumed
to have been written in 1871,
though later revisions were made

---

* A later version replaced the second half of the fourth verse with the following:

S'ils obstinent, ces cannibales,	If these cannibals persist
A faire de nous des héros,	In making heroes of us,
Ils sauront bientôt que nos balles	They'll soon find out that our bullets
Sont pour nos propres généraux!	Are for our own generals!

APPENDIX 3

Appeal to the Women Citizens of Paris

Paris is blockaded, Paris is bombarded.... *Citoyennes*, where are our children, our brothers and our husbands? ... Do you hear the cannon rumbling and the tocsin ringing the sacred alarm?

To arms! The Fatherland is in danger! ... Is it the foreigner returning to invade France? Is it the combined legions of the tyrants of Europe who are massacring our brothers, hoping to destroy with the great City the very memory of the immortal conquests that for a century we have been buying with our blood, and which the world calls Liberty, Equality, Fraternity? ...

No, these enemies, these assassins of the people and of Liberty are Frenchmen! ...

This fratricidal vertigo that has seized hold of France, this fight to the death is the final act of the eternal antagonism of Right against Might, of Work against Exploitation, of the People against its Executioners! ... Our enemies are the privileged of the present social order, all those who have always lived off our sweat, those who have always fattened off our wretchedness....

They have seen the people rise up crying: 'No duties without rights, no rights without duties! ... We want work, but in order to keep its product.... No more exploiters, no more masters! ... Work is the welfare of all, the government of the people by itself, the Commune means to live free by working or to die fighting! ...'

The fear of seeing themselves called before the tribunal of the people has pushed our enemies into committing the greatest of crimes, civil war!

Citoyennes of Paris, descendants of the women of the great Revolution who, in the name of the people and of justice, marched on Versailles and brought Louis XVI back captive, we, mothers, wives, sisters of the French people, shall we endure any longer that misery and ignorance turn our children into enemies, so that father against son, brother against brother, they come to kill each other under our very eyes according to the whim of our oppressors, who want the destruction of Paris after having sold it to the foreigner!

Citoyennes, the decisive hour has come. The old world must be ended! We want to be free! And it is not only France that has risen, all civilized peoples have their eyes on Paris, awaiting our triumph so that they can in their turn liberate themselves. Even Germany, whose princely armies were devastating our Fatherland, swearing death to democratic and socialist tendencies, she herself is shaken and moved by the breath of Revolution! Thus, for six months she has been under martial law, and her workers' representatives are in jail! Even Russia is only watching the defenders of liberty perish so that she can salute a new generation, in its turn ready to fight and die for the Republic and for social change!

Ireland, Poland, who are dying only to be reborn with a new energy; Spain and Italy, who are regaining their lost vigour so as to be able to join the international struggle of peoples; England, whose entire proletarian and wage-earning mass is becoming revolutionary due to its very social position; Austria, whose government has to repress simultaneous revolts inside the country itself and against the Slav regimes; is not this perpetual shock between the governing classes and the people a sign that the Tree of Liberty, watered by torrents of blood shed over the centuries, has at last borne fruit?

Citoyennes, the gauntlet has been thrown down, we must conquer or perish! The mothers and wives who say 'What do I care about the triumph of our cause, if I have to lose those I love!', let them realize finally that the only way of saving those who are dear to them – the husband who supports her, the child in whom she puts her hope – is to take an active part in the struggle, so as to end once and for all this fratricidal struggle, which can only be ended if the people triumph, for otherwise it will soon have to start again!

Woe to mothers if once again the people succumb! It will be their children who will pay for the price of defeat, because the heads of our brothers and husbands are at stake, and Reaction will have free rein! . . . As for clemency, neither we nor our enemies want it! . . .

Citoyennes, all resolved, all united, let us look to the security of our cause! Let us prepare to defend and to avenge our brothers! At the gates of Paris, on the barricades, in the *faubourgs*, no matter! Let us be ready when the time comes to join our efforts to theirs; if the infamous men who shoot prisoners, who murder our leaders, mow down a crowd of unarmed women, so much the better! The cry of horror and indignation from France and the world would destroy those who had attempted it! . . . And if the guns and bayonets are all being used by our brothers, we shall still have the paving stones to crush the traitors. . . .

A group of *citoyennes.*

[from *Journal Officiel* of the Commune, 11 April]

Bibliography

Unpublished documents

Archives de Paris [AP]:
    series D 2R^4: 'Garde Nationale de la Seine'
    series VD^3: 'Administration générale de la Commune'
    VO (NC) 234: 'Voie publique, Commune de 1871'

Archives de la Préfecture de Police [APP]:
    series Ba: Correspondance of Prefect of Police
    series Db: 'Commune de Paris'

Institut Français d'Histoire Sociale:
    14 AS 99 bis (Fonds Eudes)

Service Historique de l'Armée de Terre [SHA]:
    series Li: 'Armée de Paris'
    series Lu: 'Armée de Versailles'
    series Ly: 'Commune de Paris'
    'Commune de Paris 1871: Conseils de Guerre [CG]' (dossiers)

Published documents

Annales de l'Assemblée Nationale (1871) (Versailles, 1872)

Atlas statistique de la population de Paris, ed. Toussaint Loua (Paris, 1873)

Enquête sur les actes du gouvernement de la défense nationale [EGDN], in *Annales de l'Assemblée Nationale: compte-rendu in extenso des séances: annexes*, vols 20–6 (Journal Officiel, Versailles, 1874–75)

Enquête parlementaire sur l'insurrection du 18 mars, no. 740, Assemblée Nationale 1871, 3 vols (Versailles, 1872)

Journal Officiel of the Commune [JOC], in *Journal des Journaux de la Commune*, 2 vols (Paris, 1872)

Les Murailles politiques françaises (1870–71), 2 vols (Paris, 1873–74)

Procès-verbaux de la Commune de 1871 [PVC], eds Georges Bourgin and Gabriel Henriot, vol. 1 (Paris, 1924), vol. 2 (Paris, 1945)

Rapport d'ensemble de M. le général Appert sur les opérations de la justice militaire relatives l'insurrection de 1871, no. 3212, Assemblée Nationale, annexe au procès-verbal de la séance du 20 juillet 1875 (Versailles, 1875)

La Situation industrielle et commerciale de Paris en octobre 1871: rapport de l'enquête faite par une fraction du conseil municipal (Paris, 1871)

Contemporary newspapers

La Commune
Le Cri du Peuple
Le Père Duchêne
La Révolution Politique et Sociale

Reference works

DUBOIS, JEAN (1962) *Le Vocabulaire politique et social en France de 1869 à 1872* (Paris)

LE QUILLEC, ROBERT (1997) *La Commune de Paris: Bibliographie critique, 1871–1997* (Paris)

MAITRON, JEAN and EGROT, MADELEINE (1967–71) *Dictionnaire biographique du mouvement ouvrier français, 1848–71*, vols 4–9 (Paris)

Unpublished dissertations

ALLNER, MICHEL D. (1978) 'The Jacobins in the Paris Commune of 1871' (PhD, Columbia University)

BIRD, STEPHEN (1997) 'The politicization of Voltaire's legacy in nineteenth-century France, 1830–1900' (PhD, Univ. of London)

CLIFFORD, DALE L. (1975) '*Aux armes citoyens!* The National Guard in the Paris Commune of 1871' (PhD, Univ. of Tennessee)

EGROT, MADELEINE (1953–54) 'La question des subsistances à Paris sous la Commune de 1871' (DES, Paris)

FREIERMUTH, JEAN-CLAUDE (1972–73) 'Un arrondissement de la rive gauche pendant le siège et la Commune: le XIIIe' (maîtrise, Paris I)

GIARD, LOUIS (1966–68) 'Les élections à Paris sous la IIIe République (doctorat de 3e cycle, Université de Dakar)

MARION, OLIVIER (1981) 'La vie religieuse pendant la Commune de Paris, 1871' (maîtrise, Paris X-Nanterre)

MARTINEZ, PAUL (1981) 'Paris Communard refugees in Britain, 1871–1880' (PhD, Univ. of Sheffield)

ROUGERIE, JACQUES (1955) 'Les elections du 26 mars à la Commune de Paris: histoire economique, sociale et politique' (DES, Paris)

SANCHEZ, GONZALEZ J. (1994) '"The development of art and the universal republic": The Paris Commune's Fédération des Artistes and French Republicanism, 1871–1889' (PhD, Columbia University)

Books and articles

Unless otherwise stated, English books are published in London, and French books in Paris. Modern editions of contemporary works are given where possible, followed by the original date of publication in square brackets.

ALLEMANE, JEAN (1981) *Mémoires d'un Communard, des barricades au bagne* [1906]

ANDRIEU, JULES (1971) *Notes pour servir à l'histoire de la Commune de Paris en 1871*

ARNOULD, ARTHUR (1981) *Histoire populaire et parlementaire de la Commune de Paris*, Lyons [Brussels, 1878]

AUDOIN-ROUZEAU, STÉPHANE (1989) *1870: La France dans la guerre*

BARRON, LOUIS (1889) *Sous le drapeau rouge*

BARRY, DAVID (1996) *Women and Political Insurgency: France in the Mid-Nineteenth Century*

BERLANSTEIN, LENARD R. (1984) *The Working People of Paris*

BERNSTEIN, SAMUEL (1971) *Auguste Blanqui and the Art of Insurrection*

BLANQUI, AUGUSTE (1972) *Instructions pour une prise d'armes [. . .] et autres textes*, ed. M. Abasour and V. Pelosse [1869]

BOIME, ALBERT (1995) *Art and the French Commune: Imagining Paris after War and Revolution*, Princeton, NJ

BOURGIN, GEORGES (1939) *La Guerre de 1870–71 et la Commune*

BOURGIN, GEORGES (1971) *La Commune*

BROCHER, VICTORINE (1977) *Victorine B . . . : Souvenirs d'une morte vivante*

BRUHAT, JEAN, DAUTRY, JEAN and TERSEN, EMILE (1970) *La Commune de 1871*

BUSCH, MORITZ (1898), *Bismarck: Some Secret Pages of His History*, 2 vols

CASTELLS, MANUEL (1983) *The City and the Grassroots: A Cross-Cultural Theory of Urban Social Movements*

CAVATERRA, ERIC (1998) *La Banque de France et la Commune de Paris (1871)*

CHARLE, CHRISTOPHE (1991) *Histoire sociale de la France au XIX siècle*

CHAUVAUD, FRÉDÉRIC (1991) *De Pierre Rivière à Landru: La violence apprivoisée au XIXe siècle*, Brussels

CHAUVAUD, FRÉDÉRIC (1997) 'L'élision des traces: l'effacement des marques de la barricade à Paris (1830–1871)', in Alain Corbin and Jean-Marie Mayeur, eds, *La Barricade*, pp. 269–81

CHEVALIER, LOUIS (1950) *La Formation de la Population parisienne au XIXe siècle*

CHOURY, MAURICE (1967) *La Commune au coeur de Paris*

CHOURY, MAURICE (1971) *La Commune au Quartier Latin*

CHRISTIANSEN, RUPERT (1994) *Tales of the New Babylon: Paris 1869–1875*

CLAYSON, HOLLIS (1998) 'A wintry masculinity: art, soldiering and gendered space in Paris under siege', *Nineteenth-Century Contexts* 20, 4, pp. 385–408

CLUSERET, GUSTAVE PAUL (1887–88) *Mémoires du général Cluseret*, 3 vols

CORBIN, ALAIN (1992) *The Village of Cannibals: Rage and Murder in France, 1870*, Cambridge

CORDILLOT, MICHEL (1991) *Eugène Varlin: chronique d'un espoir assassiné*

COURBET, GUSTAVE (1992) *Letters of Gustave Courbet*, ed. and tr. Petra ten-Doesschate Chu, Chicago

DA COSTA, GASTON (1903–5) *La Commune vécue*, 3 vols

DALOTEL, ALAIN (1997) 'La barricade des femmes', in Alain Corbin and Jean-Marie Mayeur, eds, *La Barricade*, pp. 341–55

DALOTEL, ALAIN, FAURE, ALAIN and FREIERMUTH, JEAN-CLAUDE (1981) *Aux Origines de la Commune: le mouvement des réunions publiques à Paris (1868–1870)*

DAUTRY, JEAN and SCHELER, LUCIEN (1960) *Le Comité Central Républicain des vingt arrondissements de Paris (Septembre 1870–Mai 1871)*

DECOUFLÉ, ANDRÉ (1969) *La Commune de Paris (1871)*

DERFLER, LESLIE (1991) *Paul Lafargue and the Founding of French Marxism, 1842–1882*, Cambridge MA

DU CAMP, MAXIME (1878) *Les Convulsions de Paris*, 3 vols

DUVEAU, GEORGES (1946) *La Vie ouvrière en France sous le Second Empire*

EAGLETON, TERRY (1988) 'Foreword', in Kristin Ross, *The Emergence of Social Space: Rimbaud and the Paris Commune*, pp. vi–xiv

EDWARDS, STEWART (1971) *The Paris Commune 1871*

FEHER, FERENC, ED. (1990) *The French Revolution and the Birth of Modernity*, Berkeley, CA

FERGUSON, PRISCILLA P. (1994) *Paris as Revolution: Writing the Nineteenth-Century City*, Berkeley, CA

FIAUX, LOUIS (1879) *Histoire de la guerre civile de 1871, le gouvernement et l'assemblée de Versailles, la Commune de Paris*

FLOURENS, GUSTAVE (1863) *Histoire de l'homme: cours d'histoire naturelle des corps organisés*

FLOURENS, GUSTAVE (1871) *Paris livré*

FREDERICK OF PRUSSIA (1927) *The War Diary of the Emperor Frederick III*, ed. A.R. Allinson

FURET, FRANÇOIS (1992) *Revolutionary France 1770–1880*, Oxford

GAILLARD, JEANNE (1960–61) 'Les usines Cail et les ouvriers métallurgistes de Grenelle, 1848–1871', *Le Mouvement Social*, 33–4 (Oct.–Mar.), pp. 35–53

GAILLARD, JEANNE (1966) 'La Ligue d'union républicaine des droits de Paris', *Bulletin de la Société d'Histoire Moderne*, 13th series, 5, pp. 8–13

GAILLARD, JEANNE (1971) *Communes de province, Commune de Paris, 1870–1871*

GAILLARD, JEANNE (1977) *Paris la ville, 1852–1870*

GENET-DELACROIX, MARIE-CLAUDE (1997) 'Donner un corps à l'histoire (1830–1848–1871)', in Alain Corbin and Jean-Marie Mayeur, *La Barricade*, pp. 113–24

GIBSON, REV. WILLIAM (1895) *Paris During the Commune*

GIRARD, LOUIS, ED. (1960) *Les élections de 1869*

GIRARD, LOUIS (1964) *La Garde nationale 1814–1871*

GIRARD, LOUIS (1981), *Nouvelle histoire de Paris: la Deuxième République et le Second Empire, 1848–1870*

GIRARDET, RAOUL (1984) 'Les trois Couleurs', in Pierre Nora, ed., *Les Lieux de mémoire*, vol. 1, pp. 5–35

GONCOURT, EDMOND DE (1969) *Paris Under Siege, 1870–1871: From the Goncourt Journal*, ed. G.J. Becker, Ithaca, NY

GONCOURT, EDMOND DE (1978) *Pages from the Goncourt Journal*, ed. Robert Baldick, Oxford

GOULD, ROGER V. (1991) 'Multiple networks and mobilization in the Paris Commune, 1871', *American Sociological Review*, 56 (Dec.), pp. 716–29

GOULD, ROGER V. (1995) *Insurgent Identities: Class, Community and Protest in Paris from 1848 to the Commune*, Chicago

GUILLEMIN, HENRI (1956–60) *Les Origines de la Commune*, 3 vols

GULLICKSON, GAY L. (1991) 'La pétroleuse: representing revolution', *Feminist Studies*, 17, 1, pp. 241–65

GULLICKSON, GAY L. (1996) *Unruly Women of Paris: Images of the Commune*, Ithaca, NY

HALÉVY, LUDOVIC (1935) *Carnets*, ed. Daniel Halévy, 2 vols

HARVEY, DAVID (1985) *Consciousness and the Urban Experience*, Baltimore

HORNE, ALISTAIR (1965) *The Fall of Paris: The Siege and the Commune 1870–1*

HOWARD, MICHAEL (1967) *The Franco-Prussian War: The German Invasion of France 1870–1871*

HUARD, RAYMOND (1996) ' "Rural": La promotion d'une épithète et sa signification politique et sociale des années soixante aux lendemains de la Commune', in Michael Adcock, Emily Chester and Jeremy Whiteman, eds, *Revolution, Society and the Politics of Memory: The Proceedings of the Tenth George Rudé Seminar on French History and Civilisation*, Melbourne, pp. 214–20

HUGO, VICTOR (1862) *Les Misérables*

HUGO, VICTOR (1870) *Les Châtiments*

HUTTON, PATRICK H. (1981) *The Cult of the Revolutionary Tradition: The Blanquists in French Politics, 1864–1893*, Berkeley, CA

JOHNSON, CHRISTOPHER H. (1975) 'Economic change and artisan discontents: the tailors' history 1800–1848', in Roger Price, ed., *Revolution and Reaction: 1848 and the Second French Republic*

JOHNSON, MARTIN P. (1994) 'Citizenship and gender: the Légion des Fédérées in the Paris Commune of 1871', *French History*, 8, 3 (Sept.), pp. 276–95

JOHNSON, MARTIN P. (1996) *The Paradise of Association: Political Culture and Popular Organizations in the Paris Commune of 1871*, Ann Arbor, MI

JONES, KATHLEEN and VERGÈS, FRANÇOISE (1991) ' "Aux citoyennes!": Women, politics and the Paris Commune of 1871', *History of European Ideas*, 13, pp. 711–32

JUDT, TONY (1986) *Marxism and the French Left: Studies in Labour and Politics in France, 1830–1981*, Oxford

KRANZBERG, MELVIN (1950) *The Siege of Paris, 1870–1871: A Political and Social History*, Ithaca, NY

KULSTEIN, DAVID I. (1969) *Napoleon III and the Working Class: A Study of Government Propaganda under the Second Empire*, Los Angeles

LAFARGUE, JÉROME (1997) 'La Commune de 1871 ou l'ordre improbable', *Désordre(s)*, pp. 85–107

LA GORCE, PIERRE DE (1930) *Histoire du Second Empire*, 7 vols

LAVISSE, ERNEST and RAMBAUD, ALFRED (1904) *Histoire générale du IVe siècle à nos jours*

LEFEBVRE, HENRI (1965) *La Proclamation de la Commune*

LEFEBVRE, HENRI (1978) 'La Commune: dernière fête populaire', in James A. Leith, ed., *Images of the Commune*, Montreal, pp. 33–45

LEFRANÇAIS, GUSTAVE (1972) *Souvenirs d'un révolutionnaire* [1902]

LEHAUTCOURT, PIERRE (1898) *Siège de Paris*, 3 vols

LENIN, VLADIMIR I. (1970) *V.I. Lenin on the Paris Commune*, Moscow

LESMAYOUX, ABBÉ [Louis] (1871) *Le 25 mai à l'avenue d'Italie*

LEVISSE-TOUZÉ, CHRISTINE (1994) *Paris libéré, Paris retrouvé*

LIGER, CHRISTIAN (1998) *Le Roman de Rossel*

LISSAGARAY, PROSPER-OLIVIER (1972) *Histoire de la Commune de 1871* [1876]

LISSAGARAY, PROSPER-OLIVIER (1886) *History of the Commune of 1871*

MCADAM, DOUG, TARROW, SIDNEY and TILLY, CHARLES (1997) 'Toward an integrated perspective on social movements and revolution', in Mark I. Lichbach and Alan S. Zuckerman, eds, *Comparative Politics: Rationality, Culture and Structure*, Cambridge, pp. 142–73

Macmillan's Magazine (1871) 'A victim of Paris and Versailles', vol. 24, pp. 384–408, 487–96

Macmillan's Magazine (1892) 'What an American girl saw of the Commune' vol. 45, pp. 61–6

MAITRON, JEAN (1972) 'Etude critique du rapport Appert, essai de contre-rapport', *Le Mouvement Social*, 79, pp. 95–122

MALON, BENOÎT (1968) *La troisième défaite du prolétariat français* [1871]

MARX, KARL (1966) *The Civil War in France*, Peking [1871]

MARX, KARL and ENGELS, FRIEDRICH (1971) *On the Paris Commune*, Moscow

MENAGER, BERNARD (1988) *Les Napoléon du peuple*

MERRIMAN, JOHN M., ED. (1975) *1830 in France*

MOLINARI, GUSTAVE DE (1871) *Les Clubs rouges pendant le siège de Paris*

MOLTKE, HELMUT VON (1922) *Moltkes Briefe*, 2 vols ed. W. Andreas, Leipzig

NORD, PHILIP G. (1987) 'The Party of Conciliation and the Paris Commune', *French Historical Studies*, 15, 1 (Spring), pp. 1–35

PAZ, MAURICE (1972) 'Le mythe de la Commune: les deux reproches majeurs', *Est et Ouest*, 482 (1–15 Feb.), pp. 23–8

PAZ, MAURICE (1984) *Un révolutionnaire professionel, Blanqui*

PELLETAN, CAMILLE (1880) *La Semaine de Mai*

PERENNÈS, ROGER (1991) *Déportés et forçats de la Commune: de Belleville à Nouméa*, Nantes

PERROT, MICHELLE (1979) 'La femme populaire rebelle', in Christiane Dufrancatel, ed., *L'Histoire sans qualités*, pp. 126–53

PIGENET, MICHEL (1997) 'L'adieu aux barricades: du Blanquisme au Vaillantisme', in Alain Corbin and Jean-Marie Mayeur, eds, *La Barricade*, pp. 367–79

PINKNEY, DAVID H. (1958) *Napoleon III and the Rebuilding of Paris*, Princeton, NJ

PINKNEY, DAVID H. (1988) *La Révolution de 1830 en France*

PLESSIS, ALAIN (1985) *The Rise and Fall of the Second Empire, 1852–1871*, Cambridge

PRENDERGAST, CHRISTOPHER (1992) *Paris and the Nineteenth Century*, Oxford

REBÉRIOUX, MADELEINE (1984) 'Le Mur des Fédérés', in Pierre Nora, ed., *Les Lieux de mémoire*, vol. 1, pp. 619–49

RÉMY, TRISTAN (1970) *La Commune à Montmartre: 23 mai 1871*

RENDALL, JANE (1985) *The Origins of Modern Feminism: Women in Britain, France and the United States, 1780–1860*

Revue Blanche, La (1897) 'Enquête sur la Commune' vol. 12, pp. 249–305, 356–88 (reprinted edition, Geneva, 1968)

RIALS, STÉPHANE (1985) *Nouvelle histoire de Paris: de Trochu à Thiers, 1870–1873*

RIFKIN, ADRIAN (1979) 'Cultural movement and the Paris Commune', *Art History*, 2, 2 (June), pp. 201–20

RIHS, CHARLES (1973) *La Commune de Paris 1871: sa structure et ses doctrines*

RIVIALE, PHILIPPE (1977) *La Ballade du temps passé: guerre et insurrection de Babeuf à la Commune*

ROBERTS, J.M. (1973) 'The Paris Commune from the Right', *English Historical Review*, supplement 6

ROSS, KRISTIN (1988) *The Emergence of Social Space: Rimbaud and the Paris Commune*

ROSSEL, LOUIS (1960) *Mémoires, procès et correspondance*, ed. Roger Stéphane

ROUFFIAC, J. (1873) *Souvenirs historiques sur le siège de Paris et le commencement de la Commune*

ROUGERIE, JACQUES (1960) 'Belleville', in Louis Girard, ed., *Les élections de 1869*, pp. 3–36

ROUGERIE, JACQUES (1961) 'Comment les Communards voyaient la Commune', *Le Mouvement Social*, 37, pp. 58–67

ROUGERIE, JACQUES (1964) *Procès des Communards*

ROUGERIE, JACQUES (1971) *Paris libre 1871*

ROUGERIE, JACQUES, ED. (1973) *1871: Jalons pour une histoire de la Commune de Paris*, Amsterdam

ROUGERIE, JACQUES (1976) 'Notes pour servir a l'histoire du 18 mars', in *Mélanges d'histoire sociale offerts à Jean Maitron*, pp. 229–48

ROUGERIE, JACQUES (1988) *La Commune*

ROUGERIE, JACQUES (1995) *Paris insurgé: la Commune de 1871*

SANCHEZ, GONZALEZ J. (1997) *Organizing Independence: The Artists' Federation of the Paris Commune and Its Legacy*

SARCEY, FRANCISQUE (1871) *Le Siège de Paris*

SARREPONT, H. DE (1872) *Le Bombardement de Paris par les Prussiens en janvier 1871*

SAWER, MARION (1978) 'The Soviet image of the Commune: Lenin and beyond', in James A. Leith, ed., *Images of the Commune*, Montreal, pp. 245–63

SCHULKIND, EUGENE, ED. (1972) *The Paris Commune: The View from the Left*

SCHULKIND, EUGENE (1978) 'The historiography of the Commune: some problems', in James A. Leith, ed., *Images of the Commune*, Montreal, pp. 319–32

SCHULKIND, EUGENE (1985) 'Socialist women during the 1871 Paris Commune', *Past and Present*, 106, pp. 124–63

SEIGNOBOS, CHARLES (1921) *Histoire de la France contemporaine: depuis la révolution jusqu'à la paix de 1919: t. VII: Le déclin de l'empire et l'établissement de la 3e République (1859–1875)*

SERMAN, WILLIAM (1986) *La Commune de Paris (1871)*

SEWELL, WILLIAM H. (1980) *Work and Revolution in France: The Language of Labor from the Old Regime to 1848*, Cambridge

SHAFER, DAVID A. (1993) '*Plus que des ambulancières*: women in articulation and defence of their ideals during the Paris Commune (1871)', *French History* 7, 1 (March), pp. 85–101

SIMON, JULES (1879) *The Government of M. Thiers*, 2 vols

SKOCPOL, THEDA (1979) *States and Social Revolutions*, Cambridge

SORIA, GEORGES (1970–71) *Grande Histoire de la Commune*, 5 vols

SUTTER-LAUMANN (1891) *Histoire d'un trente-sous*

TARTAKOWSKY, DANIELLE (1991) 'Le mur des fédérés, ou l'apprentissage de la manifestation', *Cahiers d'Histoire de l'IRM*, 44, pp. 70–9

TARTAKOWSKY, DANIELLE (1998) 'Le Père-Lachaise: espace politique', *Délégation Artistique de la Ville de Paris*

THOMAS, EDITH (1967) *The Women Incendiaries*

THOMAS, ROGER (1997) 'Enigmatic writings: Karl Marx's *The Civil War in France* and the Paris Commune of 1871', *History of Political Thought*, 18, 3 (Autumn), pp. 483–511

THOMSON, DAVID (1968) *France, Empire and Republic 1850–1940: Historical Documents*, New York

TILLY, CHARLES and LEES, LYNN H. (1975) 'The people of June 1848', in Roger Price, ed., *Revolution and Reaction: 1848 and the Second French Republic*, pp. 170–209

TOMBS, ROBERT (1981) *The War Against Paris 1871*, Cambridge

TOMBS, ROBERT (1984) 'Harbingers or entrepreneurs? A workers' cooperative during the Paris Commune', *Historical Journal*, 27, 4, pp. 969–77

TOMBS, ROBERT (1986) 'Paris and the rural hordes: an exploration of myth and reality in the French civil war of 1871', *Historical Journal*, 29, 4, pp. 795–808

TOMBS, ROBERT (1991) 'Prudent rebels: the 2nd *arrondissement* during the Paris Commune of 1871', *French History*, 5, 4, pp. 393–413

TOMBS, ROBERT (1994) 'Victimes et bourreaux de la Semaine Sanglante', *1848: Révolutions et Mutations du XIXe siécle*, 10, pp. 81–96

TOMBS, ROBERT (1997) 'Les Communeux dans la ville: des analyses récentes de l'étranger', *Le Mouvement Social*, 179 (avril–juin), pp. 93–105

TROTSKY, LEON (1921) preface to Charles Talès, *La Commune de 1871*

VACHER, L. (1871) *La mortalité à Paris en 1870*

VALLÈS, JULES (1972) *L'Insurgé* [1886]

VARIAS, ALEXANDER (1997) *Paris and the Anarchists: Aesthetes and Subversives during the Fin de Siècle*

VERMOREL, JEAN (1911) *Un enfant du Beaujolais: Auguste Vermorel, 1841–1871*

VÉSINIER, PIERRE (1971) *Histoire de la Commune de Paris* [1871]

VIDALENC, JEAN (1948) 'La province et les journées de juin', *Etudes d'Histoire Moderne et Contemporaine*, 2, pp. 83–144

VINCENT, K. STEVEN (1984) *Pierre-Joseph Proudhon and the Rise of French Republican Socialism,* Oxford

VINCENT, K. STEVEN (1992) *Between Marxism and Anarchism: Benoît Malon and French Reformist Socialism,* Berkeley, CA

VINOY, GEN. JOSEPH (1872) *Campagne de 1870–1871, l'armistice et la Commune*

VIZETELLY, ERNEST A. (1914) *My Adventures in the Commune*

VUILLAUME, MAXIME (1971) *Mes Cahiers rouges au temps de la Commune* [1909]

WINOCK, MICHEL and AZÉMA, PIERRE (1964), *Les Communards*

WOOD, J.S. (1978) 'La Commune dans le roman', in James A. Leith, ed., *Images of the Commune,* Montreal, pp. 69–82

WRIGHT, GORDON (1977) 'The anti-Commune, Paris 1871', *French Historical Studies,* 10, pp. 149–72

ZOLA, EMILE (1971) *La Débâcle* [1893]